T0373146

ROYAL HISTORICAL SO
STUDIES IN HISTORY
New Series

IMAGINING ROMAN BRITAIN

VICTORIAN RESPONSES TO A ROMAN PAST

Studies in History New Series
Editorial Board 2015

Professor Michael Braddick (*Convenor*)
Dr D'Maris Coffman
Professor Barry Doyle (*Economic History Society*)
Professor Emma Griffin (*Literary Director*)
Dr Rachel Hammersley
Professor Michael Hughes (*Honorary Treasurer*)
Professor Daniel Power
Professor Bernhard Rieger
Dr Guy Rowlands
Professor Alec Ryrie
Dr Selina Todd (*Past and Present Society*)

This series is supported by annual subventions from the
Economic History Society and from the Past and Present Society

IMAGINING ROMAN BRITAIN
VICTORIAN RESPONSES TO
A ROMAN PAST

Virginia Hoselitz

THE ROYAL HISTORICAL SOCIETY
THE BOYDELL PRESS

© Virginia Hoselitz 2007

All Rights Reserved. Except as permitted under current legislation
no part of this work may be photocopied, stored in a retrieval system,
published, performed in public, adapted, broadcast,
transmitted, recorded or reproduced in any form or by any means,
without the prior permission of the copyright owner

The right of Virginia Hoselitz to be identified as
the author of this work has been asserted in accordance with
sections 77 and 78 of the Copyright, Designs and Patents Act 1988

First published 2007
Paperback edition 2015

A Royal Historical Society publication
Published by The Boydell Press
an imprint of Boydell & Brewer Ltd
PO Box 9, Woodbridge, Suffolk IP12 3DF, UK
and of Boydell & Brewer Inc.
668 Mt Hope Avenue, Rochester, NY 14620–2731, USA
website: www.boydellandbrewer.com

ISBN 978 0 86193 293 1 hardback
ISBN 978 0 86193 335 8 paperback

ISSN 0269–2244

A CIP catalogue record for this book is available
from the British Library

This publication is printed on acid-free paper

Frontispiece: 'The lifting of the "Hunting dogs mosaic" discovered in
Dyer Street [Cirencester], in 1849': *ILN*, 8 Sept. 1849.

Contents

List of Illustrations

Map

Photographic Acknowledgements

Plate 1 is reproduced by permission of Burnley Borough Council, Lancashire/ The Bridgeman Art Library; plate 2 by permission of Cardiff City Council; plate 3 by permission of the Cheshire Archives; and plate 5 by permission of the National Museums and Galleries of Merseyside.

Preface

This book is about the way in which antiquarians in the mid-nineteenth century rediscovered the Romano-British past. In a detailed study of antiquarian activity in four areas of provincial England and Wales the part this discovery played in social change and contemporary debates is examined.

It looks at the processes through which national identity and Britain's role as an imperial power were influenced and shaped by comparisons with the Roman empire and how alternative models of national origins were developed.

It examines the way in which traditional social organisations appealed to the Roman past as a justification for their authority and used the objects associated with the classical Roman heritage to maintain their standing within society. The established ruling groups sought to maintain their position in the face of challenges posed by new ideas and an increasingly professional middle class. In the ensuing debates, the pre-eminence of textual accounts of the past was questioned and the foundations were laid for the new science of archaeology based on material evidence.

It discusses the importance of artefacts as the means whereby the historical imagination could be stimulated and used to create stories about the past with which individuals and communities could identify. Finally, it looks at the central role of historical remains and objects in debates concerning ownership and preservation.

The book concludes that, at a local level, the evidence of the Roman past was used to maintain traditional social structures and enhance the prestige of the local elite in a process that was relatively unconcerned with national identity. Local antiquarians were willing to use all kinds of evidence, historical, legendary and material to emphasise the importance of their locality and their position within it. In a separate process, aspiring professionals supported each other in their attempts to develop new methods of examining the past that would differentiate them from the amateurs in the provinces.

Acknowledgements

I would like to thank my research supervisors, Catharine Edwards and Neville Morley, for their tolerance and for the understanding with which they guided a stray social scientist around the complexities of the classical world and historical research.

I dedicate this book to Steve, who lived with the Romans and Victorians for many years, organised trips to Roman remains, sorted out frequent computer crises and corrected my grammar. I could not have done it without him.

Virginia Hoselitz
February 2007

Abbreviations

AC   Archaeologia Cambrensis
AJ   Archaeological Journal
Arch.   Archaeologia
GM   Gentlemen's Magazine
ILN   Illustrated London News
JBAA   Journal of the British Archaeological Association
JCAAHS   Journal of the Chester Architectural, Archaeological and
            Historical Society
MM   Monmouthshire Merlin
PCNFC   Proceedings of the Cotteswold Naturalists' Field Club
QR   Quarterly Review
TBGAS   Transactions of the Bristol and Gloucestershire Archaeological
            Society
TEAS   Transactions of the Essex Archaeological Society
VS   Victorian Studies
WGS   Wiltshire and Gloucester Standard

AI   Archaeological Institute
BAA   British Archaeological Association
BAAS   British Association for the Advancement of Science
BFC   Bath Field Club
BL   British Library
CAA   Caerleon Archaeological Association
CAAHS   Chester Architectural, Archaeological and Historical Society
CAS   Colchester Archaeological Society
CNFC   Cotteswold Naturalists' Field Club
EAS   Essex Archaeological Society
WWJ   William Wire journal

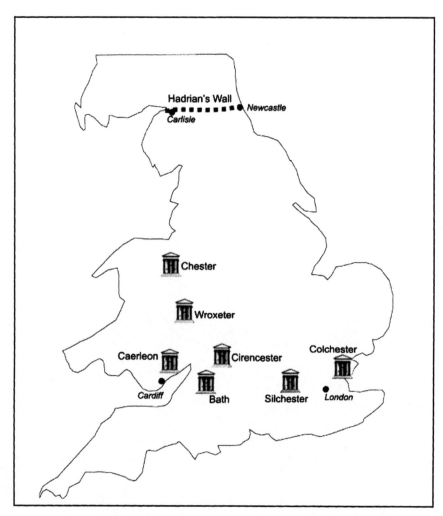

Roman Britain: sites discussed in the text.

Introduction

'To study how England and Englishmen came to be what they are, we must study first, and well, the history of the Roman occupation.'[1]

This comment by a local antiquarian in 1858 highlights the importance attached by many in mid-Victorian Britain to the relationship between the contemporary world and the Roman past. But although there have been a number of studies of responses to the city of Rome and the Roman empire, relatively little attention has been paid to responses to Roman Britain as a separate subject in its own right. This study is about that relationship and the way in which ideas about the Roman past in Britain evolved in response to both intellectual developments and changes in society at large.

There are two main aims. The first is to examine the way in which the supremacy of the classical texts as the main source of evidence for the Roman past was challenged by developments in archaeological activity and in so doing changed the way in which Roman Britain was conceptualised. With a few exceptions, such as the baths in Bath and the villa at Bignor, Roman remains in Britain were fragmentary and scattered and there was certainly nothing to compare with the Pantheon and Coliseum in Rome. However, starting in the early nineteenth century, the demands of industrialisation and urbanisation had involved large-scale excavations which had revealed more and more evidence of the Roman presence in Britain. Previously the lack of material remains had meant that antiquarians were largely dependent on the classical texts for their knowledge of the Roman period and thus their picture of that past was inevitably seen through Roman eyes. According to this view Britain was a small and insignificant island on the edge of the empire; its inhabitants, the ancient Britons, were uncivilised and in servitude and the Romano-British were totally absent. However the extent and nature of the remains that were being discovered enabled antiquarians to create a significantly different picture, one in which Roman Britain was seen as an important place in its own right and the Romano-British period acknowledged as a significant influence on national development.

The second aim is to examine the interaction between antiquarian activity and its social and intellectual context. One method for doing this is through studying the numerous organisations set up to study the past in the Victorian period. In *The amateur and the professional* Philippa Levine used this approach and argues that changes in the way the past was studied were paralleled by the creation of new organisational structures at both a national and a local level. Government-funded institutions were established nationally to

1   E. Cutts, 'Roman remains at Coggeshall', *TEAS* i (1858), 103.

1

further historical research in the universities, the Public Record Office and the British Museum, while at a local level a proliferation of societies was set up specifically to investigate the history of their own locality.[2] Levine argues that 'membership of local societies was largely restricted to those whose social characteristics were similar to those of the ruling elites in their areas and overlapped significantly with the membership of other bodies in their respective communities such as local government and the established church', thus building up a 'security of class interest' with which to maintain the *status quo*.[3]

However successful local antiquarians may have been in shoring up traditional social structures, the focus of their antiquarian activities was limited and largely separate from the activities of those on the national stage. They were increasingly regarded as 'inferior' and were the butt of jokes in magazines such as Punch. The divide between provincial and metropolitan was exacerbated by the attempts of some individuals to distance themselves from the amateurs in the shires and to gain recognition as professionals. There is a considerable body of work suggesting that the developing professions played a major part in assisting the middle class to play a more authoritative role in many aspects in British life. This was especially so in the emerging sciences, such as archaeology and ethnology, the middle-class adherents of which used their specialist knowledge to enhance their authority and distance themselves from the traditional ruling upper class.

In his study of Victorian cultural life, *Contesting cultural authority*, Frank Turner describes the intellectual debates between upholders of traditional values and those seeking new ways of understanding the world. He describes a process whereby 'groups of Victorians attempted to establish foundations for new mental outlooks, to challenge existing authority, to propose themselves as new authorities, or to resist the challenge of new comers and to preserve earlier ideas and values in novel guises and institutional arrangements'.[4] The antiquarian world also became involved in these debates and by focusing on Roman Britain rather than imperial Rome, they brought about a shift in the way both were perceived that reflected subtle changes in contemporary British society in general and in the relative authority of different groups in particular.

Levine's work is concerned with the study of the past as a whole and does not allow an examination of responses to a particular period, in this case Roman Britain and its relations with Rome. However other scholars have suggested alternative methods whereby historical debates and changing attitudes to Roman Britain can be studied. For instance, John Burrow looks at

[2] P. Levine, *The amateur and the professional*, Cambridge 1986. In appendix IV, pp. 182–3, Levine lists fifty-seven such local societies established in England between 1834 and 1886.

[3] Ibid. 4.

[4] F. M. Turner, *Contesting cultural authority: essays in Victorian intellectual life*, Cambridge 1993, p. xi.

the way in which the national past was portrayed in literature and art. His work is based on the premise that 'one of the ways in which a society reveals itself, and its assumptions and beliefs about its own character and destiny, is by its attitudes to and uses of its past'.[5] According to this view the antiquarians' descriptions of the Romans, the Ancient Britons and the Saxons offer one method whereby one can understand how they thought about themselves and the society in which they lived. This is a particularly useful tool when discussing national origins and stereotypes. Turner's analysis of the differing accounts of events in the Roman republic by nineteenth-century historians provides a literary example of the same approach.[6]

A similar premise, although this time based on art, is the basis of Sam Smiles's analysis of the romantic imagination in the first half of the nineteenth century. By tracing changes in the images of the ancient Britons and the Romans, and the relationship between them, and relating these to contemporary early Victorian society, Smiles illustrates some of the intellectual changes of the time. He argues that historians and antiquarians 'were capable of mobilising a sense of historical genealogy, provincial pride and cultural distinction of considerable importance in a world where the pressures of industrialisation were uprooting communities, engendering social mobility and upsetting the settled values vested in the old aristocratic and agricultural orders'.[7]

The case studies

All these insights have been used to inform this investigation into mid-nineteenth century responses to the Romano-British past. However they are very general and concentrate on the work of prominent individuals, what Alan Macfarlane has called 'the historically visible minority'. For instance, Levine's work presents an overall picture of organisational changes across the country and over a considerable period of time (1838–86) with the result that her discussion of local activities and institutions is unavoidably general. Macfarlane suggests that one way of avoiding this bias is to get as detailed a picture as possible of specific groups and that is what this study sets out to do.[8] It was decided to look at antiquarian activity between 1840 and 1860 in four locations where a significant Roman presence had stimulated local interest. Membership and activities are examined using contemporary accounts in

---

5 J. W. Burrow, A Liberal descent: Victorian historians and the English past, Cambridge 1981, 1–2.

6 Turner, Contesting cultural authority, 231–61.

7 S. Smiles, The image of antiquity: ancient Britain and the romantic imagination, New Haven 1994, 24.

8 A. Macfarlane, Reconstructing historical communities, Cambridge 1977, 130. See also A. Briggs, Victorian people, London 1965, 16.

journals, newspaper reports, minutes of meetings and letters in order to assess changing responses to Roman Britain.

Clearly the choice of locations was dictated to a large extent by the availability of local records. Chance plays a significant role in whether or not historical evidence is preserved and can be accessed. Some of it is in the form of official records such as minutes and proceedings which have been published and are therefore in the public domain. But where records were not published, it was serendipity whether they were saved or not and their existence can only be surmised by 'throw-away' remarks in contemporary accounts.[9] It is clear that there was often more going on 'behind the scenes' than the official records would suggest, but it was rarely recorded.[10] The intention was to use the antiquarians' own words as far as possible and in so doing to draw out the interplay of cultural and social factors involved. How was Roman Britain perceived and how much and in what way did those perceptions change? Were these views consistent across the antiquarian world or did they vary according to the location or the social position of those involved? These are the sort of questions that it was hoped a more detailed study might be able to answer.

The four areas chosen were Caerleon in south Wales, Cirencester, Colchester and Chester. Caerleon had been a legionary headquarters; the Caerleon Archaeological Association was established in 1847 by a local industrialist, Edward Lee, and the MP Octavus Morgan, and a museum of Roman antiquities was opened in 1850. Cirencester had been a major urban centre in Roman Britain. Significant mosaic pavements were discovered there in 1849 and raised through the efforts of John Buckman, a lecturer at the local agricultural college. A purpose-built museum was built by the local landowner, Lord Bathhurst. in 1856. Colchester was the original capital of Roman Britain and one of the sites sacked in the Boudican revolt. The Essex Archaeological Society was started in 1850, supplanting a Colchester Society formed a few years earlier by a local watch-maker, William Wire. Finally, Chester was another legionary headquarters; the Chester Architectural, Archaeological and Historical Society was founded in 1849 by two members of the local clergy, the Revd William Massie and the Revd A. Raikes.

All the societies were active at around the same time, in the 1840s and 1850s, and therefore local activity in each case was played out against the same national events. All four were urban sites experiencing a degree of change, although not of the same magnitude as was happening in the metropolitan cities including London. Socially however they were quite disparate. Chester was something of a backwater left behind by the industrial revolution and,

---

[9] W. T. Watkin, for instance, refers to 'Massie's notes, which I have recently inspected', but he does not say where he saw them and they do not now seem to be among the Chester records: *Roman Cheshire: a description of Roman remains in the county of Chester*, Liverpool 1886, 240.

[10] One example, concerning the style chosen for the museum building, is discussed in chapter 4 below.

possibly because of that, a haven for the retired and conservative. Cirencester was another example of a traditional society where local government was still pre-industrial and reliant on the lord of the manor, Lord Bathurst. But despite their apparent conservatism, both towns were struggling with changes which threatened to upset the *status quo*. The struggle for power between traditional authority and liberal dissent in Colchester was carried out publicly in the town's institutions, whereas in Caerleon these battles occurred in the surrounding industrial centres, apparently bypassing the town itself. In terms of this study all four towns had had a prominent position in Roman Britain and this offered the leading townspeople the opportunity to claim glory by association with a revered past. However both Caerleon, and to a lesser extent Colchester, had locally-based historical narratives which were a rich source for alternative stories of the past. It is also notable that although all four towns attracted visitors and commentators from outside, none of the officers and activists took a significant part in national archaeological activity.

Structure

Existing knowledge of Roman Britain is examined in chapter 1, together with some of the main intellectual changes which were beginning to challenge the traditional picture. Two methods of studying the past are identified: the traditional which used all the available evidence to construct a local narrative, and a modern which involved careful examination of artefacts to create an 'objective' classification scheme. The development of new national antiquarian societies is traced and the controversies surrounding the preservation of artefacts outlined, in particular the role of the British Museum in conserving and displaying the national past.

The next chapter is concerned with the way ideas of national identity developed and changed over the period. Fluctuating notions involving different characteristics and appealing to various stories of national origin reveal the extent to which a sense of national identity is a cultural construct created in the present to meet contemporary needs. In particular, Britain's growing role as an imperial power was an increasingly important factor in evaluating the Roman past. The significance of local identification and the history of their locality to the local antiquarians emerge as an important theme, serving to divide even further local activists from national bodies.

Chapter 3 examines the interplay between local social structures and antiquarian activity. The local antiquarian societies appeared to mirror the power relationships within their communities and their view of the Roman past continued to be dominated by the traditional reliance on the classical texts and a love of classical art. Those individuals who wanted to use new ideas and methods, and who were anxious to distance themselves from the dilettante, amateur image of the old-style antiquarians, gathered together and supported one another in their challenging role. The differences between the two groups throw a useful light on the underlying social structures.

The next four chapters outline the particular events and activities in the four areas chosen for detailed examination. They examine the local society, the availability of knowledge about the Roman past and the way in which each area responded to that past. As far as possible these responses are given in the words of the participants and in so doing illustrate some of the major issues discussed in the previous two chapters.

Chapter 8 looks at the meaning attributed to ancient objects and highlights their dual nature, existing both in the here-and-now while at the same time having existed in the past. It is suggested that the dual nature of objects coincides with the two approaches to gathering historical evidence outlined earlier, the here-and-now lending itself to classification and the past role assisting in the development of a rich narrative based on the imagination.

Finally, chapter 9 looks ahead to antiquarian activity in the 1860s and outlines the important developments in excavation techniques which were beginning to herald the new science of archaeology. It evaluates the extent to which local antiquarians were able to adjust their practice and acknowledges that their failure to do so would ultimately leave them in a cultural backwater.

Most of the work on nineteenth century scholars in the historical field refers to either 'historians' or 'archaeologists'. The clearest way of distinguishing between the two groups is by their methodologies, with historians dealing mainly with texts and chronological accounts and archaeologists with artefacts and accounts of systems. However, contemporary descriptions of seventeenth- and eighteenth-century scholars are more likely to refer to 'antiquarians'.[11] Arnaldo Momigliano has described an antiquarian as one 'who is interested in historical facts without being interested in history'.[12] In other words rather than seeking historical explanations through tracking changing events, antiquarians were concerned with amassing and classifying discrete pieces of information and hence were interested above all in the permanent and unchanging objects of everyday life, a procedure which probably attracted many of the more traditional and conservative in local societies. By the middle of the nineteenth century, although their techniques were still rudimentary by modern standards, some antiquarians had begun to develop the methodology that would result in the new science of archaeology and the more specialised they became in their excavating methods and collecting techniques, the less they resembled old-style antiquarians. In this study, however, they will be called antiquarians as it is the term which best describes the activities of most of the provincial workers.

---

[11] See, for instance, S. Piggott, *Ruins in the landscape: essays in antiquarianism*, Edinburgh 1976; *William Stukeley: an eighteenth-century antiquary*, London 1985; and *Ancient Britain and the antiquarian imagination: ideas from the Renaissance to the Regency*, London 1989.

[12] A. Momigliano, 'The rise of antiquarian research', in his *The classical foundations of modern historiography*, Berkeley, CA 1990, 54.

1

Changing Times

Such was the continuing importance of the classical past in cultural and intellectual life in nineteenth-century Britain that any discussion of cultural values and ideas should take Roman influence into account.[1] Indeed, according to Frank Turner, 'Victorian classicism is a topic which held a centrality for the intellectual experience for the educated Victorian elite that it is difficult for scholars at the end of the twentieth century even to begin to comprehend.'[2] Some idea of the hold that the classical past had traditionally exerted on educated men can be gauged from their portraits, such as that of Charles Townley in his library painted by Zohan Zoffany in 1783 (see plate 1). Townley chose to be portrayed surrounded by his collection of beautiful objects from the ancient civilisations of Greece and Rome. The portrait conveys the impression of a man of wealth and taste, whose seriousness as a collector is demonstrated by his employment of the well-known Pierre François d'Hancarville to catalogue his collection.[3] It is a good example of the way in which ownership of classical antiquities could be used to create a social message. To men such as Townley the classical texts were still sacrosanct and the works of Greece and Roman art were the pinnacle of artistic endeavour.

However, despite the powerful authority that the classical past continued to exert well into the nineteenth century, its pre-eminent position was beginning to be challenged by alternative narratives. For instance myths and legends appeared to offer a non-classical framework within which the past and its relevance to contemporary changes could be understood. One way in which they could be studied was through philology which provided intellectual force to what Momigliano has described as 'the desire to penetrate below the Roman surface of Western Europe'.[4] Using the newly developed skills of philology, German scholars such as Friedrich Wolfe argued that Homer's *Iliad* and *Odyssey* were composed of a series of ancient oral tales collected together

---

1   See N. Vance, *The persistence of Rome: the Victorians and ancient Rome*, London 1997; C. Edwards, 'Translating empire? Macaulay's Rome', in C. Edwards (ed.), *Roman presences*, Cambridge 1999; and Turner, *Contesting cultural authority*, pt iii.
2   Turner, *Contesting cultural authority*, 284.
3   The baron d'Hancarville had been responsible for cataloguing Sir William Hamilton's Greek vase collection. It was in the same spirit that a speaker at the BAA conference told his audience that 'There could be no more divine pleasure on earth to the man of genius and cultivated understanding than to hear the drama of Sophocles recited by the side of the Apollo or the Laocoon': presidential address, *JBAA* iv (1848), 289.
4   A. Momigliano, 'Eighteenth-century prelude to Mr Gibbon', in *Storia della storiografia metodo storico*, Rome 1975, 257.

and only written down over hundreds of years. The German scholar Barthold Niebuhr used these arguments to support his view that Livy's account of early Rome, previously assumed to be based on contemporary accounts, was also in fact constructed from oral tradition.[5] Niebuhr's theories probably owed some of their appeal to the fact that they seemed to support, and therefore justify, the new interest in epic and ballad. The British historian Edward Freeman described Niebuhr's work as 'acting like a spell ... The tale which our fathers had believed on the authority of Livy sank to the level of a myth, the invention of a poet, the exaggeration of a family panegyrist'.[6] Thomas Arnold was so impressed by Niebuhr's ideas that he wrote his *History of Rome* (1838–43) to ensure that his 'discoveries and remarkable wisdom might best be known to English readers'.[7] Thomas Macaulay's response to these new ideas was to reverse the process by which legends had been transformed into history by recreating some of the stories in Livy back into poetry in *Lays of ancient Rome* (1842).[8]

Although Niebuhr was influential among leading scholars, there are no references to his work by the antiquarians in my studies. It must therefore be supposed that they experienced his ideas at second hand through the novels of Walter Scott and the histories of Thomas Arnold.[9] Certainly by the middle of the century the idea that there were several kinds of historical evidence was becoming more acceptable. The classical archaeologist Charles Newton argued that 'every peasantry has its songs and mythic legends, its rude oral narrative of real events, blended with its superstitions. Archaeology rescues these from oblivion by making them a part of printed literature. It is thus that Walter Scott has collected the minstrelsy of the Scottish border and Grimm the traditions of Germany'.[10] The antiquarian Thomas Wright described the process through which this could happen:

[5] In Germany scholars such as Jacob Grimm, used similar arguments to justify studying early folk tales in a search for a German past free of Roman influence: S. Marchand, *Down from Olympus: archaeology and philhellenism in Germany, 1750–1970*, Princeton 1996, 154–73.
[6] E. Freeman, review of Mommsen's 'History of Rome', *National Review* (Apr. 1859), cited in W. R. W. Stephens, *Life and letters of E. A. Freeman*, London 1895, 202.
[7] T. Arnold, *History of Rome*, 1st edn, London 1838–43; 5th edn, London 1848, p. vii.
[8] Lord Macaulay gives a *resumé* of the debate on the mythical basis of Livy and refers to Scott as 'the great restorer of our ballad-poetry': *The lays of ancient Rome*, London 1842, 23. For Scott's influence on Arnold and Macaulay see H. Trevor-Roper, *The romantic movement and the study of history*, London 1969, and Edwards, *Roman presences*, 70–88.
[9] The extent of Niebuhr's influence can be gathered from such references as this from W. Smith (ed.), *Dictionary of antiquities*, London 1843: 'The history and political relations of the nations of antiquity have been placed in an entirely different light since the publication of Niebuhr's *Roman history*' (p. vii).
[10] C. Newton, 'On the study of archaeology', *AJ* viii (1851), 3. Newton worked at the British Museum and regarded himself as an historian rather than an archaeologist. He was responsible for excavating at Halicarnassus and returning the marbles he found there to the British Museum; all of which was funded by the British tax-payer: B. F. Cook, 'British

> A vast mass of popular fables, much of it of a mythical character and romances, floated during the middle ages from country to country and from mouth to mouth and these frequently taking a colouring from place and circumstance become located, and being fixed upon individuals, were handed down to us as historical facts.[11]

The expanded view of acceptable historical evidence meant that the classical past could be seen in a rather different light. Whereas in the past it had been seen as almost ahistorical, and more relevant to contemporary Britain than the intervening years, the history of Roman Britain could now be studied as just one period among many others in a continuing national history. This way of looking at the past set historians free to study the Romans with the new skills of archaeology and philology. It also allowed them to evaluate the contribution of other periods and groups to the British past: a factor that would become increasingly important in debates about English identity later in the century.

The nature of historical evidence and changes in the way the past was perceived are clearly of central importance to a study of the reception and influence of historical studies on contemporary culture. However, other intellectual developments had also begun to question some of the basic ideas underpinning the nature of the world and the place of man within that world. For instance, German scholars were looking at the evidence for the authenticity of the biblical accounts. Translations of their work were published in Britain from the 1820s and provoked both a furious reaction and considerable anxiety. At the same time two British books, Charles Lyell's *Principles of geology* (1830–3) and the anonymous *Vestiges of the natural history of creation* (1844),[12] had used the structure of rocks and fossil evidence in such a way as to throw doubt on the biblical accounts of creation. Their implied rejection of these accounts, and the suggestion that the time scales involved in geology were infinitely longer than had traditionally been supposed, called into question the very foundations of belief.[13] Charles Darwin's *Origin of species* (1859) appeared to provide evidence that species transmuted as a result of natural selection and not as a result of a pre-ordained plan of the Almighty. Darwin was careful to avoid the implications of his findings for human origins, but evidence of very early human remains discovered by Jacques Boucher de Perthes in Abbeville seemed to suggest that his ideas applied to man as well

archaeologists in the Aegean', in V. Brand (ed.), *The study of the past in the Victorian age*, Oxford 1998, 139–55.

11 T. Wright, 'Antiquarianism in England', *JBAA* iv (1848), 298.

12 The author was the Edinburgh publisher, Robert Chambers: J. A. Secord, *Victorian sensation: the extraordinary publication, reception and secret authorship of Vestiges of the natural history of creation*, Chicago 2000. Secord estimates that by 1860, 23,750 copies had been published in ten editions, a large sale for non-fiction at the time.

13 Sir Charles Lyell (1797–1875) was a wealthy lawyer turned geologist. His book was hugely influential. It disputed the cataclysmic origins of the earth and suggested that it had developed as the result of slow changes that were continuing. Darwin took Lyell's first volume on his travels on the *Beagle* and it influenced his ideas on evolution. If Lyell were correct, 4004 BCE, the date traditionally accepted as the date of creation, would have to be rejected.

as animals.[14] The new ideas meant that antiquarians would have to rethink their chronology of prehistoric human development and find alternative techniques for doing so. The implications were challenging, particularly for those who looked to the past for reassurance and evidence of continuity. The classical texts had appeared to offer an established framework of knowledge upon which antiquarians, who were interested in the Romano-British past, could rely. But the classical accounts contained only sparse references to Britain and their reliability as historical evidence was being questioned by some scholars.

Sources of knowledge

Although there are a large number of Roman texts most of them have little to say about Roman Britain. First of those that have is Caesar's account of his British campaigns in *The gallic wars* which includes a description of the native population a hundred years before the conquest. But, as Thomas Wright pointed out, such was the lack of information that 'most of the descriptions found in subsequent writers are little more than a repetition of the scanty information given by Caesar who was himself only acquainted with the south eastern part of the island'.[15] There is a general account of the Claudian conquest and expansion after the invasion in CE 43 in Tacitus' *Histories* and *Agricola*. Dio Cassius also describes the invasion and gives a detailed account of the Boudican revolt in CE 60. Dio and Herodian provide accounts of the campaigns of Septimius Severus in Caledonia and the north in the third century CE. But apart from these, references to Britain are scattered and always incidental to the main content, the history of Rome itself. Britain is seen through Roman eyes and the accounts are written to serve the purposes of Romans at the heart of the empire.[16]

Evidence of a different sort was provided in surviving military and administrative papers, such as the *Antonine itinerary*, a third-century military road book, and the *Notitia dignitatum*, a list of the chief military and civil dignitaries, compiled in CE 408. In his book *The Roman wall* (1851), the clergyman John Collingwood Bruce demonstrated the way such sources were used:

> When inscribed stones are found, bearing the name of a cohort mentioned in the Notitia, the inference is natural that, in most cases at least, the Imperial Notitia will furnish us with a key to the ancient designation of

14 The results of the French excavations were reported in 1859 to the Society of Antiquaries by John Evans. Darwin discussed human evolution in *The descent of man* (1871).
15 T. Wright, *The Celt, the Roman and the Saxon*, London 1852, 43.
16 David Braund, for example, describes Caesar's account of his campaigns as a 'polemical work of self justification as Caesar was seeking a place in Roman history': *Ruling Roman Britain: kings, queens, governors and emperors from Julius Caesar to Agricola*, London 1996, 6. Tacitus is thought to have written *Agricola*, a biography of his father-in-law, to defend his name against imperial criticism by comparing the bravery of 'barbarians' with the decadence of Roman leaders: R. Mellor, *The Roman historians*, London 1999, 79–80.

the station. The argument becomes irresistible, when, in several successive instances, the designations thus obtained correspond exactly with the order of the places as given in the Notitia.[17]

By using the Notitia, antiquarians were able to deduce that the Second Augustans had been withdrawn from the fortress at Caerleon before CE 408 and was stationed on the Saxon Shore in Kent. It was from such fragmentary and scattered references that the antiquarians attempted to build up a picture of Roman Britain.

Often the only real evidence was to be found in the remains of buildings and, in particular, the inscriptions and legionary marks they contained. Bruce based his whole account of Hadrian's Wall on such evidence: 'The plan adopted has been to make the Romans tell their own story. Scarcely a single statement is brought forward which is not directly deduced from inscriptions found upon the wall.'[18] The legionary marks that the Roman legions used as their 'symbol' on any building work they undertook enabled the antiquarians to trace the movements of the various legions. For instance the Twentieth Legion had been based in Colchester prior to the revolt in CE 61, but tiles inscribed with its name had been found along Hadrian's Wall and these had been used as evidence that for some time in the second century the legion was posted on the northern frontier.[19] The potential problem of too great a reliance on such evidence was pointed out by the antiquarian Charles Wellbeloved when he described a recently discovered Roman inscription in York: 'But, curious and interesting as it is … we can borrow no light or assistance from it in relation to the general state of Roman Britain. It relates one transaction only, limited to one Roman station; and the information it affords, even with respect to that, is imperfect.'[20] The controversies led the leading Roman antiquarian, Charles Roach Smith, to remark that 'in the absence of written history, they furnish acceptable, if not copious and connected information'.[21]

Another source of information was the accounts written after the departure of the legions in the fifth century. The first of these, widely quoted by Victorian antiquarians, was De excidio written by the British monk Gildas in the middle of the sixth century. He describes the final years of Roman rule, but stresses that he had no access to a general history of Roman Britain because no such thing existed and therefore he had to rely on oral evidence. Bede relied heavily on Gildas when he wrote his account a century later.[22]

17 J. C. Bruce, The Roman wall, London 1851, 61. Bruce was the main populariser of the Roman remains along the wall.
18 Ibid. p. v.
19 Ibid. 247.
20 C. Wellbeloved, 'Roman inscriptions found at York', GM xxxiii (1855), 296. Charles Wellbeloved was Curator of Antiquities at the Yorkshire Philosophical Society's museum at York.
21 C. Roach Smith, 'Notes on Caerwent and Caerleon', JBAA iv (1848), 262.
22 For Gildas see E. A. Thompson, 'Gildas and the history of Britain', Britannia x (1979),

Both Gildas and Bede were used as sources of information by medieval chron-
iclers such as Geoffrey of Monmouth and Richard of Cirencester, but whereas
eighteenth-century antiquarians had regarded these chronicles as reliable, by
the middle of the nineteenth century their reliability was beginning to be
questioned on the basis of internal evidence of forgery.[23]

How much local antiquarians knew, or wanted to know, about the
new ideas is not clear. Books and journals contain references that suggest
some scepticism about the nature of the evidence, particularly non-Roman
evidence. For instance, in 1801 William Coxe referred to Geoffrey's *History
of the kings of Britain* as a 'romance', and in 1846 Thomas Wright thought
that 'the account of Bede can hardly be looked upon as better than a fable'.[24]
Others were less willing to relinquish the familiar and long-trusted texts.
The Kent antiquarian, Beale Poste, defended Richard, 'whose work has been
considered by some of our first historians and antiquaries so highly important
to illustrate the early history of Britain'.[25] Poste was also involved in a dispute
with the historian Thomas Wakeman concerning the authenticity or otherwise of the *Chronicle of Tysilio*, used as evidence by Geoffrey of Monmouth.
Both authors agreed that Geoffrey had used the text of the chronicle, but
whereas Poste believed the original to be genuine, Wakeman believed it was
a 'sheer pretence' on Geoffrey's part and 'could have been written at any
subsequent time between 940 and the present'.[26]

There is little evidence of the same scepticism regarding the Roman histories. It is possible that the post-Roman accounts were seen as less reliable
than the classical texts because, Niebuhr notwithstanding, many antiquarians still believed the Roman texts to be contemporary accounts and there-

203–15. For more general Celtic sources for the Roman period see D. N. Dumville, 'Sub
Roman Britain: history and legend', *History* lxii (1977), 173–90.
[23] Geoffrey of Monmouth's *History of the kings of Britain* (1135) claimed to be a Latin
translation of an early English text. In T. D. Kendrick's opinion it was 'the most significant book in the history of British antiquities': *British antiquity*, London 1950. Richard
of Cirencester's account appeared in 1747, apparently discovered by Charles Bertram.
Although no original document was ever produced, Bertram persuaded the antiquarian
William Stukeley that it was genuine and Stukeley championed it in Britain. In 1838 the
English History Society chose to reject it from amongst the received materials of English
history: W. Gunner, 'Report on Roman period in Hampshire', *AJ* iii (1846), 161. Bernard
Woodward, librarian at Windsor Castle, finally exposed it as an eighteenth-century
forgery: 'A literary forgery: Richard of Cirencester's tractate on Britiain', *GM* n.s. i. 301.
See Piggott, *William Stukeley*, 126–38. Although discredited, the information in both
Geoffrey and Richard continued to influence popular accounts of Roman Britain.
[24] W. Coxe, *A historical tour through Monmouthshire*, 1st edn, Brecon 1801, 243; T. Wright,
'On recent discoveries of Anglo-Saxon antiquities', *JBAA* ii (1846), 50.
[25] B. Poste, 'Richard of Cirencester', *GM* xxvii (1847), 377. Poste suggested that Richard's account could have been based on a text by Tacitus in a Constantinople library,
subsequently lost.
[26] T. Wakeman, 'Notes on the territories of Vortigern and the Chronicle of Tyssilio',
JBAA x (1854), 367. Poste did concede that Geoffrey had introduced 'many romancing
narratives and a whole book of prophesy ... in short he supplies a specimen of a twelfth-
century editor' (p. 231).

fore more reliable. But it is also possible that challenging the familiar classical texts required a greater leap of faith than many antiquarians were willing to take. Whatever learned scholars had to say about the origins and early history of Rome, to men who had spent years studying these works and who were accustomed to regarding them as examples of the high point of civilisation, such questioning must often have appeared as heretical.

If the reliability of the texts was challenged, the antiquarians had to use other methods to discover Roman Britain.

Old views challenged

In 1850 the soldier and antiquarian Richard Westmacott described the *virtuosi* of the past as 'accumulating scraps of antiquity, without selection, order or application ... dilettantism without definite object ... a better class in short, of curiosity shops'. But changes in contemporary archaeology meant that it 'may almost lay claim to be a science'.[27] It is clear that Westmacott saw his own activities as significantly different from those of Charles Townley and his fellow *virtuosi*. They were different partly because, unlike the connoisseurs who collected beautiful objects from foreign civilisations, nineteenth-century antiquarians were interested in the British past. Therefore they were forced to deal in the available evidence of that past which, apart from the scanty textual references, was almost entirely composed of mundane artefacts and crumbling material remains.

In the seventeenth century natural scientists had carried out their work primarily through observation and with very little analysis.[28] By the nineteenth century antiquarians realised that facts alone were not enough and that in order to gain understanding it was necessary to create a classification system that would suggest working hypotheses. As the historian John Kemble explained, 'It is necessary to collect in a very different manner and to look for answers to questions which hitherto no one had thought of putting ... Comparison and combination, these were the two layers by which the inert mass of facts was to be moved.'[29] The relative ignorance of pre-historic and non-literate societies is evident in John Akerman's *Archaeological index* (1848), which acknowledged that 'Celtic, Roman and Anglo Saxon objects are confounded with each other in a manner calculated to embarrass and

[27] R. W. Westmacott, 'Progress of archaeology', AJ vii (1850), 1–7. The article was signed 'R. W. (Jun)'. Westmacott did some excavating whilst in the Crimea as a soldier. His father, the sculptor Richard Westmacott, was responsible for the old-fashioned displays in the British Museum.

[28] See Piggott, *Ancient Britain*, 7, 24.

[29] J. M. Kemble, 'Notices of archaeological publications', AJ xii (1855), 297. Kemble was the leading Saxon scholar of the time; his book, *The Saxons in England: a history of the English commonwealth until the Norman conquest*, was published in 1849. He had also been responsible for the publication of about 1,500 Saxon documents in the *Codex diplomaticus* (1839–48).

perplex the archaeological student.'[30] But contemporary knowledge of the pre-historic societies was so limited that he grouped together all pre-Roman artefacts as 'Celtic'.

The search for more detailed observations and better empirical evidence took two forms, neither of them new. First there were the attempts to categorise historical objects as in the work of Johann Winckelmann, the French antiquarian Anne Claude Francois de Caylus and the nineteenth-century Danish archaeologists. Second were the detailed topographical accounts of local historians, whose methods were based upon those of the sixteenth-century antiquary William Camden.

Classification systems

Johann Winckelmann (1717–68) was librarian to Cardinal Alessandro Albani in Rome. He realised that many of the best statues were in fact Roman copies of Greek originals. His *History of ancient art* (1764) depicted the art of ancient Greece as developing and changing through a series of styles, which could be related to specific historical periods. His methods consisted of a very close examination of many individual pieces, which were then used to draw conclusions about the society in which they had been produced. It was this method of working that was unique for the time. His identification of one style of Greek art in the fifth century BCE as the 'sublime' was to have a profound effect on later archaeologists and historians. He argued that the art produced during this sublime period represented the highest possible aesthetic development and that all art produced since was, by definition, inferior. Winckelmann had developed both a new technique for historical dating and a theory of art history which, by suggesting an inevitable decline from an ultimate high point, was based on a value judgement that would continue to be influential in the defining of aesthetic taste. It would also continue to influence the arrangement of collections and museums well into the nineteenth century.[31]

Winckelmann's methods involved detailed comparison to achieve classification, but only of certain objects deemed to be works of art. In contrast the comte de Caylus (1692–1765) formed a collection of all sorts of objects, of all ages and from many countries that he described and illustrated in great detail. The results were published in the seven volumes of his *Recueil d'antiquities* (1752–68). De Caylus declared that he was not a collector: 'My taste for the arts has not led me to any desire for possession ... Antiquities are there for the extension of knowledge. They explain the various usages, they shed light

---

[30] J. Y. Akerman, *An archaeological index*, London 1848, preface. Akerman (1806–73) had founded the *Numismatic Journal* in 1836 and became secretary of the London Society of Antiquaries in 1853.

[31] Richard Westmacott's arrangement of the classical sculptures in the British Museum was based on Winckelmann's ideas.

upon the obscure or little known makers.'[32] He believed that the knowledge acquired through a careful examination of objects would enable the antiquarian to establish categories through which conclusions about the different groups or cultures of origin could be drawn. Although in many ways Winckelmann and de Caylus used similar methods, there were significant differences between them. Unlike Winckelmann, de Caylus made no value judgements and included all artefacts however menial. Nor did he suggest any 'supreme' point, choosing instead to follow the changes as they developed. His insistence that material evidence was as useful to the scholar as the written word released antiquarians from their potentially restricting reliance on the classical texts. This was to be particularly important for the interpretation of the remains of pre-historic man.

Since the eighteenth century a succession of Danish archaeologists had unearthed a rich reserve of early artefacts that had been preserved in peat bogs. But without any written records, such as existed in those parts of Europe that had been a part of the Roman empire, they had difficulties in explaining their discoveries. A Danish professor explained the problem: 'Everything which has come to us from heathendom is wrapped in a thick fog; it belongs to a space of time which we cannot measure. We know that it is older than Christendom, but whether by a couple of years or a couple of centuries or even by more than a millennium, we can do no more than guess.'[33]

In 1816 Christian Thomsen, the curator of the national museum in Copenhagen, developed a classification system based on the material from which the artefacts were made, and which he claimed represented a chronological sequence of development. His theory became known as the three ages of antiquities, namely stone, bronze and iron, and, once again, it was based on a minute observation of many artefacts and the detection of fine differences. Thomsen arranged the collections according to his scheme and in 1836 produced a guidebook to the displays.[34] Thomsen's assistant and successor as curator was Jens Worsaae, who wrote what came to be regarded as the first modern book on archaeology. He claimed that 'as soon as it was once pointed out that the whole of these antiquities could by no means be referred to one and the same period, people began to see more clearly the differences between them'.[35] Worsaae visited Britain several times in the 1850s and corresponded

---

32 A. C. F. de Caylus, *Recueil d'antiquities egyptiennes, etrusques, grecques, romaines et gauloises*, ii (1753), cited in A. Schnapp, *The discovery of the past*, London 1993, 240.

33 R. Nyerup, *Oversyn over faedrelandets mindesmaerker fra oldtiden*, Copenhagen 1806, cited in G. Daniel, *The origins and growth of archaeology*, London 1967, 91.

34 C. Thomsen, *Kortfattet udsigt over mindesmaerker oldsager fra nordens fortid*, Copenhagen 1836, trans. Francis Egerton, 1st earl of Ellesmere, as *A guide to northern antiquities* (London 1848). The translation was widely reviewed in the British archaeological press.

35 J. Worsaae, *Danmarks oldtid oplyst oldsager og gravhoie*, Copenhagen 1843, trans. by W. T. Thoms as *The primeval antiquities of Denmark*, London 1849, cited in Daniel, *Origins and growth of archaeology*, 99–100. Some British antiquarians were unconvinced. Thomas Wright criticised the system in *Celt, Roman and Saxon*, pp. vi–viii, and Kemble was also

15

regularly with Charles Roach Smith and so it is reasonable to suppose that his ideas were familiar to at least some British antiquarians. Again it is possible to see similarities between the methods of the Danish archaeologists and those of de Caylus and Winckelmann. They all used close observations to distinguish a range of categories into which artefacts could be divided. The difference between them lay in the Danes' exclusive reliance on objects rather than texts and Winckelmann's concentration on selected artefacts.

Topographical accounts

Other nineteenth-century antiquarians gathered together and described all that was known about a specific locality. The precedent had been set by William Camden (1551–1623), whose *Britannia*, published in Latin in 1586, provided the first detailed account of the antiquities of Britain. The 1695 edition, translated into English and edited by Edmund Gibson, became the standard text to which all future writers referred. *Britannia* was followed by a steady flow of publications, some national and others regional, that exemplify the close association which was seen to exist between the remnants of antiquity and features of the natural world such as fossils and plants. For instance, Edward Lhwyd, who was responsible for the Welsh chapters of Gibson's edition of *Britannia*, was primarily regarded as an expert on fossils, and the botanist Richard Plott apparently saw no incongruity in including descriptions and illustrations of antiquities in his *Natural history of Staffordshire* (1686). Both Lhwyd and Plott were curators of the Ashmolean Museum in Oxford and members of the Royal Society, the foremost scientific body of the time.[36]

In the eighteenth century William Stukeley was another scientist with antiquarian interests. Victorian antiquarians used his *Itinerarium curiosum* (1724) as a guide to the monuments and remains still standing in the previous century. Detailed maps of the whole country produced by the newly created Ordnance Survey were also a useful source of information. The director-general of the new body, William Roy, wrote *The military antiquities of the Romans in north Britain* (1773), widely consulted by Victorian antiquarians.[37] These books were followed by a large number of local surveys, in which

---

opposed. One effect of the three-age system was to place the existence of early man further back than had been imagined and before any written accounts were available.

[36] This was an association that continued well into the nineteenth century, as the names of some of the newly-formed archaeological societies indicate: Shropshire and North Wales Natural History and Antiquarian Society (1835); Somerset Archaeological and Natural History Society (1849); Suffolk Institute of Natural History and Archaeology (1848) and Wiltshire Archaeological and Natural History Society (1853) to name but a few.

[37] R. Hingley, *Roman officers and English gentlemen: the imperial origins of Roman archaeology*, London 2000, 39–40.

smaller areas were described in meticulous detail.[38] The men who compiled these surveys were 'the true godfathers'[39] of the Victorian antiquarians who formed the backbone of the local archaeological societies in the nineteenth century. It was this tradition that informed the work of the local antiquarians in this study.

The way in which one Victorian archaeologist used these surveys as a starting point for his own investigations is to be seen in the work of Richard Neville, 4th Lord Braybrooke, in Great Chesterford in Essex. He used Stukeley's map of the site 'though I believe Dr. Stukeley, who wrote in 1719, is no longer considered an authority to be depended upon'. Nevertheless he felt able to use the map because 'I have verified it for myself'.[40] The temple marked on Stukeley's map as Temple Umbra, Neville took to be the vestige of a fort described by another antiquarian, John Horsley, in *Britannia romana* (1732). Horsley believed that the fort had been built by the Romans and then occupied by the Saxons. When Neville excavated the 'ghost' of a temple, 'I hoped to raise up a substantial body from the ruins and present it as the fort or building indicated by Horsley'.[41] He found many artefacts including 'a fine shallow red patera, intended doubtless to catch the blood of victims slain on the altar'. This conclusion was based on a reference in the *Aeneid* to 'Aeneas applying them in this manner while engaged with a priestess in offering sacrifice'.[42]

Neville's work is a good example of the way in which Victorian antiquarians used a variety of sources including topographical accounts and classical texts. He relied on Stukeley's map, originally drawn to trace the fifth route in the Roman *Antonine itinerary*, to which he added his own finds. But although he appears to have been content to use older antiquarian references concerning the location and importance of the site, he turned to the classical texts to inform the results of his own excavation. He also used his imagination: 'I have amused myself with re-peopling the town and country with their former occupants. In an instant the walls rise from their ruins; once more are they thronged by the garrison, who parade the streets, resounding with the martial hum of Roman legions.'[43] When Roach Smith visited the site in 1848, he clearly felt that the finds did not justify Neville's vivid description:

[38] See, for instance, P. Morant, *History of Colchester*, Colchester 1748; Coxe, *Monmouthshire*; and G. Ormerod, *History of Cheshire*, Chester 1819.

[39] The term 'godfather' was used by Richard Neville in *Sepulchra exposita* (Saffron Walden 1848) to describe his relationship with the antiquarian Gage Rockwood.

[40] Idem, *Antiqua explorata*, Saffron Walden 1847, 10. Presumably Neville considered Stukeley's evidence to be unreliable because of his obsession with the Druids later in his career: Piggott, *William Stukeley*.

[41] Neville, *Antiqua explorata*, 39.

[42] Ibid.

[43] Ibid. 48. Roach Smith quoted this passage in his *Retrospections: social and archaeological*, London 1883–91, ii. 49–50. He commented that, 'the expressions "the garrison" and "Roman legions" are fanciful as applied to Roman Chesterford which was never a prominent military station'.

'Nothing was discovered that could possibly determine the original destination of the edifice, and we are only justified in styling it a temple, because
from its somewhat isolated position and the absence of all domestic features,
it would appear to have been devoted to some public purpose.'[44] When Roach
Smith considered the internal layout of the building, he felt it was misleading
to use Virgil's description because, 'they apply generally to a high class of
buildings, something remarkable even in Italy'.

Neville personifies the difficulty of attempting to categorise antiquarians
as either *virtuosi* or archaeologists. He was a wealthy, leisured member of the
upper class who owned a landed estate at Audley End which he described
proprietarily as 'my own hunting ground'.[45] His museum was composed of
an eclectic mixture that in some ways resembled 'a curiosity shop'.[46] He was
also a serious collector of, among other things, jewellery. However there was
a side to Neville's activities that distanced him from the *virtuosi*. He was a
serious, careful excavator who related the artefacts to the features of the landscape and made his results available through a series of articles and books. In
Sepulchra exposita (1848) he declared that 'The great object of all antiquarian
research is the accumulation of a number of authenticated occurrences which
by corroborating one another when collected and compared, establish data by
which may be determined certain historical facts.'[47] He emphasised the need
to 'note at the time the nature of whatever relics may be discovered, their
relative positions and most particularly their condition ... accuracy in all
these minutiae cannot be too strictly enforced and many little circumstances
which appear trifling and comparatively useless, will be found afterwards most
valuable in the mass of evidence'.[48] So although he appeared to fit the *virtuoso*
role in social terms, by inclination and method Neville chose to align himself
with the new breed of scientific archaeologists. His involvement with the
archaeological societies that were such a feature of the Victorian scene is
further evidence of this dual nature.[49]

[44] Idem, 'Discoveries at Ickleton and Great Chesterford', *JBAA* iv (1848), 367.
[45] Neville, *Sepulchra exposita*, 32.
[46] Apart from antiquities, it also contained a collection of stuffed birds. An 1845 water-
colour of the museum shows the museum cases in a room with a 'highly domestic decorative scheme, complete with wallpaper, carpet and curtains, making the overall impression
one of pleasing idiosyncrasy': K. Jeffrey (ed.), *Audley End*, London 1997, 21.
[47] Neville, *Sepulchra exposita*, 30.
[48] Ibid. 31. The excavating techniques of some leading antiquarians were frequently slip-
shod. For instance, in 1842, the excavations of Albert Conyngham and John Akerman
were criticised as 'rather recklessly conducted, and but insufficient notes were taken of
the relics in situ': Anon., 'Archaeological notices and antiquarian intelligence', *JBAA* xii
(1856), 103. Albert Conyngham was the first president of the BAA.
[49] Neville was the second president of the Essex Society and a vice-chairman of the
Archaeological Institute. He played an important part in the institute's campaign to
change the laws concerning treasure trove in the 1850s.

The archaeological societies

From the early years of the nineteenth century, industrial development and urbanisation had led to a boom in construction throughout the country. New housing, sewage systems and above all the development of the railway network, had meant excavating on an unprecedented scale. As a result foundations of ancient buildings and huge numbers of artefacts were unearthed, many of them Roman.[50] But just as the wealth and variety of the Romano-British heritage was being revealed, it was immediately put at risk by building activities which forged ahead regardless of what lay below. One particularly notorious example was the fate of the Roman theatre in St Albans (Roman Verulamium), where lack of funds and pressure from developers meant that a promising site was covered over.[51] Roman city walls, such as those in York, Colchester and Chester, were especially vulnerable, as expanding populations led to the need for more land for housing. Artefacts were either destroyed or sold to dealers and collectors and their connection with the site lost. All this was not new: Roman remains had always been used as a cheap supply of dressed stone and many 'cabinets of curiosities' contained objects found by chance. What had changed was the scale of the destruction and the anger among some interested individuals that more was not being done to preserve the relics of the nation's past.[52]

One analysis of the dangers posed to antiquities appeared in *Archaeologia Cambrensis* in 1846. The author deplored the failure of the British government to aid preservation of national monuments and hoped that the day would come when 'The needless and wanton destruction or mutilation of any ancient monument shall be considered as a public offence.' He cited the French government as an example of good practice and was particularly impressed by French action in buying the Celtic monument at Carnac to prevent the local people using it as a quarry. He identified four types of destroyers. First were 'needy or tasteless owners of property'. Second were 'government and municipal corporations', whom he characterised as 'piti-

---

[50] Excavations for the railway in York, for example, in 1837 'exposed remains of extensive Roman baths and buildings and revealed part of a large cemetery': *York Museum handbook*, 8th edn, York 1891, p. iv.

[51] The St Albans Architectural and Archaeological Society was founded in 1845 to study local churches, but switched its interest to the Roman remains when R. Grove Lowe found evidence of Roman Verulamium. The excavations were reported in the *ILN* on 29 January 1848. The theatre was thought to be the only example in Britain and therefore its loss prompted a stronger reaction than most. According to Thomas Wright the site was destroyed by a 'Freehold Land Society' whose object was 'to make small freehold estates, to create voters, to influence the county elections': 'Wanderings of an antiquarian', GM xxxviii (1852), 253.

[52] The government's destruction of nearly twenty miles of Hadrian's Wall to construct the road between Newcastle and Carlisle was described as a 'sweeping and monstrous act of vandalism': C. Roach Smith, *Collectanea antiqua: etchings and notices of ancient remains, illustrations of the habits, customs and history of the past ages*, London 1848–80, ii. 179.

less and ruthless monsters'. Third were 'public companies, whether railroads, canals or any other similar works'. Finally there were 'the beautifiers, the repairers and the restorers ... who have done their full proportion of mischief to the land'. And of these he saw the companies as the 'most selfish and most impudently clamorous'.[53]

Chief among those pressing for change was Charles Roach Smith (1807–90). Too poor to go to university, he had trained as a chemist. In his spare time he started to collect Roman coins, an interest that came to include all things Roman. From his shop in the city of London he kept a vigilant eye on new developments and set up a museum in his own home to safeguard the artefacts he had salvaged. He campaigned to persuade the London Corporation to take a more proactive role in preserving ancient relics, arguing that the destruction was made worse by the lack of a co-ordinated response by the authorities and by the ignorance of the workmen. By visiting building sites regularly and offering to pay the labourers for finds, he had amassed a large collection that he called his 'London Museum of Antiquities'.[54] He became the leading figure in attempts to persuade government to protect ancient remains and travelled the length and breadth of the country, recording new discoveries and forming an informal network of connections through which the antiquarian community could be kept informed. He published the results of his enquiries in six volumes of *Collectanea antiqua* (1843–80) which remains an invaluable guide to contemporary Victorian archaeology.[55]

The destruction, and the unwillingness of the London Society of Antiquaries to act more positively, played a large part in the decision to set up an alternative national organisation.[56] The British Archaeological Association was founded in 1843 to encourage 'intelligent researches into British antiquities and vigilant care for their preservation'.[57] Roach Smith was among the founding members, along with his friend, Thomas Wright, and Albert Way. Wright too was from a poor background and a wealthy family friend paid

---

[53] H. Longueville Jones, 'On the study and preservation of national antiquities', AC i (1846), 3–10. Longueville Jones was one of the editors of the *Archaeologia Cambrensis*.

[54] The London Corporation took him to court, accused of receiving stolen goods. He won his case but the Corporation continued to harass him and refused to renew the lease on his shop.

[55] For more on Roach Smith see M. Rhodes, 'Some aspects of the contribution to British archaeology of Charles Roach Smith, 1806–1890', unpubl. PhD diss. London 1993. G. R. Gomme, the editor of the *Gentleman's Magazine*, emphasised the important role that Roach Smith had played in the rediscovery of Romano-British remains: 'One name stands out so prominently ... that it would be almost unpardonable not to mention that Mr Roach Smith was among the first of the pioneers of a careful and systematic system of excavation and observation': *The Gentleman's Magazine library, Romano-British remains*, i, London 1887, p. xxi.

[56] The London Society of Antiquaries was founded in 1717 and William Stukeley was an early secretary. By the middle of the nineteenth century it was a moribund organisation, with a dwindling membership, poorly attended meetings and its journal, *Archaeologia*, in debt: J. Evans, *A history of the Society of Antiquaries*, Oxford 1956.

[57] A. Way, 'Introduction', AJ i (1844), 1.

for his education at Cambridge, where John Kemble aroused his interest in the Anglo-Saxons. Over the next forty years he attempted to earn his living through writing. He produced a huge number of books and combined his literary activities with helping to organise various printing clubs, such as the Camden Society and the Percy Society.[58] By contrast, Albert Way (1805-74) came from a wealthy family and was Cambridge-educated. He was a member of the London Society of Antiquaries and its director from 1842 to 1846. The society's historian, Joan Evans, has described him as 'an admirable example of the leisured archaeologist, the learned amateur of the old school'.[59]

It was Way who outlined the purpose of the new body, starting with an explanation for the London Society of Antiquaries' lack of action: 'Although of a national and distinguished character ... the charter of the society makes no allusion to the preservation of the national monuments by influence or direct interference, when menaced by destruction.'[60] He described how the new organisation would operate. There would be a central co-ordinating committee and a network of county members who would be able to keep an eye on potential damage to ancient remains: 'The committee's purpose, as far as may be possible, [is] to secure the careful observation and record of such discoveries and preservation of the objects found.' Where this was not possible, the committee would favour the preparation of 'a proper description, with plans and drawings'.[61] A new publication, the *Archaeological Journal*, would be the means whereby members would be kept informed of developments and would act as a conduit through which new ideas could be discussed. Wright became its first editor. The new body encouraged the development of a network of local societies and by 1870 there were at least forty such organisations in England and Wales, most of them affiliated to the national association.[62] The speed with which new societies were set up indicates the level of interest in the past generally and in particular recognition of the need to protect the remains. Common to both national and local bodies was a belief that the best way to ensure the preservation of artefacts was by the creation of museums: as a result many local museums were created during the period.[63]

Despite these common aims, it was not long before differences between the

58 The Camden Society (1838) printed and distributed historical documents and the Percy Society (1840) specialised in early English ballads and popular literature. Wright also wrote articles for many magazines including the *Illustrated News of the World*, the *Cornhill Magazine*, the *Literary Gazette*, and the *London Review* to name but a few.

59 D. Wetherall, 'From Canterbury to Winchester: the foundation of the Institute', in B. Vyner (ed.), *Building on the past: papers celebrating 150 years of the Royal Archaeological Institute*, London 1994, 10.

60 Way, 'Introduction', 2.

61 Ibid. 5.

62 For a complete list see Levine, *The amateur and the professional*, appendix IV.

63 For instance Caerleon (1850), Colchester (1856) and Chester (1857). In Cirencester, where there was no formal society, a museum was built in 1856 to house the Dyer Street mosaics.

antiquarians in the British Archaeological Association began to emerge. One contested issue was the feasibility of holding a national conference to which all members were invited and, as a result, only half the leaders took part in the first meeting in Canterbury in 1844.[64] When those who had stayed away voted not to carry a report of the meeting in the *Archaeological Journal*, Wright published an account in his own *Archaeological album*.[65] Amid accusations of 'conflict of interest' and 'packing of meetings' the subsequent row brought to the surface differences of opinion concerning the nature of the BAA and views became polarised between the 'Wright' and the 'Way' factions, as they became known in the press. The row could not be settled, and culminated in a split in 1845. Those who favoured the more traditional approach broke away, taking with them the *Archaeological Journal*, and formed the Archaeological Institute. The BAA retained the rump of the membership, including Roach Smith and Wright, and created a new publication, the *Journal of the British Archaeological Association*. Underlying these disagreements were the significant social differences that will be examined in chapter 3.

Despite their differences, all the archaeological bodies recognised the need to preserve the evidence of the past. But the acrimony ensured that there was no common voice on a range of other, but related, topics. For instance, how should the remains be protected and by whom, which in turn raised the issue of to whom did they actually belong. Should the finds from excavations be kept in their locality or should they be brought together in some central repository? And, most fundamental of all, was there a national interest and if so what part should the government play? Many of these issues were high-lighted in debates concerning the content and layout of the collection in the British Museum.

The British Museum

The British Museum had been founded in 1753 to display private collections that had been given to the nation. Its contents were divided into three departments: manuscripts, printed books and natural history. Over the next fifty years the museum acquired several important collections of antiquities including Sir William Hamilton's collection of Greek vases in 1772, the Alexandrian Egyptian antiquities acquired from the French in 1801 and the Townley marbles bought after his death in 1805. As a result of these acquisitions a separate department of antiquities was set up in 1807 and was rapidly enlarged by the Phigaleian marbles in 1815, the Elgin marbles in 1816 and the Richard Payne Knight collection of antiquities in 1824. More space was

---

[64] Peripatetic conferences were one way of involving country members, as the success of the BAAS conferences since 1831 had indicated: J. B. Morrell and A. Thackray, *Gentlemen of science: the early years of the BASS*, Oxford 1981.
[65] Wetherall, 'From Canterbury to Winchester', 14.

urgently required and in 1823 plans were approved for a neo-classical building designed by Robert Smirke (1781–1867).

By the time it was completed in 1847 the design of the building was considered out-of-date and old-fashioned.[66] But in spite of the criticisms, the neo-classical style perfectly reflected the contents of the new department of antiquities. The collection consisted of aesthetically beautiful examples of art from the classical civilisations of Greece and Rome, arranged by the sculptor Richard Westmacott (1775–1856). Trained in the traditional academic manner, as described by Sir Joshua Reynolds in his lectures to the British Academy in the previous century, Westmacott arranged the antiquities for aesthetic affect. The galleries were so structured that the visitor walked through a mixture of styles and periods to reach the climax, the Elgin marbles. The display was a graphic illustration of Winckelmann's belief in the supremacy of the sublime style.

Some idea of the way in which the classical artefacts dominated the collections is to be gathered from a handbook to the antiquities produced in 1851. After stating that he only intended to deal with the most important features of the collections, the author wrote 'best to begin with the Greek as that directly tending to form and elevate public taste'. He continued: 'the only collections omitted are those by the names of British and Anglo Roman antiquities, being as yet too insufficiently arranged to admit of classification and description'.[67] This statement indicates two important features of the collection: it was representative of great works of art and was unconcerned with British antiquities.[68] In fact official attitudes towards the need for a national collection of British antiquities had not changed substantially from those expressed by Horace Walpole fifty years earlier: 'The Roman remains in Britain are upon a foot with what ideas we should get of Inigo Jones, if somebody was to publish views of huts that our soldiers run up in Senegal or Goree … I have no curiosity to know how awkward and clumsy men have been in the dawn of arts.'[69]

However, changing attitudes that had led to the creation of the new archaeological bodies also led to demands for changes in the museum's policy. One demand was that the collections should be representative of all aspects of human development rather than just examples of great art. If comparisons were to be made as advocated by the devotees of the more 'scientific' archaeology,

66 This was in comparison with the fashionable Gothic style that had been used by Pugin and Barry for the new Houses of Parliament. The building was described as 'copyist', 'cold' and 'dead': J. Summerson, 'The architecture of British museums and galleries', in J. Chapel and C. Gere (eds), *The fine and decorative art collections of Britain and Ireland*, London 1985, 9–20.

67 W. S. W. Vaux, *Handbook to the antiquities in the British Museum*, London 1851, preface. William Vaux (1818–85) was an assistant in the Department of Antiquities. Between 1861 and 1870 he was Keeper of the Department of Coins and Medals.

68 I. Jenkins, *Archaeologists and aesthetes in the sculpture galleries of the British Museum, 1880–1939*, London 1992, 9–19, 56–74.

69 This is cited in Evans, *Society of Antiquaries*, 155.

then the collections would have to include as many examples as possible of the most mundane artefacts, however crude. As Edward Hawkins, Keeper of Antiquities in the museum, argued, 'a collector may accumulate a number of amusing and elegant specimens, but it is only by combination, concentration, and comparison, that an entertaining collection can be converted into an instructive museum and archaeology into a science'.[70] Another demand was that the national collection should have a separate display devoted entirely to British remains. Complaints that there was no provision for British artefacts had increased as interest in British archaeology had grown. Frequent disparaging comparisons were made between the generous displays in several continental countries and the lack of such provision in the British Museum. For instance, Roach Smith commented that

> While Paris, Berlin, Copenhagen, Brussels, Vienna, Petersburg, Munich, Rome, Naples, Athens and other cities and towns possess rich museums of national antiquities, founded and supported by public money, the U.K., with its boundless resources, reluctantly grants for the preservation of its ancient monuments, such inadequate doles, that foreigners ask in vain to see our museums of national antiquities, so little does any collection we yet possess answer expectations formed from an acquaintance with their own rich and well digested museums.[71]

In 1837 Algernon Percy, 4th duke of Northumberland, had offered a collection of Romano-British artefacts to the museum on condition that a separate room be set aside for their display.[72] But it was not until 1850 that Hawkins was able to report that a 'British room exclusively appropriated to the formation of a series of national antiquities had been provided'.[73] There was still considerable opposition both from outside and within the museum. As late as 1860 Sir Anthony Panizzi, the principal librarian and director, reported

[70] E. Hawkins, 'Notices of a remarkable collection of ornaments of the Roman period', AJ viii (1851), 44. Edward Hawkins (1780–1867) was a numismatist and the Keeper of Antiquities between 1826 and 1860. He was an active member of the Archaeological Institute.

[71] C. Roach Smith, 'Museum of Antiquities in Scotland', JBAA v (1849), 380. There was a competitive edge between these major national museums. During the Napoleonic period art treasures from across Europe had been taken to the Louvre in Paris and during the surge in nationalistic feeling in Germany after 1815 two major museums, both classical in style and containing significant displays of ancient Greek sculpture, had been constructed, the Altes Museum in Berlin (Schinkel) and the Munich Glyptothek (Von Klenze).

[72] Northumberland was not the first; as long ago as 1808 Samuel Lysons had offered to contribute some of his collection if 'the Trustees should think to appropriate a room for the reception of Roman and other antiquities found in this country': L. Fleming, Memoir and selected letters of Samuel Lysons, Oxford 1934, 37–8. Lysons (1763–1819) was a barrister, director of the Society of Antiquaries and the first Keeper of Records in the Tower of London. He excavated several Roman villas including Bignor in Sussex. The results were published in Reliquiae romanae (1801–17). See Evans, Society of Antiquaries, 219–24.

[73] E. Hawkins, 'Proceedings', AJ vii (1850), 296. Augustus Franks, another active member of the AI, was appointed curator.

that 'The trustees have spent eight thousand pounds on medieval antiquities ... and that is the reason that the classical ones are not progressing as
they might ... the trustees bought ivories, very fine in their way; but if you
buy medieval ivories you do not buy Greek statues.'[74] The museum trustees
continued to finance large-scale excavations overseas. Typical was Sir Austen
Layard's work at Nineveh between 1851 and 1860 during which the Assyrian
antiquities were excavated and taken back to London, amid wide newspaper interest.[75] The Halicarnassian and Cnidian marbles were discovered
and excavated by Charles Newton, a former museum employee who became
Hawkins's successor as Keeper of Antiquities in 1860. Significantly these
acquisitions still conformed to a tradition that favoured large and spectacular
objects of display; objects that were impressive more for their visual impact
than because they formed some part of a coherent series.

Against such competition, the artefacts that were being unearthed by
British antiquaries seemed mundane and ordinary and Panizzi's objections
illustrate the considerable opposition that still existed to spending public
money on British artefacts. The arguments in favour of their inclusion were
based on the assumption that a better understanding of the different periods
in the British past was only possible if a systematic collection of all types of
artefacts was available for study. In 1854 there was a storm of criticism from
the archaeological societies when the museum's trustees refused to buy the
collection of Anglo-Saxon antiquities excavated by an eighteenth-century
antiquarian, the Revd Bryan Faussett. The collection was unique because
Faussett's meticulous excavation notes meant that the finds were fully documented.[76] Roach Smith had rediscovered the collection and, as a result of
his interest, Faussett's grandson offered to sell it to the British Museum.
The archaeological societies united in an effort to persuade the trustees to
buy, and another antiquary, William Wylie, even offered his collection of
Anglo-Saxon artefacts to the museum free if they would agree to buy Faussett's collection. There was a fear that if they failed to do so it would probably
be exported to France. The antiquarians' anger was summed up by an article
in the *Archaeological Journal*. The author declared that it was a 'disgrace that
England alone amongst European states possesses no series of national antiquities', and concluded that 'In the administrative body of that institution

---

74 *Report from the Select Committee on the British Museum*, London 1860, paras 336–7, cited
in M. Caygill and J. Cherry (eds), *A. W. Franks: nineteenth-century collecting and the British
Museum*, London 1997, 38.
75 A government report showed that £1,112 had been spent on the excavations in Assyria
and transport of the marbles back to Britain: Anon., 'Notes of the month', GM xli (1854),
605.
76 Hawkins told the Society of Antiquaries that 'It does not consist of rare, valuable or
beautiful objects, picked up or purchased from dealers at various times and in various
places, with little or no record or perhaps false records of the discovery; but it consists of
all the objects found in all the graves of a particular area': Evans, *Society of Antiquaries*, 274.
This statement unintentionally throws light on the probable condition of many contemporary private collections.

[the museum] the arbitrary narrow-minded spirit of the infesta noverca has been shown towards archaeological science.'[77] In the event Joseph Mayer, a wealthy Liverpool businessman, bought the collection and placed it for public viewing in his museum. Mayer paid Roach Smith to edit Faussett's notes and they were published as *Inventorium sepulchrale* in 1856. It was probably due to the outcry provoked by this decision that the trustees agreed to buy Roach Smith's London antiquities in 1856, helped no doubt by the fact that his collection was at least made up of mainly Roman artefacts.

At issue behind these controversies was the extent to which the government should be involved in preserving the artefacts and monuments of the national past. In 1852 Edmund Oldfield told the Archaeological Institute that 'In a great and civilised community, proud of its history and jealous of its rights, some provision for protecting the trophies of ancestral genius from the injuries of time and change seems no unreasonable demand for archaeology to make on the state.'[78] But this was a controversial view, and particularly unpopular with the upper classes who regarded private property rights as sacrosanct. The president of the institute, James Talbot, described the limited areas within which 'government interference could properly take a part'. One was the encouragement of both national and local museums, another was the publication of ancient documents and the third was action to protect ancient monuments.[79] The amount of time allocated to debating the issues surrounding 'treasure trove' at meetings during the 1850s is indicative of the difficulties involved in balancing the twin claims of safeguarding ancient artefacts on the one hand and private property rights on the other. The notion of public interest was still in its infancy and the claims of private ownership were generally given priority. As late as 1883 an article on the preservation of antiquities was still arguing that 'the key to most of our modern destruction is in the theory, a man may do what he likes with his own, and that the protection of antiquities interferes with the rights of property'.[80]

Predictably, Roach Smith blamed the government for the inertia:

> When our Government shall be composed of statesmen instead of placemen; of men who look to the credit, the prosperity, and the glory of our country, more than to the maintenance of themselves in power, and their connexions [sic] in places and in pensions, then and then only may it be expected that our national antiquities will be cared for and protected.[81]

---

[77] Anon., 'Archaeological intelligence', *AJ* xi (1854), 94.

[78] *AJ* ix (1852), 6. Oldfield was an assistant in the Department of Antiquities from 1848.

[79] Ibid. 364–5. The government had passed legislation in 1838 to establish a Public Records office. The Historical Manuscripts Commission was appointed in 1869 to investigate records in private hands and was regarded by some as 'arbitrary interference': Levine, *The amateur and the professional*, 119–22. The first Public Monuments Act was passed in 1882, without statutory powers.

[80] Anon., 'Book review', *The Antiquary* vii (1883), 106.

[81] C. Roach Smith (ed.), *Inventorium sepulchrale*, London 1856, p. vi.

This was Roach Smith at his most combative, but he was not alone. Similar comparisons between the French and British governments had been made by other antiquarians. Indeed, Thomas Wright had even suggested that it was lack of action by the British government that had led to the formation of so many archaeological associations. But what all these complainants failed to realise was the different political agendas in the two countries. In France there had been a long period of political upheaval, culminating most recently in the dismissal of an elected government by Napoleon III. He had good reasons for his attempts to reinforce the legitimacy of his shaky regime by appeals to a great national past, rendering the protection of the remains an imperative. In Britain, increasing industry and affluence strengthened the confident belief that private enterprise and *laissez-faire* methods could be relied on as guardians of the nation's historical heritage.

One problem for the antiquarians in their quest for government support was that those individuals who were best placed to effect a change in policy, such as the museum trustees and government ministers, were frequently men whose ideas of historical taste and beauty were largely untouched by the new ideas. As a result, they were unsympathetic to the demands for change. Collections of comparatively crude artefacts, such as Faussett's, challenged some of the basic notions of beauty and taste by which ancient objects had been judged in the past. By questioning the priority previously accorded to the classical treasures of Greece and Rome, such collections appeared to undermine the values that such artefacts seemed to represent.

Roach Smith was aware of the mixed feelings evoked by new ideas:

> It need never be apprehended, that where, as in this country, refinement of taste and a sound system of education prevail, classical antiquities will ever be neglected or be in danger of being superseded. It would be as unreasonable to dread such a result as to fear a decadence of esteem for the noble literature of Greece and Rome.[82]

The power and appeal of the classical texts and the beauty of the artefacts continued to exert a strong pull; although the old values and approaches were being challenged, this did not mean that they were rejected. This can be seen from the way in which Roach Smith managed to combine new skills and a taste for controversy with a continuing regard for old values. No one did more to encourage the new institutions and the broader horizons necessary to further the knowledge of the past. But he still believed in

> the immense superiority of the ancient fictile vessels over similar work in the middle ages, it is only necessary to place them in juxtaposition, when the latter will appear positively uncouth and barbarous. When good taste was revised in later times, nothing of consequence was achieved that was not in imitation of the classics.[83]

82 Ibid. p. x.
83 Idem, 'Discoveries at Ickleton and Chesterford', 363.

Though he embraced the new methodology, Roach Smith was still fascinated by the classical world: a fascination that had started with a collection of Roman coins, visits to the Roman villa at Bignor and re-readings of Gibbon's *Decline and fall of the Roman empire* when he was a boy in the 1820s.[84]

But while Roach Smith was able to combine his passionate interest and regard for the Roman past with an equally strong belief in the need for new methods and techniques, it is arguable how representative he was of British antiquarians as a whole. For many of them there was an inherent contradiction between, on the one hand, admiring an ancient civilisation and wishing to uphold and imitate the values it represented, and, on the other, embracing new techniques which appeared to place those values at risk. The split in the British Archaeological Association, and arguments about the purchasing policy of the British Museum, are indicative of the underlying tensions between the traditional antiquarians and the men who were confident and adventurous enough to welcome and use innovative ways of studying the past. It is significant that those who were most anxious to distance themselves and their activities from the amateur antiquarians and their cabinets of curiosities were the same as those who called themselves archaeologists and described their activities as scientific. However, as the description of Richard Neville indicates, there was no straightforward division between one group and another, antiquary or scientist. In fact, most British antiquarians had to find some way in which to balance these apparently contradictory points of view and many other factors, including patriotic feelings, social position and economic interests played a part in influencing attitudes to the past.

[84] Idem, *Retrospections*, i.100–3.

2

A Question of Identity

Some sense of the difficulties inherent in attempts to define national identity are to be found in a speech to the British Association for the Advancement of Science in 1855 during which Thomas Wright struggled to find a name for fourth-century Britons:

> If we call them Romans the term is correct politically but incorrect ethnologically. If we call them Britons the name is incorrect both politically and ethnologically and correct only geographically. The population was neither Roman nor British but an extraordinary mixture of all the different races who had been reduced by the arms of Rome.[1]

Wright's dilemma illustrates the difficulties involved in any discussion of national identity, as definitions of 'nation' and 'race' were, and still are, notoriously slippery. Geographical boundaries, linguistic differences and cultural inheritance are just some of the criteria that can be used to identify a nation. In Britain, where there had been significant movements of different groups over long periods, identification became even more problematic. Indeed, John Burrow argues that a chief motive in the writing of English history in the Victorian period was the desire to define a national identity out of the confusion created by successive waves of invasions and conquests.[2]

In the early Victorian period there were a number of different versions of British origins that reflected the different influences that had played a part in the national past: the Celt, the Roman and the Saxon.[3] Sam Smiles has argued that the features of the chosen identity arise out of a 'romantic projection into the past … in which we construct lineages to keep ourselves afloat in the choppy waters of indeterminacy and anonymity which threaten to swamp a sense of self'.[4] In other words, the choice of a group with which to identify is dictated by present needs and therefore a study of the choices made by different individuals can help to throw light on the way in which people thought of themselves at different times. Furthermore, the story of the

[1] T. Wright, 'The ethnology of England', GM xliv (1855), 523.
[2] Burrow, A Liberal descent, 9. Edward Cutts referred to 'the intermixture of races, and consequently of religions, and manners, and customs and ideas which then took place in England'. To which he added the footnote, 'which is far greater than is commonly imagined; for the soldiers who occupied Britain were by no means all Italians; they were gathered from every part of the world which was subject to the Imperial power of Rome': 'Roman remains at Coggeshall', 100.
[3] This was the title chosen by Thomas Wright for his popular account of the British past.
[4] Smiles, Image of antiquity, p. ix.

past can be adjusted and changed to meet current requirements. The truth or otherwise of the stories do not matter, their importance lies in their ability to suggest versions of the past within which individuals can place themselves.

A sense of the way in which a 'British national identity' evolved and changed is to be gathered from various pictorial and literary images of well-known events in the country's past. For example, in 1751 Nicholas Blakey portrayed Julius Caesar's landing in Britain as a contest between equals and the accompanying note described the 'brave and obstinate resistance of the ancient Britons'. But by 1847 William Linnell's picture of the same event is dominated by the towering figure of Caesar and gives greater prominence to the might of Roman conquest.[5] It is not always clear however, whether these images reflect changes in contemporary perceptions of national identity or whether they were themselves active agents of change.

Richard Hingley also uses comparison between groups as a way of defining national identity, but rather than comparing foreigners with the British, he compares class with class. So his 'Celtic subaltern' is inferior in class to the Roman officer and English gentlemen.[6] Hingley's juxtaposition is based upon a definition of 'other' that cuts right across any simplistic division between Romans and ancient Britons. It draws attention to the very fluid and ambiguous nature of all these comparisons, as no one edition of the past presents an ideal ancestor and each contains its own contradictions. The concept of the 'other' by comparison with whom an identity is achieved, can be only a partial explanation for the formation of a national identity. It suggests a possible process, but it does not explain the particular form or the changes undergone by that form over a period of time. As the nineteenth century progressed, parallels between the Roman and British empires became ever easier to draw. But the ambiguity surrounding the nature of Britain as a modern-day imperial power and a subject race of the old Roman empire became increasingly difficult to reconcile. It was partially due to these difficulties that Saxon origins became more popular, as they appeared to offer a way out of the dilemmas presented by either Roman or ancient British lineage.

Two points need to be emphasised. The first is that the terms 'British' and 'English' were frequently conflated by the Victorian antiquarians, thus obscuring the internal differences between the nations within the United Kingdom. The term 'British' implied a national cohesion that, in many instances, was more apparent than real. The second point is the way in which the results of historical and archaeological research could be used to justify and legitimise contemporary events. What is important is that the facts revealed by historical research were only the 'building bricks', the design of the edifices in which they were used reflect contemporary political concerns. It is difficult

5 Ibid. 134–7, 113–29.
6 Hingley, *Roman officers and English gentlemen*, 61–109. Hingley defines the 'Celtic subaltern' as 'those of an inferior rank who are subject to a hegemony of a ruling class' (p. 10). His study covers a period rather later than most of the material in the case studies in this book.

to determine the influence of such political machinations on the activities of local antiquarian groups, but insofar as they were a part of the national and cultural scene, they will have helped to shape the context within which the antiquarians operated. Their traces can be detected as forming the structure within which individual and group action took place.

Ancient British ancestry

The most influential descriptions of the original ancient Britons came from Roman accounts, such as Julius Caesar's *Gallic wars* and Tacitus' *Agricola* and *Annals*. They portray a primitive but brave people who possess few of the attributes of 'civilised life', most notably literacy. Early illustrations of the native peoples of North America by Theodore De Bray had been used as the basis for illustrations of ancient British men and women in John Speed's *Historie* (1611).[7] These pictures were still being used in Victorian books, such as an 1858 *Chester guide*, to provide readers with an image of the ancient Britons, with the obvious inference that ancient Britons closely resembled native populations discovered as a result of European voyages of discovery.[8] Archaeological papers contain several references suggesting that the reports of native peoples were regarded as useful aids to the study of ancient Britons. For example, Richard Neville thought that because he had found most ancient British remains in open country 'they indulged their fondness for horses and frequented the plains after the manner of Red Indians, denizens of the great Western plains of the present day',[9] while the Colchester antiquarian, William Wire, wanted to obtain curiosities from New Zealand because 'antiquarians have very few tangible remains of ancient Britons and their manners and actions are to be studied analogically [sic] by those of the inhabitants of New Zealand'.[10] Underlying these comments was an assumption that the ancient Britons, like the overseas natives, were at an earlier stage of development than the Europeans and just as the ancient Britons had been civilised by contact with Rome, so would contemporary natives be civilised by contact with British colonial rule. As the Revd Edward Cutts told the Essex Archaeological Society, 'to study how England and Englishmen came to be what they are, he [the antiquarian] must study first and well the history of the Roman occupation'.[11]

Cutts's analysis makes the important assumption that people are capable of developmental change through a process of mediation, in which one group acquires the social and cultural features of another. In the context of Roman

7   Smiles, *Image of antiquity*, 129.
8   H. Roberts, *Chester guide*, 2nd edn, rev. J. Hicklin, Chester 1858.
9   Neville, *Sepulchra exposita*, 8. Neville had been a soldier in Canada in the early 1840s and so had possibly encountered native Americans.
10   William Wire to (unnamed), 21 Aug. 1851, William Wire letter book, ERO.
11   Cutts, 'Roman remains at Coggeshall', 100.

Britain it was a process that came to be known as Romanisation.[12] The term itself was not actually used by the antiquarians in this study, but it is clear that they did envisage some sort of process whereby Britons became Romans. For example, Roach Smith called Hadrian's Wall 'a great work of defence ... for protecting the growing civilisation of Romanised Britain'.[13] Similarly, Joseph Mayer thought that 'the Romanised Briton differed little from the provincial Roman', and John Buckman considered that the Cirencester mosaics were 'the work of Romano-Britons, who were of course inferior artists when compared with the mother country'.[14] The use of the term 'mother country' is significant as it suggests the parent-child relationship that was basic to the concept of Romanisation, and it was to become a commonly used expression to describe relations between Britain and her colonies later in the century. Buckman also drew a clear distinction between Romans from outside and the Roman-Britons who were native born: 'The evidence left to us of Roman sepulture in this neighbourhood show us that cremation was the custom with the *Roman-British*, as well as with the Greeks and Romans themselves.'[15] It is clear that the antiquarians' evidence for the changes brought about through Roman rule was heavily influenced by Tacitus' account in *Agricola*: 'The nation which used to reject the Latin language began to aspire to rhetoric: further, the wearing of our dress became a distinction, and the toga came into fashion, and little by little the Britons were seduced into alluring vices: to the lounge, the bath, the well appointed dinner table.'[16]

Although the distinctions they drew between the different groups are clear, the antiquarians do not elaborate on the implications of the way in which cultural change was brought about. An author in the *Quarterly Review* appears to suggest that it is a one-way process, in which one culture dominates another and there is no room for mutual exchange: 'Wherever the Roman inhabited he carried with him the comforts and luxuries of his own country,

---

[12] The term owes its prominence to the archaeologist Francis Haverfield, who presented his ideas in a paper to the British Academy in 1905. His views, much influenced by Mommsen, continued to dominate archaeological attitudes for much of the twentieth century. More recently the term has been the subject of much criticism on the grounds that it ignored social meanings: D. J. Mattingly, 'Dialogues in Roman imperialism: power, discourse and discrepant experience in the Roman empire', *Journal of Roman Archaeology* s.s xxiii (1997), 7–24. For a more recent study of the way cultural change was brought about in the provinces of the Roman empire see G. Woolf, *Becoming Roman: the origins of provincial civilisation in Gaul*, Cambridge 1998.

[13] Roach Smith, *Collectanea antiqua*, iii.154. Roach Smith was such an influential figure that his use of the term will have given it greater credibility. For instance, it was used by John Buckman in his book on Roman Cirencester and Edward Lee in an address to the Woolhope Naturalists' Field Club in 1875.

[14] *Proceedings and papers of the Historical Society of Lancashire and Cheshire*, Liverpool 1848–9, 28; *WGS*, 24 Sept. 1849.

[15] J. Buckman and C. Newmarch, *Remains of Roman art in ancient Corinium*, London 1850, 111.

[16] Tacitus, *Agricola* xxi.

and scorned to descend to the ruder habits of his subjects.'[17] Another contributor to the *Archaeological Journal* suggested that it was an active and conscious policy on the part of the Romans to 'implant among the conquered the seeds of civilisation and thus mould them into peaceful subjects'.[18] Underlying the concept of Romanisation was an implicit assumption that Roman society was superior to the local societies, probably inevitably, as all the textual evidence had been provided by the Romans themselves. Romanisation was therefore not merely describing a process through which Britons became 'civilised Romans', but it also implied a value judgement that was so taken for granted that there was no need to spell it out. Romanisation was a concept with a strong attraction for men who were naturally inclined to give priority to the classical civilisations for a whole range of reasons associated with their background, education and social pretensions.[19]

In spite of seeing Roman superiority as a 'given', it is important to note that Romanisation was based on an assumption that culture was not necessarily dependent upon race. It allowed less developed people, such as the ancient Britons, to change and progress until they were like the Romans, an imperial nation. But as new ideas began to influence opinion, race increasingly came to be seen as synonymous with culture and, therefore, doubt was cast on the notion that one race could be 'civilised' through contact with another. The reports about 'natives' sent back to Britain by explorers, traders and migrants were an influential factor in these changing views.[20] Whereas previously other races had been portrayed as noble but undeveloped, more recent travellers' accounts presented a different picture, as in Darwin's description of the natives he encountered in Tierra del Fuego: 'These poor creatures were stunted in growth, their hideous faces bedaubed with white paint, their skin filthy and greasy, their hair entangled, their voices discordant, their gestures violent and without dignity. Viewing such men, one can hardly make oneself believe they are fellow creatures, and inhabitants of the same world.'[21] If British ancestors were seen as similar to these natives, then such reports made disturbing reading.

The desire to understand the basis of human behaviour and the belief that

[17] J. H. Merivale, 'The Romans at Colchester', QR cxciii (1855), 88.
[18] [J. Buchan], 'Notice of the barrier of Antonus Pius', AJ xv (1858), 26.
[19] Undergraduates in Cambridge were given essay topics such as 'the best means of civilising the subjects of the British empire in those parts of India controlled by the East India Company' and 'The probable design of the Divine Providence in subjecting so large a portion of Asia to the British dominion': L. Colley, *Britons: forging the nation, 1707–1837*, London 1992, 169–70.
[20] Linda Colley provides interesting evidence of the extent to which attitudes to racial differences were mediated through the experience of Britons in contact with North American Indians: *Captives; Britain, empire and the world, 1600–1850*, London 2002, 162–71.
[21] C. Darwin, *The voyage of the Beagle* (1839), London 1989, 177–8. Accounts of cannibalism featured prominently in engravings used to illustrate missionary accounts of native people. These were distributed widely and did much to enhance the perception that these people were heathen, base and incapable of further development: B. Smith, *European vision and the South Pacific*, New Haven 1985.

this was possible through the study of so-called primitive people and societies had led to the creation of an Ethnology Society in 1842. Several antiquarians began to call themselves ethnologists, including Thomas Bateman whose main antiquarian interest was in opening long barrows in Derbyshire in order to find the remains of the pre-literate ancient Britons. The new science was recognised by the British Association for the Advancement of Science which had a separate ethnology section at their conferences to which Thomas Wright gave papers on British origins. The members of the Ethnology Society believed that 'the various tribes of men are of one origin'[22] and therefore capable of advancement, a view rejected by others who saw race alone as responsible for the poor physical and cultural characteristics observed by travellers. Although scorned by many leading intellectuals, such as Darwin and Huxley, the idea that race alone was responsible for differences in development gained wide acceptance, as it appeared to justify Britain's role as a colonial power.[23]

Another development that appeared to support the separate development of the races was the 'science' of craniology that came to prominence in the 1840s. Exponents of the new science purported to show that the brain capacity of different races varied, and that brain size could limit potential development. The antiquarian John Thurnam and the anthropologist Joseph Davis used skulls found in ancient burial mounds to illustrate *Crania britannica* (1856) in which they argued that 'the forms of the cranium are permanent and not transmutable between the different races'.[24] Davis extended the argument even further when he claimed that there was 'striking evidence of the essential differences in the moral constitution of the people from European nations [as compared with the Chinese]'.[25] The associated science of phrenology became enormously popular and although many of its findings were disputed, it is hard to believe that the huge interest it attracted did not have some influence on changing attitudes towards racial difference.[26]

[22] J. C. Pritchard in a paper on 'The contributions made by philology and anatomy to the human species', delivered to the BAAS in 1832. This is cited in Morrell and Thackray, *Gentlemen of science*, 284.

[23] Darwin's ideas were used as evidence by both sides in the controversies, but Darwin himself was cautious: 'It is very difficult to say why one civilised nation rises, becomes more powerful and spreads more widely than another.' This is cited in A. McDougall, *Racial myths in English history*, Montreal 1982, 124. See also G. Stocking, Jr, *Victorian anthropology*, London 1987.

[24] J. B. Davis and J. Thurnam, *Crania britannica: delineations and descriptions of the skulls of the early inhabitants of the British Isles*, London 1856. This quotation is from a review of the book in *AJ* xiii (1856), 422. See also an article by Davis in the same number of the *AJ*: J. B. Davis 'Bearings of ethnology upon archaeological science', *AJ* xiii (1856), 315–27.

[25] Davis, 'Bearings of ethnology', 322.

[26] In 1844 Wire reported that 'For some time past phrenology has been all the rage in this town': WWJ, entry for 17 Feb. 1844. In Cirencester T. C. Brown reported the discovery of several skulls. 'There is a uniform type in the skulls – smooth, well developed, expanding towards the occiput – excepting two varying remarkably from this type': 'Recent discoveries at Cirencester', *JBAA* iv (1848), 71. See also Secord, *Victorian sensation*, 69–74, and

Although these matters continued to be hotly debated, the overall effect was to ensure that contemporary native people, and by implication ancient Britons, were perceived very differently in the 1860s from the way they had been conceived earlier in the century. Amid the plethora of new data, the simplicity that had allowed the idealisation of the 'noble savage' had been lost. In its place was a hierarchy in which the ranking was determined by race, into which culture was subsumed. Probably inevitably, the Europeans who developed this theory saw their own culture at the top and native cultures at the bottom. Thus, the hierarchy of development was both a description and a justification for the attitudes to which it gave rise. It was only a relatively short step from these ideas to the notion that it was the duty of the 'superior' race to govern the 'lesser'. To people who were becoming accustomed to their role as colonialists governing different races around the world,[27] it was difficult to consider themselves as descended from similar native groups, and the more involved with empire Britain became, the less acceptable this analogy proved to be.[28]

Boudica and Caractacus

Some of the ambiguity surrounding the Victorian's view of the ancient Britons is to be seen in the various representations of native leaders, such as Boudica and Caractacus. Much of their symbolic power was derived from the ease with which they could be used in a variety of different interpretations, helped by the fact that the classical texts themselves offered opposing views, especially of Boudica.[29] Differences in the way they were depicted give some

M. Cowling, *The artist as an anthropologist: the representation of type and character in Victorian art*, Cambridge 1989. The new 'science' had many critics, however. For instance, a comparison of the heads of Apollo, a black man and a chimpanzee was criticised in the *Athenaeum*, 17 June 1854: 'It ought not to have been suffered in a work professedly scientific', cited in Cowling, *The artist as an anthropologist*, 61.

[27] There are frequent references to the demands of the British imperial role. For instance, 'It is our duty to prepare ourselves for the right use of that vast power that England sways, a power over the fortunes of mankind such as no people or potentate ever before possessed': E. S. Creasy, *The spirit of historical study*, London 1840, cited in Levine, *The amateur and the professional*, 161.

[28] Charles Kingsley warned his Cambridge students that 'we must be careful how we compare our forefathers with these savages': *The Roman and the Teuton*, London 1864, 9. He thought that British ancestors must have been superior: 'If our forefathers in the German forests had been like Powhatton's people as we found them in the Virginian forests, the Romans wouldn't have been long in civilising us off the face of the earth' (p. 10). Recent research by David Finkelstein has shown how the reports of the explorer John Speke on his travels in Africa were drastically rewritten to promote a view of Africans living in a 'dark continent and in need of Christianity and colonial protection': *The Guardian*, 13 Aug. 2001.

[29] Tacitus presents her as a wronged woman and puts virtuous speeches into the mouths of her British subjects, whereas Dio Cassius presents the whole revolt as a Roman victory over vicious native barbarians.

indication of the changing views of the ancient British inheritance. In 1782 Thomas Cowper described Boadicea[30] as 'the British warrior queen, bleeding from the Roman rods ... with matchless wrongs', and the Romans as 'ruffians, trampling on a thousand states'.[31] His version emphasised Roman cruelty and the British love of freedom and is clearly based on the account in Tacitus. However in 1859 Tennyson described her as a force of savage, uncivilised nature, wreaking horrible retribution on the Roman citizens of Colchester: 'Mad and maddening ... Yelled and shrieked between her daughters.'[32] Tennyson's interpretation, using Dio Cassius' version of events, probably reflected some of the powerful, negative emotions aroused by the Indian Mutiny two years before, in which Indian troops had murdered British citizens.[33]

The notion of a female monarch was a particularly useful symbol when another woman was on the throne. In Hollingshed's Chronicle of 1577, Boudica is portrayed reviewing her troops in an image which, with the exception of a hare under her arm, could be Elizabeth I reviewing her troops before the Armada. The two women had been conflated into one image of the warrior queen defending the liberties of her realm. This version of the Boudica story was the basis for the famous statue in London, by Thomas Thornycroft, in which she is shown in her chariot, spear in hand, leading her troops into battle, every inch the warrior queen.[34] Although it was not implied that the statue resembled Victoria, honour could be done to a contemporary queen by reference to another powerful queen in the past. But Boudica could also be used in a more conventional representation of the female role. For example, a statue by James Havard Thomas shows her as the mother, on foot, unarmed, and with arms protectively held around her daughters, possibly a more fitting tribute to Victoria, the mother of the nation (see plate 2).[35]

Hence, the story of Boudica was open to many interpretations. In the eighteenth century, when Britain feared invasion, she had been seen as the patriot leading her people against foreign domination. As Britain became

[30] Boudica was the Celtic word for victory. However the Victorians invariably referred to her as 'Boadicea'. I will use Boudica for my comments, but where I am quoting others I will use their spelling.
[31] W. Cowper, Poetry and prose, ed. H. S. Milford, London 1968. The poem celebrates the British empire in 'the regions Caesar never knew'.
[32] Alfred Lord Tennyson, Poems, ii, ed. C. Ricks, London 1987.
[33] The Royal Academy Exhibition in 1858 showed a painting by Joseph Noel Paton 'In Memoriam'. It portrayed armed Indian soldiers advancing on English women and children at Cawnpore. A critic complained that 'The subject is too revolting for further description ... it ought not to have been hung': J. Treuherz, Victorian painting, London 1993, 114. The picture was repainted with Highlanders coming to the rescue and a new inscription read 'Designed to commemorate the Christian heroism of the British ladies in India during the mutiny of 1857, and their ultimate deliverance by British prowess.'
[34] Thornycroft is reported to have emphasised the symbolic nature of Boudica at the insistence of Prince Albert, who was no doubt aware of the propaganda value offered by the parallels between a contemporary female monarch and a great patriotic queen of the past.
[35] The statue is in the City Hall in Cardiff.

an imperial power, she was portrayed as the almost demented leader of a savage revolt. Finally, when Britain stood confidently at the zenith of imperial power, she reappeared as the personification of Britannia, 'regions Caesar never knew thy prosperity shall sway'.[36] The bare bones of the story were the same. What had changed was the way in which the events had been interpreted to best suit the symbolic requirements of contemporary events.[37] Antiquarians in Colchester were particularly interested in the accounts of Boudica: the local implications of her story will be discussed in chapter 6.

Caractacus was less problematic. He was male and therefore did not cause the confusion created by the image of a female warrior. His portrayal in the classical texts as a brave and dignified figure was very familiar, as Thomas Wright pointed out: 'The story as related by the historian Tacitus, is the theme of every school boy.'[38] But that he remained an ambiguous symbol is illustrated by the reactions to Watts's painting of 'Caractacus led in triumph through Rome' (1843). On the one hand the *Illustrated London News* described him as 'the grand old man, firm as a riven rock, and in his barbaric pride, as grim and unconquerable as a mastiff, strides through the crowded streets with more the air of a victor than of vanquished'.[39] But others criticised the picture for depicting the British hero as a 'chained savage, led in humiliating procession by his captors'.[40] Another intriguing image of Caractacus was used to illustrate Hugh Roberts's *Chester guide* in 1858 (*see* plate 3). It depicts Caractacus standing erect and proud, while at his feet there is a kneeling Roman soldier releasing the chains from his feet. It could almost appear that the Roman is kneeling in homage. The juxtaposition of the two figures lends a different interpretation to the relative position of conqueror and conquered, Roman and Briton, owner and slave.[41]

---

36 The lines are from Cowper's poem of 1782 and are inscribed on the statue's plinth. The sense of Roman parallels could not be more explicit.

37 See S. Macdonald, 'Boadicea: warrior, mother and myth', in S. Macdonald, P. Holden and S. Ardener (eds), *Images of women in peace and war*, London 1987, 40–61, and R. Samuel, *Patriotism: the making and unmaking of the British national identity*, III: *National fictions*, London 1989, p. xxvii.

38 Wright, *Celt, Roman and Saxon*, 25.

39 Anon., 'Exhibition of cartoons in Westminster Hall', *ILN*, 8 July 1843, 18.

40 The review was in the *Athenaeum* and is cited in Smiles, *Image of antiquity*, 158. The painting won a prize in the competition for the frescoes in the new Houses of Parliament: T. S. R. Boase, 'The decoration of the new Palace of Westminster, 1841–63', *Journal of the Warburg and Courtauld Institutes* xvii (1954), 319–59.

41 The picture was published in the second edition of Roberts's *Chester guide*. It is an engraving by Hollis from a daguerreotype by Beard from the original by C. Panormo. I have not seen this picture anywhere else and I have not been able to find out anything about Panormo.

Roman ancestry

An alternative British identification was with the Romans themselves through the Romano-Britons. This was the traditional view that Britain had achieved 'civilisation' and owed her contemporary pre-eminence in the world to the experience of 400 years of Roman rule that had 'Romanised' the ancient Britons. Edward Cutts's article describes the benefits of Roman rule: 'Much of our existing institutions and habits and modes of thought has its [sic] roots far back in Roman times.'[42] Although he does not suggest a genealogical connection, he does draw close parallels between the Romans and the Britons, 'conquering, civilising and practical, so like in many traits of their personal and national character to us Englishmen'.[43] Cutts was most concerned with the institutional heritage of the Romans, whereas in Cirencester John Buckman was more impressed with the evidence of architectural splendour. He described the remains of houses and other buildings and says that although the exteriors were plain, 'the internal arrangements and decorations ever betokened the presidency of a spirit of elegance and refinement'.[44] By using such words as 'comfort', 'good taste' and 'luxury', Buckman creates a picture of civilised Roman living that probably owed as much to the magnificent remains in Rome and Pompeii as it does to life in Roman Cirencester.

But there were aspects of Roman society and behaviour that were repugnant to the moral conscience of the mid nineteenth-century observer, differences that had been highlighted by Gibbon: 'The untutored Caledonians, glowing with the warm virtues of nature, and the degenerate Romans polluted with the mean vices of wealth and slavery.'[45] Rather than highlighting similarity such comparisons tended to emphasis the distance between the Romans and contemporary Britons. Probably the most important of these were the Romans' pagan beliefs and their persecution of the early Christians, attitudes that were particularly difficult for a Victorian audience for many of whom religion was still central to society. There was a feeling of abhorrence at the supposed superstition and cruelty associated with paganism, although some archaeologists did acknowledge that the later Roman empire's conversion to Christianity had facilitated that religion's rapid spread. Others pointed out that the British empire now played much the same role in taking Christianity to her colonies: 'When I look at some of our heathen altars of the fourth century, I feel encouraged to hope, that now that the tide of heathenism in some of our colonies – India for example – has been somewhat checked, it

---

[42] Cutts, 'Roman remains at Coggeshall', 101.
[43] Ibid. 100.
[44] Buckman and Newmarch, *Remains of Roman art*, 25.
[45] E. Gibbon, *The decline and fall of the Roman empire*, abridged D. M. Low, London 1960, 65.

may be entirely stemmed back and those sunny lands be flooded with divine light.'[46]

An added complication was the association of Rome with Roman Catholicism and the papacy. In 1850 widespread disquiet about the reintroduction of the Catholic hierarchy in Britain had led to riots.[47] In a period of increasing national pride and confidence, in which the Protestant allegiance played an important role, this was another factor rendering association with Rome problematic.[48] The Roman enthusiasm for games and gladiatorial contests was also alien. Contemporary fiction, such as Edward Bulwer-Lytton's *Last days of Pompeii*, emphasised the physicality of the contests between man and man, and man and beast.[49] Most references to the games emphasised the more lurid aspects, as in a description of the embossed figures on a Colchester vase: 'It is well known how passionately fond the Romans were of the venatio, in which criminals, captives or hired bestiari hazarded their lives in conflicts with ferocious animals.'[50] Even a piece of pottery could offend Victorian susceptibilities: 'Despite our knowledge of the unrestrained sensual habits of the Romans, we are surprised to see evidence of their licentiousness paraded forth upon the domestic board.'[51]

Although these factors ensured that the Roman analogy could be uncomfortable, it was the comparisons between the Roman and the British empires that proved to be the most troubling. Edward Cutts maintained that the demise of the Roman empire 'forms a problem which we shall do well to study, even in this nineteenth century of the Christian era'.[52] Most commentators emphasised the difference between the supposedly benign influences of British imperial rule and those of 'decadent' Rome. For instance, the authors of an article on Roman roads compared them with those built by the British: 'Theirs were to bind the nations of the earth in one entire chain of servility, ours to carry forth liberty to the nations and emancipation to the world.'[53] The antiquarians' eagerness to demonstrate the ways in which the two empires differed can be seen as an attempt to assuage the anxiety to which such comparisons gave rise. British imperial expansion in Africa and, above all, in India, had meant that Britain was now ruling huge numbers of

---

46 J. Collingwood Bruce, 'Observations', *AJ* xvii (1860), 347, and Lord Neaves proclaimed that 'The noble character of our missionary enterprise rivals or even excels the far famed propaganda of Rome herself': Lord Neaves, 'The Ossianic controversy', xiv (1857), 36.
47 Some antipathy to Catholicism was noted by Wire in Colchester. But Kristina Jeffes has suggested that disturbances involving aggression towards Catholics in England were prompted as much by fears that Irish migrants would take jobs away from indigenous workers as they were by religious differences: 'The Irish in early Victorian Chester: an outcast community?', in R. Swift (ed.), *Victorian Chester*, Liverpool 1996, 102–9.
48 For the importance of Protestantism in British identity see Colley, *Britons*, 18–54.
49 He uses such phrases as 'the people were warmed into blood' and 'the interest had mounted up to the desire of sacrifice'.
50 Anon., 'Notices of archaeological publications', *AJ* xviii (1861), 96.
51 C. Roach Smith, 'Red glazed pottery of the Roman', *JBAA* iv (1848), 9.
52 Cutts, 'Roman remains at Coggeshall', 100–1.
53 J. Just and J. Hartland, 'Roman Ribchester', *JBAA* vi (1850), 251.

'coloured' people who, according to the new racial theories, were regarded as inherently inferior; so just as comparisons with the Roman empire appeared to be increasingly apposite, changes in theories of race made such comparisons worrying. As Collingwood Bruce remarked, 'another empire has sprung into being of which Rome dreamt not. In that island where in Roman days, the painted savage shared the forest with a beast of prey, a lady sits upon her throne of state, wielding a sceptre more potent than Julius or Hadrian ever grasped'.[54] The problem for the Victorians was to explain just how the painted savage had become an agent of imperial power and if that had been possible in Britain, what was to stop the same switch in the balance of power between rulers and ruled in British India?

Britain's dual role as both a subject nation under Roman rule and as the imperial power in contemporary India is nicely demonstrated in a description of the subject matter of the frescoes for the central corridor in the new Palace of Westminster: 'Six subjects have been selected: in three Britain appears sunk in ignorance, heathen superstition and slavery; in the other three she appears instructing the savage, abolishing barbarous rites and liberating the slave.'[55]

Much of the anxiety evoked by these comparisons was focused on the decline of the Roman empire, a decline that was vividly underlined by the physical presence of ruined buildings and fragments of artefacts revealed by antiquarian activity and written about by poets and writers, including Pope and Wordsworth.[56] Bruce talked about the dilemmas presented by such evidence in his book on the Roman wall, the whole tenor of which can be seen as a commentary on imperial decline: 'In the wall we have evident traces of the might of Rome, but it is the might of a giant laid prostrate ... the mistress of nations is no more and the eternal city is buried in her own debris.'[57] Gibbon's suggestion that internal decadence had been one of the reasons for Roman decline had raised the possibility that the same could occur in Britain, a possibility discussed further by Anthony Trollope in 1855. He analysed what he regarded as the possible decline of the British empire: 'What is left of Rome? We have to acknowledge that its noblest buildings and monuments were built during its decadence. Will the same have to be said of us? Is our present wealth and glory, our increasing luxury, our love of art, our polished intellect of which we are so proud; are these things but signs of our decay?'[58] It is perhaps hardly surprising that Bruce should conclude his

54 Bruce, The Roman wall, 41.
55 This is cited in Boase, 'The decoration of the new Palace of Westminster', 341. The subjects of the pictures were defined by parliament in PP xxxiii (1847), 275.
56 For instance, Alexander Pope, 'See the wild wastes of all devouring years, how Rome her own sad sepulchre appears', quoted by Lord Bathurst in his speech to the BAA in 1869: 'Presidential address', JBAA xxv (1869), 23, and William Wordsworth 'On Roman antiquities discovered at Bishopstone Herefordshire', quoted by Professor Marsden in his address to the EAS in 1852: 'Inaugural lecture', TEAS i (1858), 14.
57 Bruce, The Roman wall, 40.
58 A. Trollope, The New Zealander (written in 1855–6), Oxford 1972, 10. This was origi-

book by emphasising the responsibility of imperial rule: 'The sceptre which Rome relinquished, we have taken up. Great is our honour, great our responsibility.'[59]

Saxon ancestry

In 1856 Thomas Bateman, referred to 'the Roman legions, impelled by craving lust of power [that] reduced the painted Briton to a state of slavery'.[60] His words illustrate the problem faced by British antiquarians and historians in their attempts to construct a version of the national past that did not involve either of these unappealing models of British origins.[61] Hence a version of the past that viewed British origins as Saxon provided an acceptable alternative and was to prove very useful to British antiquarians and historians as they strove to liberate themselves from the troublesome analogies presented by a Roman or ancient British past. An early, and very influential, picture of Saxon England was Walter Scott's Ivanhoe (first published in 1820 and frequently reissued), in which he portrayed 'a striking contrast betwixt the Saxons, by whom the soil was cultivated, and the Normans, who still reigned in it as conquerors'.[62]

Eighteenth-century scholars in Germany and Britain had used folk tales and oral traditions in order to construct a version of the past that was not based exclusively on the classical past. Another very important source of information about the German tribes who opposed Rome was a classical text, Tacitus' Germania. It is a rather idealised description as his intention had been to provide a contrast through which life in Rome could be criticised. But his picture of independent self-governing communities was very attractive and an important source of information for those searching for alternative versions of the past. It also served as a useful reminder that German tribes were among those that had helped to bring about the eventual defeat of the Roman empire. In a European continent in which several countries including

nally written as a response to Macaulay's review of Ranke's 'History of the popes', in the *Edinburgh* Review cxiv (Oct. 1840), 228. Trollope uses characteristics of British civilised living that could be seen as just those attributes inherited from Rome.

59 Bruce, *The Roman wall*, 450. Vance has drawn attention to the way leading political figures used Roman analogies in the debates concerning the creation of imperial India in the 1870s. For instance, Robert Lowe warned that 'The power of imperial Rome was broken in conquering the world': Vance, *The persistence of Rome*, 230.

60 T. Bateman 'Notices on archaeological publications', *AJ* xiii (1856), 421.

61 The term 'construct' is used advisedly to emphasis that national identity is always fashioned to meet contemporary demands and as a result is constantly changing. Bateman's emotive language presents the two models in more extreme language than most of the antiquarians chose to use, but his words demonstrate the potential drawbacks of both British and Roman antecedents.

62 Sir Walter Scott, *Introduction to the Waverley Novels*, XVI: *Ivanhoe* (1st pub. 1820), Edinburgh 1860, 4. This depiction of the brave and independent Saxons battling the 'foreign' Normans was to feature in many Victorian histories later in the century: A. Briggs, *Saxons, Normans and Victorians*, Hastings 1966.

Germany had been subjected to French occupation and Napoleon had chosen to present himself as a new Caesar, Tacitus' model offered welcome parallels.

The desire for independence from French rule became focused on a romantic search for an idealised heroic past free of the Roman (or French) shadow. This was clearly articulated in De l'Allemagne by the French Protestant, Madame Germaine de Stael, who had been exiled from France as a result of her opposition to the Napoleonic regime. She suggested that the independent institutions, through which the German people were organised, had their origins in the institutions described by Tacitus in Germania. This demonstrated that the Germanic (or Teutonic) model was as old and tried as its Roman counterpart, but still possessed sufficient energy and enthusiasm to contribute to the birth of the Reformation, and hence Protestantism. By demonstrating the links between past and present in Germany, de Stael offered another tradition to which those fighting for independence could look for inspiration. She had originally written her analysis of the differences between the cultures based on Roman classical forms and those based on the folk traditions of the north to give coherence to a number of anti-classical reactions that she termed Romanticism. But her opposition to the Napoleonic adventures, and her friendship with German intellectuals, led her to revise her script in order to increase its propaganda value as a rallying call for a free and united country.[63] Germany had never been a united nation, but had consisted of a disparate collection of small states and free cities bound together by a vague allegiance to the Holy Roman Empire. In de Stael's book it was described as an admirable, coherent nation and given a central position in her analysis of European history.[64]

By the middle of the nineteenth century this alternative Saxon version of ancestry had begun to emerge in Britain. For example, an 1844 article in the Penny Magazine remarked that 'Two nations only have left permanent impression of their laws, civil polity, social arrangements, spirit and character, on the civilised communities of modern times, the Romans and the handful of Northern people from the countries beyond the Elbe, who had never submitted to the Roman yoke.'[65] But the classical texts presented conflicting pictures of the 'northern people'. For instance, Tacitus' Germania, with its emphasis on German independence and courage, was very different

---

[63] The first edition of the book was pulped by French troops in 1810 and it was finally published in Britain in 1813 when it sold out within days. It was to be re-published frequently in both Britain and France: J. Isbell, The birth of European romanticism: truth and propaganda in Stael's De L'Allemagne, 1810–1813, Cambridge 1994.

[64] I have found only one direct antiquarian reference to de Stael's work and that was in a paper given to the BAA conference in 1849 by Dillon Crocker on the advantages of archaeology to the study of history. Crocker was an Irishman who was keenly interested in the folk tales and stories of Ireland, another country on the Celtic fringe untouched by direct Roman influence.

[65] Penny Magazine, 7 Aug. 1844.

from the account of Ammianus Marcellinus. His description of the Goths'
attack on Rome used phrases such as 'wild beasts threatening cruel carnage',
'barbarians like savage beasts that had broken their cages, poured raging
over the wide extent of Thrace', and 'this madness of times, as if the furies
were confounding the whole world'.[66] Gibbon had used Ammianus in his
Decline and fall and, as a result, these vivid descriptions will have been well
known.[67]

Knowledge of the Saxons and their role in English history had begun to
change as German scholarship, itself partly motivated by the concern to find
roots for German nationalism, became better known in Britain. Barthold
Niebuhr's work on the origins of Roman history was much admired by Thomas
Arnold, who gave his version of national identity to his Oxford students in
1842: 'Our history clearly begins with the coming over of the Saxons; the
Britons and the Romans had lived in our country, but they are not our fathers
... Our English race is the German race.'[68] And Grimm's student, John
Kemble, published *The Saxons in England* in 1849, in which he emphasised
that it was the Saxons who had laid the foundations of English government,
to which he attributed its subsequent stability.[69] Arguments about the extension of the franchise had led to an increased interest in the British constitution and therefore Kemble's emphasis on the Saxon 'mark-community' (that
it was supposed they had brought to England) was particularly apposite.[70] By
stressing that English government was modelled on small, local, self-governing
units, Kemble underlined the difference between English government and
those with a more centralised (and sometimes despotic) administration, such
as France and, by implication, Rome: 'It cannot be without advantage to us
to learn how a state so favoured as our own has set about the great work of
constitution and solved the problem, of uniting the completest [sic] obedi-
ence to the law with the greatest amount of individual freedom.'[71] In 1849
Edward Freeman wrote that 'We have at last learned where to look for our
own fathers: we have at last discovered that we owe not more to Athenian

---

66 Ammianus Marcellinus, trans. John C. Rolfe, Cambridge, MA 1938, XXI.ix.9; XXI.viii.9;
XXXI.x.1.
67 In his first lecture at Cambridge, Charles Kingsley told his students that 'I suppose you
all to be acquainted with the *Germania* of Tacitus and with the 9th chapter of Gibbon':
The Roman and the Teuton, 1.
68 T. Arnold, *Introductory lecture on modern history*, 4th edn, London 1849, 23, 26.
69 Almost all the accounts of history at this period talk of 'England'. I will use the word
when they use it, but otherwise refer to Britain. This is a tale of continual national redefi-
nition. Kemble was making a political point about stability as his book was published in
1849, only one year after revolts had broken out in several European countries. He attributed Britain's robust ability to avoid such difficulties to the Saxon inheritance. He was a
very active member of the Archaeological Institute until his death in 1855.
70 J. W. Burrow, 'The village community', in N. McKendrick (ed.), *Historical perspectives:
studies in English thought and society*, London 1974, 260–1.
71 Kemble, *The Saxons in England*, p. vi, cited in Levine, *The amateur and the professional*,
85.

forms of beauty, to Roman laws and government, than to those seeds of liberty and glory which the despised "barbarians" planted in his German forest.'[72]

The lack of material evidence and knowledge of the Saxon period was reflected in the small number of Saxon artefacts in museum collections. Augustus Franks's 1853 report on the contents of the recently opened British Room in the British Museum stated that 'The additions to the Saxon antiquities have not been very numerous, and that branch of national archaeology is the most deficient in the whole collection.'[73] But under the stimulus of historical work like that of Kemble and Freeman the situation began to change. Increased interest in the Saxon inheritance led to the creation of several important collections of Saxon artefacts by, among others, Richard Neville in Essex, William Rolfe in Kent, William Wylie in Oxfordshire and John Akerman.[74] Roach Smith's rediscovery of the Faussett collection of Saxon grave goods was particularly important both for its contents and for the interest it stimulated as a result of the controversy surrounding its ownership.[75] By the time that Thomas Wright gave his lecture to the British Association for the Advancement of Science in 1855 the possibility of Saxon origins had become well established. He thought that the mixed population that had resulted from centuries of Roman rule had facilitated the amalgamation of the Saxon invaders that had followed their departure. In Wright's opinion, the towns became 'Saxonised' [sic] and the early Celtic population was very small. He concluded that 'The popular story that the people who resisted the Saxons was the ancient Celtic population and that it retired before the conquerors until it found a last refuge in Wales is a mere fiction.'[76]

What emerged was a picture of Anglo-Saxon society that was far removed from the old stereotype of the barbarian hordes as depicted by Ammianus Marcellinus. After Thomas Wright had seen the Faussett collection for the first time he wrote that 'We are accustomed to regard them as half savages, without refinement, rude in their manners, and skilful only in the use of their weapons. But here the followers of Hengist and Horsa seem to rise up before us ... our previous notions vanish ... we see at once the refinements of Saxon life ... and the skill and taste of Saxon workman.'[77] Roach Smith's preface to the catalogue of the Faussett collection, *Inventorium sepulchrale* (1856), is a further indication of changing views of the Saxons and is all the more striking

---

[72] This is cited in Stephens, *Life and letters of Freeman*, 120. Freeman's attempts to substitute 'Saxon' words for those based on Latin were to become notorious.

[73] A. Franks, 'Additions to the collection of national antiquities in the British Museum', *AJ* x (1853), 8.

[74] Neville's work was published in article form in the archaeological journals. Akerman published *Pagan Saxondom* (London 1852–5), which was widely reviewed in the journals. Wylie offered his collection free to the British Museum if they agreed to buy the Faussett collection. Rolfe's collection was bought by Joseph Meyer.

[75] See introduction above.

[76] T. Wright, 'The ethnology of England', *GM* xl (1855), 523.

[77] Idem, *The archaeological album*, London 1845, 10, cited in Rhodes, 'Charles Roach Smith', 221.

because Roach Smith himself was so attached to the Roman inheritance. After giving a fairly standard description of the destruction wrought by the Saxon invasions, he still had to admit that they had 'laws of their own and all the elements of civilisation'. Further, that their artefacts were 'so ingeniously and tastefully constructed and bespeaking skill of a high order that were not at all compatible with a state of barbarism'.[78] He also questioned the traditional view that the departure of the Roman legions and the arrival of the Saxons represented a dramatic cut-off point. In fact the evidence suggested that 'at least a century was required to transform Britain after the Romans into a heptarchy of Teutonic kingdoms' and furthermore the close proximity of Roman and Saxon burial places were 'the result of a close relationship'.[79] In Roach Smith's view, the paucity of information and lack of interest in Saxon remains were all the more surprising precisely because of the frequent references that were made to the Saxon-based foundations of British institutions and laws.[80]

By the middle of the century the importance of the Saxons as the ancestors of choice was well established; they even offered a national hero, King Alfred. In 1849 an Alfred Medal was commissioned to commemorate the thousand-year anniversary of his birth. On one side was his portrait and on the other were the words 'And his children, The British Empire, United States and Anglo Saxons everywhere, 1849'.[81] As the image of the ancient Britons and the Romans became more ambiguous and troublesome, so did the Saxons appear ever more attractive as potential ancestors. As Edward Freeman remarked, 'Men's minds had at last waked to the fact that Greece and Rome did not exhaust the world's stock of wisdom and greatness.'[82] Charles Kingsley presented it as a battle between the old world of the Romans and the new world of the Teutons: 'The Teuton had at last tried his strength against the Roman. The wild forest child had found himself suddenly at death grips with the Enchanter whom he had feared, and almost worshipped for so long; and behold, to his own wonder, he was no more a child, but grown into a man.'[83] This grown man was the ancestor of choice for the Victorians.

[78] Roach Smith, *Inventorium sepulchrale*, p. xx.
[79] Ibid. pp. xii, xiix. The antiquarian Lord Neaves told the Archaeological Institute that 'I believe that most of the traditions that assign fixed dates to ancient immigrations are inaccurate. The invasions of Hengist and Horsa are a myth': 'The Ossianic controversy', 33.
[80] Most academic historical research over the next half century was to be concerned with the growth of the British constitution from its supposed Saxon origins; for instance W. Stubbs, *Constitutional history*, Oxford 1873–8.
[81] Anon., 'The Alfred medal', *ILN*, 27 Oct. 1849, 285. The article also described the Anglo-Saxon jubilee held at Wantage that included divine service, an address and music in the town hall, the distribution of food to the poor, a dinner followed by a ball in the evening; altogether a thoroughly Victorian affair. The article described Alfred's likeness: 'It exhibits the royal philosophic and philanthropic countenance, deeply imbued with Christian virtues.'
[82] This is cited in Stephens, *Life and letters of Freeman*, 120.
[83] Kingsley, *The Roman and the Teuton*, 81.

Local studies and nationalism

The argument so far could seem to suggest that the different versions and interpretations of the past formed a neat series of choices: classical versus romantic; ancient Britain versus Roman; Roman versus Saxon. In practice, of course, this was not the case and it is probably only with the benefit of hindsight that such choices are apparent. Most of the localities had more than one version of the past: an historical one, based on written records, and a popular one, based on local traditions and folk tales, and the two accounts frequently bore little relation to one another. In fact the most conspicuous feature of a local group's activities was its deep concern with its own locality. Concentration on the local is perhaps rather surprising but it is consistent with local antiquarians' apparent lack of interest in national events and debates.

Ambiguity and choice

In general the antiquarians' responses to national origins were ambiguous and inconsistent, not just between group and group or from individual to individual, but frequently within one speech or paper. In reality, the views expressed by almost all the local antiquarians were a mixture. Thus, for instance, Arthur Raikes in Chester could describe the Romans as 'The instrument of God's providence for taming the wilderness and reducing the world to order ... who brought the blessings of eternal peace and of regular government and civilisation.' Then, in the same lecture, 'Our country must have been under the iron sway of Rome and the valour of its unarmed natives must have bowed before the discipline and weapons of its conquerors.'[84] Similarly the author of an article in the *Quarterly Review* described a Roman general as both a 'noble savage' and a 'gallant Roman' in the same paragraph.[85] And the Revd Barton Lodge described the Romans as having both 'barbarous habits' and 'great mental accomplishments' in the same sentence.[86] Some of these apparent inconsistencies arise because of the frequent use of stock adjectives and phrases, for instance 'master of the world', 'conqueror' or 'barbarian' as a sort of shorthand in which one or two words are used to evoke a more complex image. They seem to have been used as rhetorical devices and without much thought, and as a result the modern reader may attribute meaning that was not necessarily intended.

What the inconsistencies do suggest, however, is that apart from general patriotism, local antiquarians had no clearly articulated theories of national origins. Instead, several antiquarians dealt with the mixed origins of the British by suggesting that contemporary Britons were the result of all the best

---

84 A. Raikes, 'Inaugural lecture', *JCAAHS* i (1849–55), 16.
85 J. H. Merivale, 'The Romans at Colchester', *QR* cxciii (1855), 84.
86 B. Lodge, 'Remarks upon a Roman urn', *TEAS* (1858), 132.

qualities of the many nations who had conquered the country throughout its history. For example the Revd David Jones spoke of the contribution made by the four nations that had settled in Caerleon: the ancient Britons were 'quick in thought', the Romans were 'the go ahead people of their day', the Saxons were 'tenacious' and the Normans were 'dignified'.[87] By not excluding any group, these antiquarians were able to explain Britain's contemporary pre-eminence in the world by picking the most favourable aspects of all groups, while excluding the defects that caused so many tensions.

There was general agreement that the Romans had brought 'civilisation' to Britain and, whatever the drawbacks of their rule, the benefits to Britain had been to lay the foundations of contemporary success. Where the groups differed was in regard to the supposed contribution of the ancient Britons and the Romano-Britons, left behind after the Roman withdrawal. In Colchester there was strong support for the idea that the indigenous British population had been well organised and relatively wealthy before the arrival of the Romans. A local antiquarian, Dr P. M. Duncan, thought that the coins produced for the British king, Cunobelin, were strong evidence in favour of a British civilisation before the Romans.[88] He drew a distinction between Cunobelin's coins and much cruder examples from earlier periods 'which in all probability puzzled the youthful Cunobelin quite as much as it did the modern antiquary'.[89] During the controversy surrounding the location of the Tribantine capital of Camulodunum, William Wire supported Duncan's views. He wrote to Roach Smith that 'I cannot conceive of a place to have been the chief town and residence of royalty and to have left no vestiges of its former occupancy.'[90] It is clear that Wire and Duncan were envisioning a more developed and sophisticated society than the crude picture depicted by some other antiquarians.

An author in the *Quarterly Review* was also inclined to see the Trinovantes as civilised:

> The successor of Cassivellaunus [who had led the resistance to Julius Caesar] was not a mere wild man of the woods dwelling in a stockade at the centre of a morass. The court of Cunobelinus, called by Shakespeare

---

[87] D. Jones, 'Address', MM, 24 June 1848. Dean Farrar used a similar approach in a lecture to the Harrow Literary Institute in 1857:'The Briton bequeathed us his faith and awe; the Roman his laws and order; the Saxon his freedom and manliness; the Dane his strength and intrepidity; the Norman his cultivation and enterprise. They died and passed away; and we, the children of all of them, are nobler than any. We are the heirs of all the ages in the foremost files of time.' This is cited in J. H. Plumb, *The death of the past*, London 1969, 87. Farrar was a teacher at Harrow and the author of several books for boys.

[88] P. Duncan, 'History and description of the walls of Colchester', TEAS i (1858), 26.

[89] Ibid. 27. This comment demonstrates the antiquarians' increasing ability to differentiate between the tribes encountered by Caesar in 55 BCE and the more advanced society defeated in the Claudian invasion a hundred years later.

[90] Wire to Charles Roach Smith, 1 Dec. 1851, Wire letter book. In another letter he remarked that they would only have left so little behind if 'they were in so rude a state as to lap water with their tongues and eat food of leaves': Wire to Roach Smith, 8 Dec. 1851.

Cymbeline, was not perhaps, much less refined than it appears in the poet's strange medley of fact and fancy. It was the resort of Italians no less than Gauls; and the chamber of the king's daughter may well have been adorned with stories from Southern mythology, for the coinage of the king of the Trinobantes, the only monument of his civilisation we might expect to survive, is not unworthy in style and execution of a Roman mint.[91]

Wire, Duncan and the anonymous author in the *Quarterly Review* were agreed that the defeated Britons, in spite of leaving no written record, were not primitive in terms of their social organisation and skills. But it is interesting that they measured the tribes' level of civilisation using Roman standards. This would seem to suggest that they were more influenced by the classical world than they were willing to admit.

Thanks to the high profile of the Essex tribes in the classical texts, more was known about them than about the tribes in any other part of the country. The antiquarians were aware that they were looking at the vestiges of a more developed society introduced by recent migrations from the continent. It is perhaps not surprising, therefore, that these positive attitudes to the ancient Britons should occur in Colchester. What is surprising is that although the antiquarians describe the town's destruction during the revolt, they hardly mention Boudica. A possible explanation for this could be that the lurid details of murder and revenge found in Dio Cassius were difficult to connect with their generally more positive view of the British tribes and, as a result, Boudica's part in the drama was ignored. If the more detailed knowledge of Colchester's past allowed a fuller and less stereotyped picture, it also high-lighted the ambiguities presented by an apparently civilised society led by a woman behaving with cruel barbarity. What is clear is that in the Essex society, attitudes towards the different groups of origin were divided. Cutts's views were representative of those who felt that Roman influence was the dominant factor in British civilisation. But others disagreed and William Wire, for instance, makes no reference to the debt owed to the Romans. It is possible that Wire's lack of a conventional classical education enabled him to appreciate more easily the contribution of other ancestral groups, but it is also likely that differences of opinion regarding the origins of British society were a reflection of the social divides within the Essex group itself.[92]

The Caerleon society was another group that gave a prominent place to non-Roman origins, namely the ancient Britons and the Romano-British in the person of King Arthur. David Jones described

---

[91] Merivale, 'The Romans in Colchester', 71–105. In his journal Wire reported that 'I have been credibly informed that the author is the Rev. Merivale of Lawford': WWJ, entry for 21 July 1855.

[92] Norman Vance makes the point that the controversy surrounding the possible Roman origins of the Norman castle arose from 'unacknowledged reluctance to confront the evidence of conquest despite genuine fascination with the relics of Empire': *The persistence of Rome*, 241.

The four distinguished nations who have in turn occupied the ground upon which we now stand the Ancient Britons, the Romans, the Saxons and the Normans ... Of the four which have each in turn been the familiar tongue of this place, the two which have survived have been the language of the oppressed and of the conquered, not the language of the conquerors.[93]

He went on to identify himself as an ancient Briton and, although he does not say so, it is probable that he spoke Welsh, the language of an oppressed people. His description was a useful device to emphasise the mixture of different peoples coming together in contemporary south Wales.[94] But his use of language is provocative since he was speaking at a time when the central government in London was actively trying to discourage the Welsh language. The notorious blue books on Welsh education had just been published and had dramatically illustrated the fear of Welsh workers felt by the ruling class.[95] The anger with which the reports were received became known as 'The treason of the blue books'. This was a reference to the treason of the long knives, an old Celtic story according to which the leader of the ancient Britons, Vortigen, had been treacherously killed by the Saxon leaders, Hengist and Horsa. The story had become useful again in the 1840s to describe the way in which Saxon England was not to be trusted in its dealings with the Welsh.[96] By proclaiming himself an ancient Briton, Jones was clearly positioning himself on the side of the conquered, whose language was under threat. It was an oblique political point, but it will not have been lost on his audience and it needs to be understood if the modern observer is to make sense of Jones's portrayal of the past and its relevance to contemporary concerns.

The interest that Welsh antiquarians showed in the details of the Roman conquest of Wales can be interpreted as one way in which resurgent Welsh nationalism found an acceptable voice in the 1840s. The journal which dealt

---

93 D. Jones, 'Stone laying ceremony, MM, 24 June 1848, 3.

94 A rather different, albeit somewhat patronising view of the Welsh is given in Lady Charlotte Guest's diary: 'All Saxon as I am, my own countrymen chill my shyness into pride. But the dear Welsh, with their ready smile and never failing welcome, make me feel amongst them as another being': The diaries of Lady Charlotte Guest, ed. Frederick Posonby, Lord Bessborough, London 1950, 182.

95 The English newspaper reports on the blue books are revealing as they illustrate the way in which Welsh workers were perceived by at least some English observers. For instance the Morning Chronicle declared that 'the Welsh are fast settling down into the most savage barbarism', and the Examiner thought that Welsh habits were 'those of animals and would not bear description': D. Williams, A history of modern Wales, London 1950, 274. Such comments would suggest that English observers saw little difference between contemporary Welsh people and the popular stereotypes of ancient Britons.

96 The Welsh language and the dissenting chapels were seen as the unifying factors around which revolt might be organised: Williams, History of modern Wales, 199–215. Williams cites a warning letter sent by 'Rebecca' during the Rebecca Riots in Wales (1839–43): 'It is a shameful [sic] thing for us Welshmen to have the sons of Hengist to have dominion over us, do you not remember the long knives, which Hengist hath invented to kill our forefathers and you may depend that you shall receive the same if you will not give up when I shall call to visit you' (based on PRO, HO/45/265).

specifically with Welsh antiquities, *Archaeologia Cambrensis*, was founded in 1846 and contained several articles that portrayed the brave Britons defending themselves against foreign usurpers.[97] For instance an article by Samuel Meyrick in 1848 maintained that the Romans, 'While they appeared to be only putting an end to the horrid rites of human sacrifice, they were in reality undermining the powers assumed by the Druids and riveting more firmly the chains of those they had subdued.'[98] Caractacus proved useful as a symbol of independence and resistance to outside occupation and as such he was 'adopted' by some Welsh antiquaries. In an article on a supposed site of his final battle with the Romans, one author describes him as 'Caractacus the renowned leader of the Silures [who] made his last stand in defence of the liberties of his country.'[99] Another article about the site of the same battle illustrates the ambiguity at the heart of all these conflicts between Rome and the ancient Britons: 'Whether we view it with the patriotism of a Briton, or with a grateful sense of Roman benefaction, we must regard that event as the commencement of an important era in the history of Wales.'[100] The fact that Caractacus was not a member of the Silures tribe and that there is no evidence that this last battle was in Wales was not allowed to interfere with these fanciful references.

Alternative histories
What the articles illustrate is that there were many differing versions of what happened in the past and that the accuracy of such stories mattered less than that they should satisfy the particular needs of the audience for whom they were intended. According to Raphael Samuel 'myth and history are not incompatible, but coexist as complementary and sometimes intersecting modes of representing the past'.[101] Certainly, all four areas had their own versions of the local past. In each case there was the history based on evidence, contained in texts and artefacts (what could be termed the professional account), and then there were the unofficial accounts, based on myths, legend and stories passed from one generation to another, often by word of mouth. Towards the end of the nineteenth century, as historians and archaeologists struggled to gain acceptance for themselves as professional academics, one of the methods they used to distinguish their work from the amateur activities of the antiquarians

[97] The joint editors of the *Archaeologica Cambrensis* were the Revd H. Longueville Jones and the Revd John Williams. The latter's main interest was philology and he was a fanatical supporter of Welsh nationalism, preferring to call himself by the Welsh name, Ab Ithel. His views eventually led to disagreements and he resigned as editor. It is probable that his opinions were shared by at least some of the journal's subscribers.
[98] S. Rush Meyrick, 'On the Druidic religion in Britain', AC iii (1848), 14.
[99] J. Davies, 'British and Roman encampments of Herefordshire', AC n.s. ii (1851), 45. Davies was a Herefordshire solicitor.
[100] W. Foulkes, 'Site of the last battle of Caractacus, AC n.s. ii (1851), 122.
[101] Samuel, *Theatres of memory*, ii. 14.

was to scorn the contribution and relevance of these other accounts. But in the mid-Victorian period many antiquarians were still debating and giving credence to these other histories, as happened in the debates about Geoffrey of Monmouth's account of British origins.[102] Another example was when Roach Smith excavated the fallen walls at the Roman fortress at Lymne. He found that 'popular tradition had attributed the destruction to an earthquake; and this belief, it is now proved, was nearer the truth than the notion of those who attributed its overthrow to the Saxons'.[103]

These alternative versions allowed local individuals and events to play a part although they might well be excluded from more official records. As Richard Neville pointed out, 'where authentic narrative fails, popular tradition is the ground work of history'. In Essex there appears to have been a strong local tradition that the Danes had played a significant role and that the local Bartlow Hills 'owed their elevation to the Danes, being raised to cover the bodies of those slain in battle between Canute and Edmund Ironside'.[104] Although Neville's excavations came to the conclusion that the mounds were Roman, the appeal of the Danish stories continued, presumably because they involved events that had had a major impact on the locality and had therefore been retained in oral accounts. Neville recognised that these local traditions were both popular and resistant to analysis: 'Some antiquarians may be dissatisfied with my endeavours to penetrate the mist that floats around these gigantic fosses, since by throwing light upon their construction and eliciting their true date the stories relative to their early origins must necessarily be destroyed.'[105]

However Caerleon's claim to have been the site of King Arthur's court was the best known and most fully developed alternative version of the past. The story had been constructed, at least in part, for nationalist purposes. It had first been put forward in Geoffrey of Monmouth's *History of the kings of Britain* (1138–9) in which Arthur is described as a great British king who defeated the Saxons and created an empire. The book was written against the background of a revolt of the Welsh in south Wales against the Normans in the course of which Welsh lords recaptured most of the area, including Caerleon. A story that offered ancient origins and a leader who led his people to victory over a foreign invader was particularly welcome when the Welsh were under attack from either the Normans or the English.[106] By the beginning of the nine-

---

102 See chapter 1 above.
103 C. Roach Smith, *Report on excavations made on the site of the Roman castrum at Lymne in Kent in 1850*, London 1852, 7.
104 Neville, *Antiqua explorata*, 30.
105 Idem, *Sepulchra exposita*, 55.
106 See R. Howells, 'Roman survival, Welsh revival: the evidence of re-use of Roman remains', *Monmouthshire Antiquary* xvii (2001), 58. Howells argues that the Welsh used the extensive Roman remains to enhance their prestige in their fight to regain independence from the Normans. It was to ensure that this could not happen again that the Normans destroyed most of the remaining Roman buildings when they recaptured the town in 1217.

teenth century many antiquarians were beginning to question the account in Geoffrey's history, but local people did not agree. According to William Coxe in 1801 'the natives of Caerleon… point out the remains of the Roman amphitheatre, under the name of King Alfred's Round Table, from a supposition that a military order was here instituted, which first raised the spirit of chivalry in Europe'.[107] The power and appeal of the Arthur legend is apparent from the number of times it was retold, for instance in the Celtic epic The Mabinogion that Lady Charlotte Guest translated into English in 1843 and again in Tennyson's The idyll of the kings. The Geraint and Enid section of the poem includes a reference to the tension between cultures that is personified in the ruins of Caerleon:

Who swept the dust of ruin'd Rome
From off the threshold of the realm, and crush'd
The Idolaters and made the people free?
Who should be king, save him who makes us free?[108]

The appeal of the Arthur story lay in the way it lent itself to be used as a symbol of resistance to outsiders, be they Roman, Norman or English.

The importance of place

It had always been maintained that the objective of the local antiquarian societies was to discover and illustrate all aspects of the history of their own locality, as the bishop of Llandaff reminded the Cambrian Archaeological Association:

The local antiquary was ever the only effective purveyor of local materials; he was animated by the keen zeal of local affections; and in investigating the history and remains of his own district, felt himself really engaged in elucidating the bygone fortunes of his own immediate ancestry; he alone possessed that full and accurate knowledge of local details which others must want.[109]

Whereas an increasingly professional body of historians and archaeologists concerned themselves with detailed accounts of specific aspects of the national past, it was the minutiae of local events and the local topography that fired the imagination of the local antiquarians. And nowhere is this more apparent than in the lack of interest that the local societies showed in the national organisations. Although they all subscribed to either the Archaeological Institute or the British Archaeological Association, and frequently both, the individual local members were largely uninvolved in national

107 Coxe, Monmouthshire, 102.
108 Tennyson, 'The idyll of the kings', in Tennyson poems, ii.
109 [Alfred Olivant], bishop of Llandaff, 'The antiquities of Glamorgan', AC iv (1849), 299.

campaigns. Indeed it would be possible to read local journals and accounts of meetings and be left totally unaware of national debates, such as the founding of a British Room in the British Museum or the fate of the Faussett collection, issues that loomed so large in the national bodies. The only exceptions were those individuals who were already involved in other arenas of public life. For example, Octavius Morgan was an MP and chaired meetings of the London Society of Antiquaries and Richard Neville, who as Lord Braybrook sat in the House of Lords, was a vice-president of the Archaeological Institute. But in most cases even those men who were most active at a local level, such as Edward Lee in Caerleon and William Massie in Chester, did not comment on national affairs. This is not to say that they were uninterested or unpatriotic, merely that they had different agenda and used different methods to achieve their ends.

The antiquarians' local pride and patriotism is apparent in the links that they attempted to draw between their own locality and well-known figures and events in national history. In effect, they 'borrowed' national figures and pictured them against the backdrop of their own area. This could involve imagining the march of events in a particular location, as Mr J. Hicklin told the Archaeological Institute's meeting in Chester: 'The walls of Chester have echoed to the tramp of the legions of Rome; here the raven standard of the Danes floated amidst scenes of carnage and tumult; here the Barons of the Norman court have displayed all the chivalry of history.'[110] In other instances, the antiquarians imagined single, well-known figures acting out their historical role against a particular local scene. For example, Raike claimed that Agricola's headquarters for his Welsh campaigns might have been at Chester: 'The very spot on which we are met, the point where the streets intersect was doubtless the Praetorium … Agricola may have held his councils and issued his orders to the twentieth legion from this, the central part of the city.'[111] As John Marsden, Disney Professor of Archaeology at Cambridge, remarked 'we are bound by association to the scenes which were once frequented by great and good men'.[112] He illustrated his argument by describing a grassy slope outside the walls of Colchester where the commanders of the royalist garrison had been shot after the town fell to parliamentary troops in 1648: 'An interest deep and sad is at once created in regard to the spot on which he would not otherwise have bestowed a single thought.'[113]

Marsden believed that these associations were one advantage of living in an old country: 'The Americans who visit England have no such reminiscences at home, are found in many instances to show as much interest in these of their mother country as we do ourselves.'[114] It is a pity that he did

[110] J. Hicklin, 'Proceedings', AJ xiv (1857), 366.
[111] A. Raikes, 'Inaugural address', JCAAHS i (1849–55), 16.
[112] J. Marsden, 'Inaugural lecture on archaeology', TEAS i (1858), 23.
[113] Ibid. 24.
[114] Ibid. Marsden's use of the phrase 'mother country' is interesting: could he be making an oblique reference to America's former colonial status?

not choose to elaborate on the particular nature of the advantage, but we could speculate that he was suggesting that a sense of belonging to one place that had remained intact over a long period was reassuring to its inhabitants. In France, Germany and Italy, where there had been major political changes involving the very existence of the nation state, governments had attempted to create a national past with which individuals could identify. In effect, these national myths were a means of shoring up shaky regimes, what Michael Dietler has called 'a highly politicised construction of national memory and identification'.[115] In Britain, by contrast, the difficulties had been created for individuals, brought about by the massive social changes involved in industrialisation and urbanisation. One way of dealing with these upheavals was for individuals to create a sense of belonging to a specific locality through involvement with its past. And if that locality had played some conspicuous part in national events or had been particularly splendid, then some of that prominence and prestige could still be attached to the contemporary town and, by association, to its inhabitants. What the local antiquarians were doing, maybe unknowingly, was tracing local origins and in the process giving local people a sense of pride and identity with 'their' town. The function of the numerous local societies was to provide an arena in which they could do so.

[115] M. Dietler, 'A tale of three sites: the monumentalization of Celtic *oppida* and the politics of collective memory and identity', *World Archaeology* xxx (1998), 76. Dietler quotes Napoleon III in 1866: 'In honouring the memory of Vercingetorix, we must not lament his defeat. Let us admire the ardent and sincere love of this Gallic chief for the independence of his country, but let us not forget that it is due to the Roman armies that we owe our civilisation; our institutions, our customs, our language, all this comes to us from the conquest.' Picking the best attributes of all national origins was not an activity confined to the British antiquarians. Napoleon III was a great admirer of Julius Caesar, an authoritarian ruler who replaced a chaotic political situation. The parallels are obvious.

3

Gentlemen and Scientists

Philippa Levine has described antiquarians in the nineteenth century as 'a highly motivated self-taught elite on familiar and friendly terms with one another and sharing a common body of knowledge'.[1] She argues that 'it was this coalescence of community and class that prompted perception of their common experience as binding and correct, as possessed of an authority and a code of practice largely unspoken but none the less powerful'.[2] In other words a common interest in the past of their locality was not the only characteristic shared by group members, although its investigation and preservation were the publicly stated objectives.

Most groups have both overt and covert aims; a truism which was as apt in the Victorian period as it is now as several studies of intellectual and scientific groups in provincial society of the period make clear.[3] For instance, in a series of papers on the relationship between ideas and their social context, Ian Inkster has argued that 'science has social functions in the social system and social uses for the individuals comprising it'.[4] According to this view, the subject matter or overt aim is only one function of a group; its social roles are equally important although rarely spelled out. Michael Neve has examined the ways in which ideas can be utilised socially. Either they can be used 'among marginal men as a means of social legitimisation', or 'they can play a decisive role within established elites in the manufacture of a new language of authority and political power'.[5] In other words, new ideas and their associated organisations could be used as a vehicle either to attack or to confirm the social *status quo*. They had an important role to play in the confrontation between the growing numbers of the professional middle class and the traditional social networks of authority and control.[6] The ruling group could assimilate aspiring new members and make use of their skills and knowledge to strengthen the *status quo*, as was the case in the careers of Edward Lee in Caerleon and John Buckman in Cirencester. Alternatively, such individuals could be ostracised as happened in the case of William Wire in Colchester. The excluded individuals could, in theory, create alternative groups to challenge the traditional ruling networks.

---

1 Levine, *The amateur and the professional*, 7.
2 Ibid. 4.
3 I. Inkster and J. Morrell (eds), *Metropolis and province: science in British culture, 1780–1850*, London 1983; Morrell and Thackray, *Gentlemen of science*, 1–35.
4 I. Inkster, 'Introduction', to Inkster and Morrell, *Metropolis and province*, 14.
5 M. Neve, 'Science in a commercial city: Bristol, 1820–1860', ibid. 179.
6 See D. Fraser, *Power and authority in the Victorian city*, Oxford 1979.

This study's findings would seem to support the view that the local societies and their committees were composed of individuals who played a major part in all aspects of town life. The same individuals formed a complex network of overlapping contacts operating in many facets of society and frequently rein-forced by marriage and family ties. It was through their dominant position that these socially cohesive groups were able to retain and control local power. Even in the case of Cirencester, where no group emerged, this appeared to be a consequence of the community's acceptance of Lord Bathurst's pre-eminent position.

In Caerleon, Colchester and Cirencester, ownership was in the form of collections and museums, whose changing location and form often symbol-ised changes in the locus of control. This close identification between place and the ruling group meant that anything that enhanced the supposed impor-tance of a locality also increased the prestige of its governing body. In much the same way that nation states sought to increase national pride by laying claim to a glorious history, so a town's leading citizens were eager to embrace evidence of the importance of their locality in the national past. It follows that the findings of the local archaeologists' activities could be seen as not only important to the town, but also as increasing the standing of its leaders. Local archaeology and the interests of the ruling group were thus mutually reinforcing. Moreover, in the case of the local groups in this study, specifi-cally chosen because they had played a conspicuous part in the unearthing of Roman Britain, the material evidence of that association with the clas-sical Roman past could be seen as endowing those involved with some social advantage. Precisely because knowledge of the classical world and, in partic-ular, an ownership of classical artefacts, had been taken as a manifestation of gentility, the evidence of such associations could only confirm the social standing of those involved and thus justify their position.

The local groups

There is only very limited information about membership of the groups in general and it is therefore difficult to gauge the extent of individual members' involvement. Most of the available evidence describes the committee members and therefore it has to be assumed that the social characteristics of the membership were broadly similar to those of the committees and the analysis is based on this assumption. In all the groups the same names appear year after year as both committee members and authors of the journal arti-cles and the names of those in general membership are conspicuous only by their non-appearance.[7] We could speculate that one possible difference was that the committee members were more interested in the study of the past,

---

[7]   This appears to have caused some annoyance. See Lee's reports to the CAA reported in the MM, 14 July 1849, and Massie's obituary notice in *JCAAHS* i (1849–55), 401.

whereas the ordinary members were more interested in being identified as members of the ruling elite. There was some evidence in Chester that this was the case.

Some idea of group composition can be gathered from the limited lists that have survived, for instance the list of subscribers to the fund for building the Museum of Antiquities in Caerleon.[8] It contains forty-eight names and in a few cases the town where they live is identified. Of the forty-eight, one is a bishop, five are Anglican ministers, two are identified by their rank as ex-soldiers and two are members of parliament. There are only three women. By 1863 the membership had risen to 149, most of them living locally. The list includes many members of the leading county families as well as the most prominent business and industrial names from nearby Newport. The numbers of Anglican ministers had risen to about a quarter of the total membership and there were twenty-four women. The number of leading citizens suggests that the society was regarded as one of the bodies which they considered worthy of their patronage.[9]

Social events played an important role in creating group cohesion and fostering shared interests. They demonstrated the social importance of the members and in so doing confirmed their sense of superiority and security to both themselves and the community at large. Society journals and local newspaper reports provide numerous examples of group outings and activities that emphasised group solidarity as much as they helped the furtherance of archaeological knowledge. One example is a report of a bazaar held by the Caerleon group in 1848 to raise money for the new museum: 'The bells rang their best peal, the town wore quite a gala appearance, and the leading inhabitants kept open house and furnished hospitable tables, terminating the day with a dance.'[10] Or, in a very different vein, this was a journal account of William Massie's funeral in Chester: 'To the solemn music of The Dead March, and a funeral peal from the muffled bells, the mournful procession, composed of clergy, magistrates, citizens and soldiery moved on towards the cemetery.'[11] In both cases the leading citizens' involvement with archaeology and with the town seems to merge into one, each part indivisible from the other.

The Chester society was the only group to hold regular monthly meetings open to all the membership. The impression gained from their journal is that many of these meetings were regarded more as pleasant social events than anything to do with archaeology. It is possible that the covert function of the Chester society, namely that of providing another forum in which the

---

[8] G. Jones, 'John Edward Lee: a Monmouthshire antiquary', unpubl. MA diss. University of Wales 1991, contains a photocopy of the list. Its whereabouts are not given.
[9] The second list appears as an appendix to a report by Morgan and Wakeman on local castles. Most of the women were relatives of the male members, which underlines the importance of the social aspects of the group's activities.
[10] MM, 28 July, 1848.
[11] Anon., 'The late Rev. W. H. Massie', JCAAHS i (1849–55), 404.

members could meet other in the same social circle, had been so successful that its stated antiquarian aims were in danger of being lost. This problem was not confined to Chester; the Archaeological Insitute was told in 1858 that 'the business of the Institute must not be confined to the study of archaeology by means of hospitable entertainments, however pleasant that course might be. But the scientific department however dry or tedious should be strictly followed up'.[12] The ruling committees, on the other hand, met regularly and thus probably reinforced their dominance within the groups.

Antiquarians also maintained links with each other through regular meetings with other societies. Many of these took place at the annual meetings of the national archaeological bodies that met over five days in a variety of British cities. When the Archaeological Institute visited Caerleon in 1851, the whole party of eighty guests sat down to a picnic in the middle of the Roman amphitheatre. At the Chester meeting in 1857 a large party went by special train to Liverpool, where a long day of sightseeing was rounded off with 'a brilliant conversazione to which they had been invited by the Historic Society of Lancashire in the Town Hall'.[13] Less formal gatherings were also used to identify members of the elite group. The *Wiltshire and Gloucestershire Standard* reported that an excursion train had brought a number of visitors from London to see the contents of the new museum in Cirencester. The article listed the names of all the visitors, evidence of the way in which such reports could allow fellow antiquarians to identify each other and share the same information.[14]

Another practice that assisted both the spread of information and the identification of fellow enthusiasts was through the lists of subscribers to archaeological books and journals. It was common practice at this time to print books for subscription only. The prospective author would advertise his intention to write a book and invite those interested to subscribe. The names of the subscribers would subsequently be listed in the publication. Apart from the obvious advantage of assured sales, these lists could serve to demonstrate to contemporary society the interest and taste of those named. Many archaeology books were published in this way, including most of Roach Smith's volumes of *Collectanea antiqua* and Richard Neville's on Roman archaeology in Essex.[15] In these relatively small social circles many of the names will have

---

[12] J. Talbot, 'Presidential address', *AJ* xiv (1858), 369. In his study of the Leeds Philosophical and Literary Society Jeremy Morris describes a similar situation: 'For many members, the Phil. and Lit. became one aspect of their leisure and relaxation with only a thin veneer of education': *Class, sect and party: the making of the middle class in Leeds*, Manchester 1990, 232.

[13] Anon., 'Proceedings', *AJ* xiv (1858), 378.

[14] *WGS*, 4 Aug. 1860. The importance of the railways in enabling easy access to archaeological sites should not be underestimated.

[15] Roach Smith, *Collectanea antiqua*, i–vi; Neville, *Antiqua explorata* (1847) and *Sepulchra exposita* (1848) both printed privately in Saffron Walden.

been familiar and the lists will have enhanced the sense of belonging to a group with shared intellectual tastes and similar social position.[16]

These shared social and intellectual activities were based upon fundamental similarities that were common to most (although not all) the group leaders and members. These were money, leisure and an acknowledged position within their local communities, generally based on shared political and religious views. These three characteristics were so closely related to each other that, although there were individual exceptions, they apply to the majority of the members. Antiquarianism was essentially an amateur pursuit and therefore it was necessary that an individual should have other sources of income in order to allow sufficient free time to devote to antiquarian activities. All the local leaders discussed in this book had either private means or a career or business that rendered an income without demanding a full-time commitment. Sir Digby Mackworth, Octavius Morgan and Thomas Wakeman in Caerleon, John Taylor and Henry Vint in Colchester and the architects, James Harrison and M. Penson in Chester are all examples of such men, as are the large numbers of ministers.[17] The career of Augustus Franks provides a fascinating mirror reflection. He was a wealthy man of leisure and so when he was offered a paid post at the British Museum he had to consider 'whether it would not be infra dig for me to take a post'.[18]

Chester provides the best example of a socially cohesive group that faithfully reflected the main features of the local society. Its committee was intentionally composed of representatives of the powerful Anglican hierarchy connected with the bishopric. Whose idea this was is not known, but it is possible that it was the accepted and normal way of doing things in a city so heavily dominated by the Church. Because Chester had largely avoided major industrialisation, its middle class was more traditionally based in the professions, rather than in the innovating world of industry and science, as in the larger cities of the north-west, including Liverpool and Manchester. It was a society that still represented in many aspects the older structures of power and authority pre-dating the industrial revolution. In 1880 a local councillor commented on the city's lack of enterprise: 'I am afraid there is a spirit in the council that would push Chester into a corner and make it little better than a village.'[19] According to a local historian in 1831 it was a town which actively traded on its stability and unchanging aspects in order to attract

---

[16] For the modern researcher the subscribers' lists give some indication of the audience for particular books and subjects. Many names appear repeatedly, for instance Roach Smith, Lee, Neville, Bruce and Way. Just as informative is the absence of other names. For instance, I have never seen Buckman's name on a subscribers' list, which would suggest that he confined his interests to antiquities in his own area.

[17] Levine, *The amateur and the professional*, appendix v, 'Clerical membership of local societies'.

[18] D. M. Wilson, *The forgotten collector: Augustus Wollaston Franks of the British Museum*, London 1984, 12.

[19] This is cited in J. Herson, 'Victorian Chester: a city of change and ambiguity', in Swift, *Victorian Chester*, 40.

the more conservative-minded to come and live in it. The concentration on architecture and the desire to retain the ancient-looking façade are indicative of more than mere economic interest. They also suggest a conservative outlook that sought reassurance in the continuity of the religious institutions and the physical manifestations of the city's links with the past. Unlike Colchester, where new developments were leading to a polarisation of many of the town's institutions, in Chester there was an apparent social harmony that did not require its citizens to proclaim allegiances or to position themselves as belonging to one social class rather than another. It was not that social divisions did not exist, rather that they were so generally accepted as to render the polarisation of interests relatively unnecessary.

The Chester group also illustrates the way in which certain leading citizens played a variety of different roles, in which their membership of the antiquarian society was only one part of a multi-faceted involvement with the town's civic life. Massie's obituary in the society's journal praised his work with the poor during the 1849 cholera epidemic, a concern that found expression in his work as a member of the Sanitary Committee and as an active campaigner for sanitary reform. Raikes was very involved in the creation of a Ragged School Institution to provide schooling for the poorest children in the town. Another committee member, and curator of the society's informal museum, Thomas Pullen, had helped to set up the public baths, the Mechanics' Institute and the Water Tower museum and its associated gardens. It was through their involvement with a number of bodies, operating in all aspects of the town's life, that these citizens confirmed their position as natural leaders in Chester. Seen in this context, their involvement with the Chester Archaeological Society was just one connection amongst many. Members of the Chester society were so confident of their stable social position that they offered membership to the working men of the city, something that no other society felt able to do. But as the nature of their activities in setting up 'improving institutions' such as a mechanical institute suggests, their involvement with working people was almost akin to civilising the natives overseas.[20] The noticeable lack of response to this traditional, paternalistic gesture might suggest that social harmony was not quite as complete as the city fathers might have hoped.[21]

If Chester is an example of a group that successfully upheld and reinforced social cohesion, then the Essex antiquarians illustrate a society attempting to contain social dissent. The manner in which the Essex Archaeological

[20] David Cannadine argues that the traditional hierarchy of power at 'home' was reproduced in the empire, in such a way that the factory workers were equated with native people abroad. The assumption was that both groups were inferior and had to be controlled: *Ornamentalism: how the British saw their empire*, London 2001. See also R. J. Morris and R. Rogers (eds), *The Victorian city: a reader in British urban history, 1820–1914*, New York 1993, 34–5.

[21] A similar lack of enthusiasm on the part of the workers was evident in the Mechanics Institute in Newport.

Society took over the original Colchester group and, in so doing, marginalised William Wire, is an example of the way in which a less confident group
dealt with the aspirations of those who could be seen as a possible threat to
their interests. Again it is the context in which these events were played out
that helps to explain them.

In Colchester every aspect of social and religious activity in the town was
divided along both political and religious lines, reflecting in microcosm many
of the disputes in contemporary British society. On one side were the Tories,
who had traditionally dominated the corporation and had links with the
county gentry. Their mouthpiece was the *Essex Standard* and they upheld the
favoured position of the Anglican Church. The Liberal opposition was based
in the many dissenting chapels in the town and their failure to win control of
the council meant that they had to bring their influence to bear through such
bodies as the Poor Law Guardians and the Sanitary Committee.

In this polarised society, every local organisation was perceived as on one
side or the other, and the fate of the Colchester Archaeological Society,
founded in 1850 by William Wire, seems to bear this out. The new body
never really got off the ground and it was only in 1852, when a new society
for the whole county was proposed, with the support of the local gentry, that
a local antiquarian society really began to flourish. The allegiance of the
new body was clear. The initial planning meeting was held in the library of
the Revd J. Round, who had opposed the town museum and whose brother,
Charles, owned the castle building. Half of those present were Anglican
ministers. The rules of the new society stipulated that the vice-presidents
should be noblemen and members of parliament, and that the bishop and
lord lieutenant were to be patrons. County men dominated the proceedings.
Two of the most active members were the Revd John Marsden and Richard
Neville. Both men were typical of the old-style antiquarian, with money and
leisure, leaving them free to follow other pursuits. In addition, they both had
links with other organisations of the ruling group – in Marsden's case to the
University of Cambridge and in Neville's to the House of Lords. It is quite
clear that William Wire, working man, Chartist sympathiser and dissenter,
would not fit into the new body.[22]

It is probable that the need to earn a living interfered with Wire's ability
to manage the original Colchester society. But this does not explain what
appears to have been his almost total exclusion from the new county body.
Wire was quite sure that it was his lack of the usual attributes of a gentleman,
namely money and a classical education, that had made him the outsider,
even though he was frequently better informed than those who excluded
him. Petty personal jealousies were doubtless a part of the explanation. But
if a longer-term view is taken, and the disagreements are put into the wider
context of the fractured and troubled society of Colchester in the middle

[22] Sources for Wire include his journal, an unpublished notebook in the possession of
Colchester Museum, which also has a number of letters from Roach Smith to Wire. Wire's
own letters are in his letter book (1847–53) which is in the Essex Record Office.

years of the nineteenth century, then these events would appear to be a good example of group interests protecting their position. It is interesting to speculate whether the relatively more cohesive society in Chester would have been able to assimilate this intelligent and knowledgeable man without regarding him as a threat. But it is probable that Wire was just too different in too many ways to be easily assimilated into any group organised by the ruling interest.

On the other hand, Edward Lee, in Caerleon, is an example of an individual who, while differing in several significant ways from the usual membership of antiquarian societies, was none the less both accepted and became a pivotal figure. This was due in part to the manner in which he chose to present himself. It was also a consequence of the differences between the social context of south Wales and that of the other three areas. After a visit to Caerleon in 1856 Alfred Lord Tennyson described the town as 'a most quiet, half ruined village', and described Lee as 'a landed proprietor'.[23] But appearances can be deceptive and both his descriptions were inaccurate.

Although Caerleon was little more than a village, its close proximity to the expanding and prosperous communities in the east Gwent valleys and the sea at Newport, meant that its apparently rural appearance was misleading. With the exception of Sir Digby Mackworth and some Anglican ministers, most of the Caerleon Archaeological Association's committee members had links with this industrial activity. There were the owners of the two local tinplate works, John Jenkins and John Butler, and a railway surveyor, Francis Fox. Octavius Morgan, despite his antiquarian tastes and close association with the leading families, owed his income and lifestyle to the Tredegar estate's domination of the transport routes through which coal was shipped to the world. Lee himself was a partner in a large nail works in Newport, as was another committee member, Frederick Mitchell.[24] These were not men living in a rural backwater, passing the time with antiquarian enquiry; rather they were closely involved with those very forces of innovation and technology which in other parts of the country were seen as threatening an old way of life. But although they were involved in economic changes, they did share many of the social characteristics of antiquarian leaders in other, more conservative, areas, such as Chester and Cirencester.

Edward Lee, as a man from outside the locality, and a dissenter, could have appeared as a potential threat. He came to Newport in 1841 in order to become a partner in the nail works. He invested a considerable sum of money in the business, but he was not to be a sleeping partner for the agreement between himself and the owner, J. J .Cordes, stipulated that they would run the business together.[25] But whereas Cordes's large house overlooked the works in Newport, Lee did not want to identify himself so closely with the

[23] Alfred Lord Tennyson to Emily Sellwood Tennyson, 16, 17 Sept. 1856, in *Letters of Alfred Lord Tennyson, II: 1851–70*, ed. C. Y. Lang and E. F. Shannon, Oxford 1987, 158.
[24] Mitchell joined the CAA committee in 1854 and his son, F. J. Mitchell, became joint secretary with Lee in 1871.
[25] The agreement, dated 1 June 1841, is in the Gwent Record Office (D 169.000).

place in which he worked and he chose instead to live in Caerleon, several miles away, in a large house, where he could live the life of a gentleman.

In many respects Lee would appear to illustrate the attributes of a 'gentleman of science' as described by Arnold Thackray and Jack Morrell in their study of the British Association for the Advancement of Science. They note that the first generation of industrial entrepreneurs were not from, and were not interested in joining, the landed gentry. But by the 1840s 'industrialists of the second and third generation' were more interested in joining these elites.[26] In the face of civil unrest at home and reports of revolution abroad, they sought reassurance and support by associating themselves with authority. Lee had already experienced the way in which outsiders could be assimilated through his early contact with the British Association for the Advancement of Science and in particular, through his friendship with its first secretary, John Phillips.[27] His acceptance and apparently easy assimilation into Caerleon society is an example of the factors which Thackray and Morrell describe, here at work in an antiquarian setting.

Another, and in many ways more powerful illustration of the complex relationship between archaeological knowledge and discoveries on the one hand, and the traditional social order on the other, is to be found in Cirencester. One of the most striking features of archaeological activity in that town was the failure to establish a society to act as its focus. Despite the huge interest created by the discovery there of very fine, well-preserved Roman mosaics in 1849, there does not appear to have been any suggestion that a society be formed. This is even more remarkable in view of the large numbers of such societies created throughout the country in both urban and rural areas. It might have been supposed that the very striking nature of the discoveries would have been enough in itself to prompt a typical response, namely the creation of a group to ensure their preservation. There are two factors that could help to explain why this did not happen. One was the very traditional nature of the town's social structure and the other was the particularly rich nature of the artefacts themselves. Both helped to ensure that no society would emerge.

In Caerleon the energy and enthusiasm of Edward Lee had brought about the formation of a group comprising the leading citizens of the town. Together they had raised funds to build a museum in which to house the relics of the town's past. Its name, the Caerleon Museum of Antiquities, and the building's grand classical style, symbolised the group's hopes that, in the words of Sir Digby Mackworth it 'would be the first step in restoring the town to its

---

[26] Morrell and Thackray, *Gentlemen of science*, 14.

[27] Phillips was a self-made man who had used his contacts with the BAAS to further his career as a professional geologist. The two men remained friends and probably travelled together in Italy in 1869. Phillips wrote an article on the relationship between archaeology and geology: 'The relationship of archaeology to physical geography', *AJ* xi (1853), 179–86.

ancient importance'.[28] As a leading local citizen he was proclaiming not only his own, but the group's pride in their town and their belief that its reputation could only be enhanced by a reminder of its previous greatness. In fact, the museum's collection comprised a large number of small articles, none on their own particularly striking, but which, taken together, indicated that the town had been a considerable centre of Roman activity. The whole exercise had served to underline local pride in, and local ownership of, Caerleon's past.

In many respects the situation in Cirencester was exactly the opposite, and the differences between the two could help to explain the absence of group activity in the town. The importance as was discussed earlier, attached to the ownership of the Roman past and its symbolic value as an indicator of social standing and aesthetic taste meant that who owned what and who should have access to the artefacts was of considerable significance. Cirencester provides a good example of the way in which these issues played a part in social standing and perceived authority in a specific social structure.

As in Caerleon, it was an outsider, John Buckman, who took a leading role in preserving the remains of the Roman past. When the mosaics were discovered in Dyer Street he had organised the local effort to assist in clearing the debris and lifting them out of the ground. But it was at this point that the local magnate, Lord Bathurst, made his offer to pay for the mosaics' preservation and to build a museum in which to house them. In effect, he took them over and claimed them as his own. This ownership was underlined when the mosaics were eventually put on display in the 'Bathurst Museum', built on Bathurst land, the building itself forming a part of the wall which surrounded the estate, maintaining a boundary between estate and town. This represented more than the lord of the manor playing a leading role, as was the case in Caerleon, where Digby Mackworth was also lord of the manor. This was a pre-modern society making a last stand and asserting a right of ownership, excluding all other possible contenders. It was a response which was quite different from the conservative, but none the less modern, responses elsewhere, for instance in Colchester.[29]

The Bathurst family had dominated Cirencester since they bought the estate in the sixteenth century. They owned almost all the land and the patronage of all local positions was in their gift. The offer to provide a museum for the pavements, although universally proclaimed as 'generous', had the effect of ensuring that the Bathurst name was perceived as being synonymous with the town's Roman past. This could help to explain the reluctance on the part of many local people to donate their finds to the museum. The creation of the Cripps Museum later in the century is only the most extreme example of a more general trend as many townspeople were reluctant to donate their finds to a local museum. When Buckman compiled his list of artefacts in 1856, he wrote on the front page that 'the articles belonging to J .B. [James Buckman]

---

[28] Anon., 'Caerleon Archaeological Association', MM, 24 June 1848, 4.
[29] I am grateful to Neville Morley for pointing this out.

are deposited in this museum for the benefit of science. They can be removed by him if not properly taken care of. And in fact most of the objects in the museum were described as 'on loan'. This apparent unwillingness to donate objects to the museum in Cirencester is unusual. In Colchester and Caerleon, where local museums had been established at approximately the same time, collectors appeared eager to donate objects to a local collection. Indeed in Chester the eagerness to give artefacts outstripped the society's ability to house them and provided the committee with a problem. It is possible that the reluctance to do so in Cirencester could be due to a perception that the museum, rather than being owned by the town itself, was seen as the property of the lord of the manor in the person of Lord Bathurst.

The Bathurst dominance is evident from a report in the *Archaeological Journal* in which Charles Newmarch described the recent discoveries: 'Mr Newmarch warmly eulogised the liberality of Earl Bathurst, who had determined to erect forthwith a museum, for the secure reception of these remains discovered on his property. Mr Morgan [Octavius Morgan of the Caerleon Association] proposed cordial thanks to the noble proprietor of the ancient Corinium.'[30] Even bearing in mind the rather effusive style in which these journal articles were written, it is not difficult to understand how Bathurst and the mosaics came to be linked together in the minds of those concerned. The antiquarians had revealed the importance of the Roman town, the pavements had demonstrated the wealth of its citizens, but Bathurst owned them and this ownership legitimised his social position in Cirencester.

Bathurst's willingness to provide for the mosaics would seem to indicate more than a desire to claim what he quite clearly regarded as his property. It can only be speculation, but it is possible that it was the very nature of the artefacts concerned that made him willing to go to the expense of erecting a purpose-built museum, bearing his name, in which to house them. The mosaics were remarkably well preserved, as can still be seen in the Corinium museum today. They were colourful, stylish and beautiful examples of classical art, redolent of wealth and a luxurious way of life. As such they appealed to a traditional appreciation of works of classical art that had been held up as the ultimate achievement to which later ages could only hope to aspire. All these were features with which the old ruling order had sought to associate itself as indicative of social position. It is quite possible that if the work in Dyer Street had unearthed a large cache of more mundane artefacts, Lord Bathurst would not have been so eager to claim and house them. The value of the mosaics lay as much in the associations they suggested in the present as in the information they conveyed about the past.

If he had wanted to start a local society Buckman, an outsider, might have been in a better position to act as the catalyst for group activity than if he had always been subject to the restraints imposed by feudal Cirencester. We

---

30 Anon., 'Proceedings', AJ vi (1849), 396.

know he was interested in further excavation as he appealed through the archaeological journals for financial support to carry on.[31] It is also quite probable that he wrote *Remains of Roman art* in order too raise money for the same purpose. But none of these efforts elicited any organised support, as they had done in Caerleon and, to a lesser extent, in Colchester. Clearly, the dominance of the Bathurst interest was one factor in this situation, but Buckman himself was another. He did not share the attributes that would have marked him out as a natural member of the ruling order. In fact to the contrary, rather than studying the classics at Oxford or Cambridge, he had been trained in the natural sciences and was attempting to make his way in the world as a professional scientist. He would almost undoubtedly have felt more at ease in the company of fellow natural scientists in the Cotteswold Naturalists' Field Club than in a more conventional antiquarian group. It is noticeable that his book's references to the artistic merits of the mosaics are, in fact, quotations from traditional authorities, such as Richard Westmacott. Buckman's emphasis on the physical properties of the mosaics, rather than on the classical allusions they depict, would seem to support this view.

Like others in the same position, Buckman needed to find support and paid employment, and in the 1840s and 1850s patronage still played an important part in such attempts. No references to the nature of the relationship between Lord Bathurst and Buckman have been found, but bearing in mind that Bathurst chose all subsequent curators of the museum, it is highly unlikely that he would have sanctioned Buckman in the post if he had not approved of him. In other words, even had he wanted to do so, it was not in Buckman's interest to challenge Bathurst's authority.

Buckman was forced to resign his professorship at the agricultural college in 1863. The new principal, in his desire to change the ethos of the college to one more closely resembling the traditional centres of education, forced the resignation of many of the professors. It is ironic that someone who played such a significant part in revealing Cirencester's Roman past should lose his professional job as a scientist because he lacked a formal classical education.[32]

Exclusion

In the archaeological societies examined so far, group activity appeared to confirm the position of the ruling groups within their local communities. Common outlook and shared activities allowed the members to feel secure, even when the boundaries of society appeared to be shifting. One way in which this process operated was to allow socially aspiring individuals to be assimilated into the group. But this was only possible if the ambitious 'would

---

[31] For example, J. Buckman, 'A.I. proceedings', GM xxxv (1851), 410.
[32] Idem, *An address to E. Holland Esq. M.P., chairman of the Agricultural College, Cirencester*, Cirencester 1863; R. Sayce, *History of the Royal Agricultural College*, Stroud 1992, 59–60.

be' member was not too different from the majority and was prepared to accept most group norms. Those like William Wire, who differed in too many respects, were excluded. Problems could also be created if there were so many aspiring outsiders that to allow them entrance would significantly alter the nature of the group itself. If that happened, it could be unclear who was assimilating whom. In this section the ways in which potentially disruptive individuals were excluded from the exclusive archaeological world will be examined. Certain events at the centre, in London, will also be considered because it was through national activities that some of these 'misfit' individuals sought to gain recognition and support from like-minded others.[33]

When the British Archaeological Association was founded in 1843, many people saw it as a response to the numerous criticisms levelled at the existing national antiquarian body, the London Society of Antiquaries. The society had become increasingly moribund, there were few papers for the meetings, it appeared unmoved by the threat to ancient monuments and the membership policy was seen by many as unnecessarily exclusive. It was typical of the society's approach that, despite their extensive archaeological activity, both Roach Smith and Wright experienced difficulty in being accepted as members. Roach Smith observed of Wright's application that 'he was never encouraged; and his contributions were accepted more as favours conferred on him than as a credit and honour to the society'. And Roach Smith's own nomination, in 1836, was challenged on the grounds that he was 'in business'.[34]

The first volume of the *Archaeological Journal*, in 1844, carried an article in which the author, W. Jerdan, talked about the ways in which he thought the British Archaeological Association should develop. He stressed the need to include all those who were interested in the past:

> Science and literature are the only true republics impervious to 'class' doubt or censure... The simple fact of being devoted to pursuits of this description ought to be admitted as proof of intellectual ability and respectability, which should make the candidate, lowest perhaps in the gifts of station and fortune, an eligible associate for the most exalted in rank and the most powerful in wealth.

He hoped that such a body would foster good relations in which 'peers would have no dislike to meeting with well-informed husbandmen, nor the heads of the church with the un-presuming lay-brother'.[35]

Jerdan's comments suggest that at least some of the original founders of

---

[33] It could be argued that archaeological organisations in the big cities, where professional networks were better established and the interpenetration of commerce and scholarship was probably taken more for granted, would reveal a different picture. I would like to thank Peter Mandler for this suggestion.

[34] Roach Smith, *Retrospections*, i. 81. Smith's friend, Joseph Clarke, was also blackballed: Thomas Wright to Joseph Mayer, 7 Mar. 1855, BL, MS Add. 3347.

[35] W. Jerdan, 'The British Archaeological Associaion', *AJ* i (1844), 298.

the association were anxious to create a body in which distinctions of class and wealth would not constitute a barrier to membership. But it soon became apparent that this view was not shared by all. The association was becoming irrevocably split over one of the issues that defined the opposing points of view concerning the manner in which antiquarian pursuits could, or should be carried forward, namely amateur status. Antiquarianism had always been regarded as essentially an amateur pursuit, carried on by men of independent means, wealth and leisure. To allow individuals differing widely from this description the official status of membership of antiquarian bodies was to strike a blow against the class interests that underpinned them. And that is precisely what one of the founding members, Thomas Wright, was believed by some to be doing.

The split in the British Archaeological Association and the row between the 'Way' and the 'Wright' factions brought to the surface deeply held differences of opinion concerning the nature of the new society. Views became polarised between those who supported Wright (and by implication all those who did not fit the organisations' idea of a 'leisured gentleman') and those, like Way, who felt that archaeology should remain an amateur activity, carried out by gentlemen. In the ensuing row the opposition to Wright was supported by several national journals, including the *Gentleman's Magazine* and the *Athenaeum*. An article in the latter stated that

> It was high time for the 'better spirits' of the council to look ahead, and see that they did not lend their names a second time to the traders associ-ated with them ... The Treasurer must be a man of business habits ... The Secretaries must be disinterested men, of name and standing ... who can write good English, and speak it correctly when it was written.[36]

In his memoirs, the publisher J. H. Parker supported the notion that this was essentially a dispute about class. He wrote that

> the Society consisted of two distinct classes of persons – the one, gentlemen of property and amateurs of Archaeology, who wished to have the opportu-nities of communicating to others the information they had collected, that it might not die with them, as had frequently been the case with many of their friends. The other party consisted of 'would be' professional archae-ologists.[37]

These differences were reflected in the attitudes taken towards the choice of

---

36 *Athenaeum*, 1 Mar. 1845.
37 This is cited in Wetherall, 'From Canterbury to Winchester', 17. It is necessary to treat Parker's use of the word 'professional' with some caution. However his assessment was supported by Wright's friend, the antiquarian and actor, James Planche. He noted that the social tensions in the BAA offered 'Opportunities for nobodies to become somebodies ... duties became enviable when they were discovered to be passports into society and tickets for turtle soup': *Recollections and reflections: a professional autobiography*, London 1872, 304.

subject matter deemed appropriate for study. The report in the *Athenaeum* of the association's first congress expressed a traditional view that valued examples of classical art over other more mundane artefacts, and saw Romano-British artefacts as inferior to those produced in Rome itself: 'A careful survey of Roman remains in Britain will add little or nothing to our stock book of architectural models; and the remains of Roman sculpture in Britain are in the very worst of taste of expiring and degraded art.'[38] A BAA member, Alfred Dunkin, rebutted these arguments, stressing that all evidence was of value if a full understanding of the life of the past was to be achieved: 'The true antiquary does not confine his researches to one single branch of archaeology; but in a comprehensive view surveys every fact; and aims to bring in every object to serve the great end and purpose of knowledge of man and his habits and customs in past ages.'[39] As these passages demonstrate, there were not only major social differences between the two groups, but also a different basic interpretation as to what constituted the subject matter of archaeology.

The row could not be settled and culminated in a split. Those who favoured the more traditional approach broke away, taking with them the *Archaeological Journal*, and formed the Archaeological Institute. The membership of the institute gives some indication of the type of person opposed to the inclusion of a wider membership. It included several cathedral deans, masters of Oxford and Cambridge colleges and hundreds of Church of England clergy. The president was the marquis of Northampton, who was also president of the Royal Society. It was indeed a representative cross-section of 'the great and the good', men who exemplified the ruling groups in society and who might have felt themselves threatened by the aspiring middle class.

The BAA retained the rump of the membership, including all the founders who had favoured a wider and more inclusive membership. But Roach Smith complained that the association was still dominated by 'persons of social position and influence who [were] flattered by elevation into the foremost ranks of science and literature'. He complained that the president, Lord Albert Conyngham, had packed the committee with nineteen noble patrons

> with the best of intentions and under the belief that it would counterbalance the clerical banners of the Institute. But I have ever considered it a blemish upon English scientific, literary, and artistic institutions that they should have so little self-dependence as to feel it necessary to place the phantom of patronage over their muster rolls.[40]

Roach Smith's comments draw attention to his growing disaffection with all aspects of the organised archaeological groups at both national and local levels. This was due in part to the usual personality clashes that are a feature of most organisations. In the case of the British Archaeological Association

[38] This is cited in Roach Smith, *Retrospections*, i. 11–12.
[39] Ibid. i. 12.
[40] Ibid. i. 38.

these were exacerbated by the difficult nature of Thomas Pettigrew, the association's treasurer and a dominant figure throughout this period. Pettigrew's high-handed methods led to the dismissal of the secretary, Thomas Hugo, at a public meeting in 1854. The row was caused by letters Hugo wrote to members in Gwent concerning the association's proposed excavations at Caerwent. Other letters written by Hugo to Pettigrew, and fellow committee members, indicate that there was an almost paranoid atmosphere between the members of the ruling body.[41]

It was doubtless events such as these that led Roach Smith to tell William Wire that 'I have no great faith in the utility of societies. They elevate the inefficient and science is by their means too often prostituted to mere worldly influence.'[42] Roach Smith felt that the social aspects of the local archaeological societies were so pre-eminent that they distracted attention away from archaeological matters. So when he started his excavations at the site of the Roman fort at Lymne, in 1850, he did so independently of any society. Later he wrote that 'At the time I did not notice it; but afterwards I found that my colleagues of the BAA were not altogether pleased with my independent action.'[43] He told Wire that the excavation had been very successful: 'You see how preferable they are to the indecision and jealousies of societies that talk and work not.'[44]

Disillusioned by the arguments and rivalries, a small group of like-minded outsiders began to emerge. The group was never formalised, there were no committees or rules, but it is clear from letters and other accounts that these men remained in close and constant contact with one another. Apart from Roach Smith and Wright, the core of the group consisted of the illustrator Frederick Fairholt, the gentleman farmer and curator of the Saffron Walden Museum Joseph Clarke, and the Liverpool goldsmith and jeweller Joseph Mayer. In addition, there were several others who were connected more loosely, such as the London antique dealers William Chaffers and Edward

---

[41] The letters and correspondence of Thomas Hugo (1844–75) are in the British Library (MSS Add. 30277–300). Hugo quoted the Athenaeum's description of Pettigrew: 'In any public relation he can live comfortably only in an atmosphere of disturbance; and as that is a phenomenon easy to produce, he easily contrives wherever he goes to create the moral condition in which his egotism thrives … Petulance, captiousness and jealousy are still among his characteristics. The concoction of intrigues, the packing of meetings, and the confusion of congresses are his delight. The fomenting of suspicions by misrepresentations to each of his colleagues what the rest are alleged to say in their disparagement … is still his constant habit': A letter to the late members of the BAA, London [1855], cited in Evans, Society of Antiquaries, 254.

[42] Roach Smith to Wire, 13 Feb. 1851, Colchester Museum. The Danish archaeologist Jens Worsaae, who visited England in 1843, told Roach Smith that he had been struck by the disregard shown to men of science: 'I have been most kindly received by the highest in the land, because I carried an introduction from the King; but I could not do otherwise than observe that men of the greatest eminence in science were left quite unnoticed': Roach Smith, Retrospections, ii. 154.

[43] Ibid.

[44] Roach Smith to Wire, 20 Oct. 1852.

Price, and the antiquarian collectors William Wylie and William Rolfe.[45] The railway enabled them to travel around the country to visit sites and examine collections, frequently in each other's company and when this was not possible they wrote vast numbers of letters.[46] They were united by an interest in the past generally, and in archaeology in particular. But the clearest link between them was that they did not fit easily into the organised archaeo-logical bodies. In the case of Fairholt, this was because he was a relatively poor working man, with a background that set him apart from the traditional rulers in society. Joseph Mayer, on the other hand, although he was anxious to be accepted by the Historical Society of Lancashire and Cheshire, appears to have remained something of an outsider, possibly because of his associa-tion with Roach Smith and a lingering whiff of 'trade'.[47]

One example of the way in which this informal network was linked through a myriad of interconnections is to be found in the events surrounding Mayer's acquisition of the Faussett collection, in 1854. When the Trustees of the British Museum refused to buy the collection Mayer bought it for his own museum in Liverpool, with Roach Smith and Chaffers acting as the interme-diaries with the Faussett family. Mayer then commissioned Roach Smith to compile a catalogue for the collection, which was published in 1856 as *Inven-torium sepulchrale* with illustrations by Fairholt. Mayer was widely praised for his rescue of the collection by, among many others, Joseph Clarke and Thomas Wright.[48] In 1854 Wright was invited by Mayer to give a lecture, based on the collection, to a joint meeting of the BAAS and the Historical Society of Lancashire and Cheshire in Liverpool. Finally, a friend of Clarke's from Saffron Walden, Henry Eckroyd Smith, was introduced to Mayer and became the curator of his museum.[49]

Correspondence between Roach Smith and Clarke gives some idea of the group's dislike of the way in which the traditional holders of authority domi-nated all organisations, not just archaeological societies. When Mayer offered some of his extensive collection for display in the Art Treasures Exhibition

45 William Chaffers was a leading London dealer who specialised in Roman antiquities and coins. William Wylie was a wealthy landowner who excavated Anglo-Saxon graves in Oxfordshire. William Rolfe was a farmer whose excavations at Richborough in Kent were financed by Mayer. Wire was on the edge of this group, courtesy of his friendship with Roach Smith.
46 Roach Smith's memoirs provide numerous instances of these outings to, amongst other places, Hampton Court, the Roman potteries at Upchurch and the Isle of Wight.
47 Mayer was the librarian for the Lancashire Society, but his main role in British archae-ology was the financial help he gave Roach Smith and Wright for their excavations at Lymne and Wroxeter, and his willingness to buy collections threatened by dispersal: R. H. White, 'Mayer and British archaeology', in M. Gibson and S. M. Wright (eds), *Joseph Mayer of Liverpool, 1803–1886*, London 1988, 118–36.
48 Ibid. 121.
49 Henry Ecroyd Smith was an antiquarian. He wrote *Reliquiae insurianae* (London 1851) on the Roman remains at Aldborough. He was a skilled draughtsman and his book of lithographs of Roman tessellated pavements was published in 1850. He was the curator of Mayer's museum from 1852 to 1870.

held in Manchester in 1857, he was only offered one case in which to display them. This infuriated Clarke, who told Roach Smith: 'Here are a parcel of snobs and charlatans at the head of affairs in Manchester whose vocation it occurs to be to cringe and toady to the great.'[50] Clarke was equally scathing about Richard Neville's excavations at Great Chesterford. He thought the sites had been left partially abandoned and had therefore gone to rescue what he could 'as anybody takes away whatever they may fancy. All I have picked up, but I did not start soon enough'. In another letter, Clarke described one of the outings of the Essex Archaeological Society as 'mere parties of pleasure'.[51] Their dislike was compounded, and possibly justified, by what they regarded as the societies' unwillingness to give proper weight to the importance of archaeological work. Roach Smith alluded to this when he described the difficulties involved in financing the publication of the results of his excavation at Lymne: 'It is necessary that the result of researches be printed and properly illustrated; and this can hardly be done when the councils of societies are composed as they usually are, of gentlemen who do not feel the importance of any historical antiquities what so ever.'[52] Similarly, Wright had considerable difficulty raising the money for his excavations of the Roman remains of Uriconium, in spite of appealing to 'noble men and M.Ps': he was only able to proceed because of financial help from Mayer.

With hindsight, it is possible to see the activities and thoughts of this disaffected group as evidence of a much wider struggle that was going on in many aspects of the intellectual life of the period. In effect, the struggle was between traditional authority with its associated belief systems and those newcomers who sought to contest this authority through the creation of new institutions and using new theories of knowledge. Most of the work in this area has identified professionalisation as a major factor in this process.

Professionalisation

James Moore has described the process of professionalisation in the Victorian period as 'the high road to power and authority among bourgeois intellectuals'.[53] Moore's view that it was the mechanism that allowed the new men and new beliefs to acquire legitimacy and respect has been supported by many other studies.[54] It is important to recognise, however, that when people of

[50] This is cited in White, 'Mayer and British archaeology', 133.
[51] J. Clarke to C. Roach Smith, n.d. Saffron Walden Museum, drawer 4.
[52] Roach Smith, Lymne, p. vi.
[53] J. Moore, 'Theodicy and society: the crisis of the intelligentsia', in R. Helmstadter and B. Lightman (eds), Victorian faith in crisis: essays on continuity and change in nineteenth-century religious belief, London 1990, 154.
[54] See, for instance, R. Porter, 'Gentlemen and geology: the emergence of a scientific career, 1660–1920', Historical Journal xxi (1978), 809–36; F. M. Turner, 'The Victorian conflict between science and religion: a professional dimension', Isis lxix (1978), 356–76; R. Jann, 'From amateur to professional: the case of the Oxbridge historians', Journal of

the period talk of 'professional' (for instance Parker quoted above), they do not necessarily mean what modern usage would lead us to think. As Morrell has pointed out, 'The notion of a profession has never been static. On the contrary, it has changed drastically over time; it has been a social semantic construct.'[55]

If the opportunity to earn a living through activities associated with a particular subject area is assumed to be central to the term, then archaeology and history offered very few openings to the would-be professional. There was still a general view that antiquarianism was the pursuit of gentlemen and was a virtue in itself. In a speech to the British Archaeological Association in 1850 Thomas Pettigrew declared that 'no officer of this society receives a salary ... that with us, the love of the pursuit beguiles all the labour of it'.[56] Roach Smith opposed salaried positions for national societies like the Numismatic Society or a possible government commission, on the grounds that 'I am also too well aware of how things are "jobbed" in England ever to expect being recognised in the event of the appointment of a Commission of Monuments. The persons appointed would be people of influence.'[57]

John Akerman, the man responsible for the excavations at Caerwent, was one of the few individuals who managed to earn a living through his antiquarian activities. In his early life he had a series of jobs as secretary to, among others, William Cobbett, the Greenwich Railway Company and Lord Albert Conyngham. In 1848 he became the joint secretary to the London Society of Antiquaries and editor of their journal *Archaeologia*, a post he held until his retirement in 1860.[58] Thomas Wright was another contender for the secretaryship of the Antiquaries in 1848, but he withdrew his application on the grounds that he did not wish to cause any dissent or divisions within the society.[59] Doubtless he was mindful of their reluctance to make him a member and of the split in the BAA caused by his literary activities. Both Akerman and Wright managed to earn a living through their writing and administra-

---

British Studies xxii (1983), 122–47; and J. B. Morrell, 'Professionalisation', in R. C. Olby, G. N. Cantor, J. R. R. Christie and M. J. S. Hodge (eds), *Companion to the history of science*, London 1990, 980–9.

55 Morrell, 'Professionalism', 980.

56 T. Pettigrew, 'The study of archaeology', *JBAA* vi (1850), 166. Pettigrew was justifying the fact that the BAA was not able to finance excavations.

57 Roach Smith to J. Worsaae, 6 Mar. 1848, cited in Rhodes, 'Charles Roach Smith', 215.

58 In 1848 Akerman received £100 a year and the use of furnished rooms. He was expected to be in the library for two hours a day throughout the year. He managed to combine these duties with the post of secretary to Conyngham. The salary was increased to £200 when he became the only secretary in 1855 and £250 when he took over the editorship of *Archaeologia* in 1858.

59 Wright did not apply again in 1860 because 'They require a degree of attendance which would put a stop nearly to my literary and antiquarian labours': Wright to Mayer, 9 May 1860, BL, MS Add. 33347.

tion of various societies, but it was a tenuous existence, and they were both reliant, to some extent, on the patronage of wealthy gentlemen.[60]

Paid employment was offered in the Central Record Office and in the Historical Manuscripts Commission, both of which were concerned with the textual evidence of the past. Thomas Wright was paid to edit a volume of political songs and poetry which he told Mayer 'will be the first money I have ever received from the government'.[61] However the material evidence that played so large a part in the antiquarians' interests still did not figure in any government institutions. University departments continued to be dominated by amateurs. The first Disney Professor of Archaeology at Cambridge was a clergyman, the Revd John Marsden, and another cleric, Charles Kingsley, was professor of history there during the 1860s. It was not until much later in the century that a chair of classical archaeology was created at Oxford and pre-historic archaeology was not taught until the twentieth century. Furthermore, the traditional dominance of the classical world in historical and archaeological studies was probably an important factor in the tendency of practical archaeologists to identify themselves with ethnography, rather than the older subject areas. This was partly a function of the way in which they chose to define their studies, but it might also have been because they felt that it would be easier to be accepted in the more scientific discipline of ethnology.[62]

If the opportunities for professional development at a national level were only gradually being created, there was an almost complete absence of such developments at the local level. Local activity continued to be dominated by representatives of the ruling group, either acting alone or, more usually, together through a local society. It was not until the early twentieth century that the activities of local groups became marginalised by the development of professions in the historical and archaeological spheres nationally. The only paid employment offered locally was in connection with the collections and museums. The Caerleon group decided to appoint a museum keeper at a fee of not more than three guineas a year.[63] During the excavation at the Caerwent site in 1855 a tessellated pavement was uncovered and the committee agreed to pay for an accurate drawing to be made and for the lifting of the pavement.

[60] Wright's work was subsidised by Mayer and Lord Albert Conyngham funded Akerman's Anglo-Saxon excavations.
[61] Wright to Mayer, 9 May 1858, BL, MS Add. 33346. He was paid a lump sum of £400. He complained he was 'given a work sixteen times as difficult as that given to anyone else with the same rate of remuneration': Wright to Mayer, 5 June 1858, ibid.
[62] For instance Pitt Rivers was president of the Ethnology Society. The GM reported the discussions of the ethnological section of the BAAS under 'Antiquarian researches'. In 1854 Wright told a meeting of the ethnological section that 'The proper and only correct arrangement of a museum of antiquities was an ethnological one': GM xxxii (July–Dec. 1854), 601. This was consistent with his opposition to the Danish three-age system: Celt, Roman and Saxon, preface.
[63] CAA minutes, 21 Aug. 1850. The 1863 membership list records the keeper, a Mr Powell, living at the post office, presumably his main employment.

The work cost £34, but this was a one-off payment.[64] The Chester society was more ambitious. The minutes record that a Mr Bellars was paid for 'occasional services in sketching lithographs for the journal and that he should be employed for one week only at a fee of two guineas to arrange the books, coins and other property of the society'.[65] In 1855 Bellars was being employed jointly by the society and the city library to work five hours a day in the library and reading room. In 1857 the minutes record 'Mr. Taylor, the present keeper of the city news room to be employed as curator, librarian and general officer at the salary of eight pounds a year'.[66] The Essex society was the only one to appoint a full-time curator. In collaboration with the local authority it was decided that the pay should be £35 a year, of which the society would pay £5. Whoever was appointed was judged insufficiently knowledgeable to produce a catalogue, because the society decided to pay William Chaffers £21 to catalogue and arrange the collections.[67]

Wright's letters provide an intriguing glimpse of how difficult it was for an interested man to break into paid employment. During the course of his excavations of the Roman town at Wroxeter he got to know one of the young assistants, Hilary Davies. Wright introduced him to Mayer as someone who could transcribe documents. A few weeks later Wright suggested Davies as a possible curator for Mayer's museum: 'He is a good artist who draws with extreme accuracy and I know no one who draws antiquities better ... Perhaps he could help you in the moving of the museum.' And as the excavations at Wroxeter began to falter, Wright tried again to interest Mayer in helping his young *protégé*: 'Poor Hilary Davies will be out of employment ... Could you get him some employment in your museum? ... I believe he would be well worth his pay.'[68] As there are no further references to him in Wright's correspondence we lose sight of Davies and he has to be regarded as an example of Macfarlane's 'historically invisible majority'.

In the light of this local evidence, anyone aspiring to earn a living through study of the past would have been advised to gravitate towards the centre of activities in London, where the British Museum and the national societies did at least offer some chance of employment.

If professionalism is defined more widely to include notions of standards and specialist knowledge, then the number of those who could be so described would be greater. It would include, for instance, several members of the dissident group around Roach Smith. It is doubtful whether any of them would have referred to themselves as professional, but their expert knowledge and insistence upon the importance of systematic recording and publica-

64 Ibid. 16 Aug. 1855; 5 Aug. 1856.
65 CAAHS minutes, 24 Mar. 1854.
66 Ibid. 21 May 1857.
67 EAS minutes, 10 Aug. 1860; 13 Feb. 1862.
68 Wright to Mayer, 8 Mar., 18 Apr., 30 Oct. 1867, BL, MS Add. 33347. Frederick Fairholt, who had previously been the illustrator of choice in the group around Roach Smith, had died in 1866.

tion of results provide a stark contrast to the more cavalier methods of many amateurs in the local societies.

Archaeology and the working man

One paradox about archaeology in this period is that although the activists, writers of books and members of societies, were almost entirely middle- and upper-class, the individuals who actually found most of the artefacts in the first place were working men on building sites. So how did the antiquarians regard these people who were so necessary, but who hardly conformed to the social conventions underlying the societies?

As Jerdan's article in the first edition of the JBAA suggests, there was some lip-service paid to the idea that a genuine interest in the past should be the only qualification necessary for membership of the new national body (the BAA). However all the local societies were composed of members of the ruling groups in their areas and as such were unlikely to prove particularly welcoming to those outside the group, as Wire experienced in Colchester. But despite Wire's experience there were at least two factors that ensured that the working man could not be ignored entirely. First was the need to ensure that the labourers who uncovered artefacts did not destroy them through ignorance. Second was the Victorian urge to 'improve' the working man. In some ways these overlapped and the need for the former justified the latter.

The destruction of artefacts and sites of archaeological interest that had prompted the creation of the BAA in 1843 was due to several factors, including the ignorance of the workmen. A BAA representative in Leicester pointed out the difficulties:

> Here is another sin of archaeologists and antiquaries ... they are too gener-
> ally anti-movement men, as regards the civilization of the masses, and they
> are well punished for it. If we loved such things with the right sort of love,
> and not merely as something exclusive and recherché and as elevating us
> above the *profanum vulgus*, we should, through very horror of their destruc-
> tive powers and opportunities, overflow with affection to the diggers and
> delvers of the earth, and every broad-cloth member at our sittings would
> have a fustian member at his side, and cherishing him tenderly as the very
> apple of his eye, and never be satisfied till he had indoctrinated him up to
> his own standard.[69]

But the many disputes concerning the ownership of antiquities from the town hall site in Colchester demonstrated that love of the artefacts alone was not the only or even the chief motive of those who sought to find them. It was a situation in which no one's motives were totally straightforward. Certainly the workmen on the town hall site were aware of the value of the artefacts, if

[69] Correspondence between Roach Smith and a Leicester antiquarian: Anon., 'Proceedings', *JBAA* i (1845), 259.

only prompted by the zeal of the city fathers (and others) to buy them.[70] The antiquarians spoke of a danger that they could be lost to the town, but even Wire was a trader who would sell the artefacts to collectors elsewhere. More basic still, the use of classical associations as the means whereby individuals could define themselves as part of an elite was too strongly entrenched to allow the 'diggers and delvers' into the charmed circle.

There seems to have been very little attempt to educate the workmen directly, possibly because of the fear that they would use such knowledge to their own financial advantage. There was little encouragement for working men to join the societies and thus acquire some knowledge and a sense of local pride in the area's past. The Chester Society did have a separate low membership fee for artisans and their journal stated that 'workmen have been liberally encouraged to save relics, which would otherwise have been broken up or lost',[71] but few working people took advantage of this. Many of the meetings were held during the day and the excursions that figured so prominently in activities involved expenditure on railway tickets and meals, all of which would deter those with any sort of regular employment or on low incomes. William Wire complained to Roach Smith that he felt cold-shouldered by other antiquarians because 'my circumstances will not permit me to feed them well'. Indeed the very social nature of the outings will have tended to emphasise the exclusive nature of the societies. As Wire complained 'those who were once kind to me, are now as distanced as possible, as they can be asked to luncheon and breakfast at the houses of the great ones'.[72]

Instead of attempting to involve working people in the archaeological societies, many of the leading members were involved in the creation of other organisations which aimed to improve 'artisans' and 'operatives'. At the forefront was the creation of Mechanics' Institutes, a movement that spread rapidly after the 1832 Reform Act. Institutes were formed in Colchester in 1833, in Chester in 1835, in Newport in 1841 and in Cirencester in 1844. However, they all failed to attract working men as Thomas Hughes points out in his *Stranger's guide to Chester* : 'What a marvellous fact it is, that with these benefits within their reach, so few mechanics avail themselves of this, their own institution.'[73]

The aspect of the Mechanics' Institutes that was invariably the most successful was the reading room and library. In both Cirencester and Chester these continued in operation even after the other activities had ceased.[74]

---

70 An article in *The Antiquary* pointed out the level of awareness: 'The workmen, who at first considered all the coins they met with as being merely old half penny pieces which were worth nothing, soon discovered their errors and have now become connoisseurs. They can distinguish between the coins of the Lower and Higher Empire, and even detect an Otho or an Antonine': Anon., 'Reviews', *The Antiquary* vii (1883), 273.

71 Anon., 'Introduction', *JCAAHS* i (1849–55), preface.

72 Wire to Roach Smith, 20 Feb. 1852; 21 Aug. 1851, Wire letter book.

73 T. Hughes, *Stranger's guide to Chester and its environs*, Chester 1856, 110.

74 Mayer built a library and public reading room in the grounds of his new estate in Bebington. In 1866, the year it opened, 700 tickets were issued and 12,190 volumes lent.

There was also a large increase in the number of commercial lending libraries, of which the largest and most well-known was Mudie's in London.[75] Most towns of any size had circulating libraries that were usually attached to the local book publisher. In Cirencester, Messrs Bailey and Jones took over the contents of the library and reading room from the library committee, which had gone into debt in 1847.

The spread of libraries and reading rooms, both institutional and commercial, was an indication of the huge increase in the production of periodicals and cheap books that gathered pace from the 1840s. The introduction of the steam press had allowed the price of books to fall dramatically and had coincided with increasing literacy rates among the population as a whole.[76] According to one observer, 'books are everywhere to be obtained at a cheap rate. [People] lived amongst books, and had only to shut their eyes and stretch forth their hands to the shelf, to be put upon learning made easy'.[77] Cheap periodicals such as the Penny Magazine and Chambers Journal covered a vast range of topics, including extracts from Thomas Arnold's History of Rome.[78] When the Society for the Diffusion of Useful Knowledge decided to cease production of the Penny Magazine in 1846 it was stated that the decision had been made because 'the Society's work is done, for its greatest object is achieved. The public is supplied with cheap and good literature'.[79]

One effect of the huge increase in book production was to make knowledge of the classical past and Roman Britain more widely available. In 1847 the Archaeological Journal carried an advertisement for Bohn's Antiquarian Library that included cheap versions of, among others, Bede's History, The Anglo Saxon chronicle, Mallet's Northern antiquities and six old English chronicles including Gildas, Nennius, Geoffrey of Monmouth and Richard of Cirencester.[80] Thomas Wright reviewed the library in the JBAA. He called it 'exceedingly valuable' because these works had been 'inaccessible except to the few'. He concluded that 'I am sure that no one ever dreamt that he would obtain a complete translation of Bede's History and the Anglo Saxon Chronicle for five shillings.'[81] In 1849 the publisher Charles Knight, who had produced the Penny Magazine, announced a new periodical, the Imperial

By 1876 there were 4,932 tickets and 29,494 volumes lent: Roach Smith, Retrospections, i. 75. For more on Mayer's library see R. Foster, 'Philanthropy and patronage', in Gibson and Wright, Joseph Mayer, 28–43.

75 Mudie's was founded in 1843 and expanded rapidly. The firm frequently ordered several thousand copies of new publications, with the result that books such as Wilkie Collins's No name (1862) were sold out on the day of publication because of Mudie's pre-publication order.

76 Richard Altick has calculated that about 60% of the population over twenty was literate in 1851: Writers, readers and occasions: selected essays on Victorian literature and life, Columbus 1989, 143.

77 Essex Standard, 27 Oct. 1848.

78 Penny Magazine, 10 Feb., 22 June 1844.

79 Society for the Diffusion of Useful Knowledge, Address, London, 11 Mar. 1846.

80 Anon., 'Advert', AJ iv (1847), 379.

81 T. Wright, 'Review of Bohn's antiquarian library', JBAA iii (1849), 362.

Cyclopaedia. A writer in the *AJ* welcomed the new publication because it would promote archaeological knowledge among 'A class of people who have very often opportunities of rescuing from destruction interesting relics and memorials, but which are now passed by unheeded, from the absence of any knowledge of their value.' (He was of course referring to labourers on building sites.)[82]

Once again, it is difficult to judge how many working people actually read these cheap versions of the chronicles. Opinions vary; Robert Chambers, editor of *Chamber's Weekly*, wrote that

> it was read by the elite of the community; those who think, conduct them-
> selves respectably, and are anxious to improve their circumstances by judi-
> cious means. But below this worthy order of men, our work, except in a
> few particular cases, does not go far. A fatal mistake is committed in the
> notion that the lower classes read ... Some millions of adults of both sexes,
> in cities as well as in rural districts, are till this hour as ignorant of letters as
> the people were generally during the middle ages.[83]

However the number and availability of cheaper books and periodicals and the creation of so many lending libraries suggests that, potentially, knowledge of the past was reaching a wider public than ever before. Thomas Wright's *Celt, Roman and Saxon* was only one example of a book that made available current archaeological knowledge in a form and at a price that had previously been impossible. Some complained that the result was a less rigorous regard for the subject matter, but Bulwer-Lytton refuted this argument: 'People complain of it, as though it were a proof of degeneracy in the knowledge of authors, it is a proof of the increased number of readers.'[84]

It is probable that concerns about the 'watering down' of scholarship were, in part at least, indicative of a wider concern about the social implications of an increasingly knowledgeable and assertive audience in the population as a whole. If that were indeed the case then it is more than likely that many members of the local antiquarian bodies would have shared those concerns and that the covert social aims were used to reinforce the authority of the ruling groups. Individuals who did not fit in socially could find themselves excluded by rules and practices which effectively meant that they could not participate. It is also notable that the approach to the study of the past of local antiquarians was equally traditional for there is little indication of new knowledge or techniques being discussed or used. Rather the opposite, as traditional methods and a socially exclusive membership were both at work,

---

82 Anon., 'Miscellaneous notices', *AJ* vi (1849), 100.
83 R. Chambers, 'Editorial', *Chamber's Journal* xi (1840), 8.
84 E. Bulwer-Lytton, *The last days of Pompeii*, 1st edn, London 1834; new edn 1970. Rose-
mary Jann has suggested that the attacks on the style of popular history books at the end of
the nineteenth century arose from a fear that they might diminish the authority of would-
be professionals: 'From amateur to professional', 129. There were too few professionals in
the mid-nineteenth century for this to apply.

mirroring and reinforcing each other and thus helping to ensure that the locality and the ruling group within it maintained their hegemony. Those individuals who did not conform were forced, or chose, to work outside the conventional bodies and relied on one another to justify their position as outsiders. It is not possible to describe the members of this informal group as professionals in the narrow sense of the word. However, as they placed a greater value on knowledge of their subject than they did on social position, their differences from the local groups were confirmed and it is probably most useful to regard their activities as representing an early stage in the progression from amateur to professional. This division becomes clear when the activities of the local societies are examined in detail.

4

Isca Silures

In 1845 *Delineations of Roman antiquities found at Caerleon* was published in London. The author, John Edward Lee, declared that 'The town of Caerleon in Monmouthshire has long been known as a Roman military station and as a place of great interest to the antiquarian.'[1] He described the Roman remains and emphasised their vulnerability: 'Many of them are left exposed to the open air and are daily receiving injury from the weather ... It is mortifying that by far the greater part are lost, scattered or destroyed.'[2] Lee's book was to be the catalyst for all the archaeological activity that took place in the town over the next two decades, including the formation of an archaeological association, the establishment of a museum and several excavations.

Roman Caerleon

Although Lee had said that Caerleon was well known as a Roman military station, the Roman texts make no direct reference to the fortress of Isca Silures (the Roman name for the fort). Tacitus, Dio and Herodian had all described some events during the Roman occupation of Britain, but Isca Silures does not appear in any of these narrative accounts. The only textual information was to be found in the administrative and military records. It was known that Britain had been divided into two provinces for administrative purposes and that one of these, Britannia Secunda, had a military station at Isca Silures, where the second Augustan Legion had been based. The *Antonine itinerary* located Isca Silures in south Wales, on the Via Julia between Bath and Carmarthen. Caerleon lay on the route of the Via Julia at a convenient bridging point on the river Usk and close enough to the sea to allow easy access for provisioning a large military settlement. It followed from this that if evidence of the presence of the second Augustan Legion could be located in the immediate area, then the site of the fort could be identified. An abundance of tiles with the Second Augustan's name and mascot, the Capricorn, found at Caerleon suggested that the site was indeed that of Isca Silures. Lee's book contained drawings of the tiles and he wrote that 'Fragments of tiles and bricks showing the original form and also the various impresses found

---

[1] J. E. Lee, *Delineations of Roman antiquities found at Caerleon and neighbourhood*, London 1845, preface.
[2] Ibid.

upon them, … indicate that they were the work of artificers belonging to the Second Augustan Legion.'[3]

The only hard evidence for the fortress was to be found in the remains of buildings and the inscriptions they contained. For instance, an inscription found in the churchyard in the centre of the town referred to the Emperor Severus and the possible rebuilding of the site at the end of the second century. Lee concluded that 'The knowledge we possess of the history of Caerleon under the Romans is scanty indeed, in fact it rests more on the antiquities which are found there, than on actual historical records. There can however be no doubt that for a long series of years it was the residence of the Second Augustan Legion.'[4]

For more information antiquarians had to rely on accounts written between the departure of the legions in the early fifth century and their own time: Lee referred to Bede when he discussed the possible origins of the word Caerleon. However, the most often quoted guides to Caerleon's past were Geoffrey of Monmouth's *History of the kings of Britain* and Giraldus Cambrensis's *Journey through Wales* (1188). Both these writers were thought to have visited Caerleon and therefore were regarded as eye-witnesses. It was Geoffrey who was responsible for the widespread popular belief that Caerleon had been the site of King Arthur's court. Thus he described the rise of a great British king who defeated the Saxons and created an empire:

> Arthur, who was quite overjoyed by his great success, made up his mind to place the crown of the kingdom on his head … in the city of the legions. Situated as it is on the River Usk, not far from the Severn Sea and being richer in material wealth than other townships, it was eminently suitable for such a ceremony … It was adorned with royal palaces and by the gold painted gables of its roofs it was a match for Rome.[5]

The supposed associations with Arthur were to be used by later writers, for instance in *The Mabinogion*, and in Tennyson's *Idyll of the kings* (1859). The whole Arthur saga as described by Geoffrey suggested an alternative Celtic inheritance for the Caerleon site that could be seen as challenging the Roman history.

The other medieval source had been written by the cleric Giraldus while on a recruiting journey for the Third Crusade. Lee quotes Giraldus' description of the ruins in its entirety:

> This was an ancient and highly privileged city, admirably built in former times by the Romans with walls of burnt brick. You will see here many traces of ancient grandeur, immense palaces, whole roofs once gilded, imitated the Roman splendour, it having been built by the Roman emperor

[3] Ibid.
[4] Ibid. 2.
[5] Geoffrey of Monmouth, *The history of the kings of Britain*, trans. Thorpe Lewis, London 1966, 202.

and adorned with handsome structures. Here was a prodigious high tower, noble baths, remains of temples and theatres with grand walls, parts of which are still remaining.[6]

The similarity between the two passages, written fifty years apart, would seem to suggest that Giraldus had read Geoffrey's account and that his views had been shaped, at least in part, by the earlier writer. Lee makes no comment as to whether he believes Giraldus, but the fact that he quotes him in full, and that it is the only quotation he uses apart from extracts from classical texts, would seem to suggest that he was content to let this description stand. It would certainly leave the general reader with the impression that this was how Lee wished to portray Roman Caerleon. His friend, the Monmouth-shire antiquarian Thomas Wakeman, treated Giraldus' description with more scepticism:

When Giraldus, writing of its remains as existing in his time, mentions immense palaces ornamented with gilded roofs, we may be allowed to doubt whether any roof of Roman construction could possibly have endured through the seven centuries at least which had elapsed from the departure of the Romans to his time. Henry Huntingdon, who wrote half a century before Giraldus, gives a very different account of it: he tells us that the walls were then scarcely to be seen.[7]

There were also the observations of a series of travellers. The most influential of these was undoubtedly William Camden in *Britannia* (first published in 1586). The chapter on Welsh antiquities in the 1695 edition described Caer-leon as 'The city of the legions, placed here by Julius Frontinus in garrison against the Silures'.[8] Camden described in some detail inscriptions, altars and statues, a pavement discovered in 1685, a stone coffin and pottery. All of these were illustrated. Camden quotes Giraldus and Geoffrey, but says of the latter's account, 'It seems not of entire credit, so many ridiculous fables of his own invention hath he inserted in that work.'

Finally there was *A historical tour through Monmouthshire* written by the Revd William Coxe and his friend, Richard Colt Hoare in 1799. They had been among a number of visitors attracted to the wilder and more picturesque parts of Britain as a result of the increased interest in the Celtic past.[9] Colt Hoare was an antiquarian from Wiltshire. He had translated the 1586 edition of Camden from the original Latin and was therefore very familiar with the

6 Giraldus Cambrensis, *Journey through Wales*, ed. Thorpe Lewis, London 1978, 114.
7 T. Wakeman, 'Caerleon and history', AC iii (1849), 228. Other visitors to the town, Mr and Mrs S. C. Hall, were also dubious about Geoffrey's account: 'It has long been regarded as a collection of fables, to which no value can be attached': S. C. and A. M. Hall, *The book of South Wales, the Wye and the coast*, London 1859, 118
8 W. Camden, *Camden's Wales; Being the Welsh chapter taken from Edmund Gibson's revised and enlarged edition of Camden's* Britannia, trans. from the Latin with additions by Edward Lhuyd, London 1722.
9 See Smiles, *Image of antiquity*, 46–75.

work on Caerleon. Coxe was quite sure that Caerleon had been a Roman fortress:

> There is no occasion to employ many words in proof of these facts; the remains of the walls and amphitheatre, the numerous sculptures, altars, pavements, inscriptions, coins and other antiquities discovered within the town and the vicinity, evidently prove it the site of a great Roman city. Immense quantities of Roman bricks stamped with *LEG II AUG*, testify that this was the situation of the Second Augustan legion.[10]

Coxe gave a detailed description of the remains with site plans and drawings. He remarked on the quantity of Roman bricks and tiles lying on the ground, but regretted that most of the Roman antiquities had been removed. His account was published in 1801. It was used by antiquarians in the 1840s as a guide to what had stood on the site fifty years before and therefore highlighted what had been lost in the intervening years. Awareness of the extent of the loss was to be a crucial factor in Edward Lee's determination to form an antiquarian association in Caerleon.

Roman Caerleon in 1845

Lee's book gives a clear picture of the Roman remains in 1845. It is essentially a series of drawings, with an explanatory text attached: 'The object of the following pages is not either to write a history of the place or to give a dissertation on Roman antiquities in general; but simply to afford such information as may be necessary for the illustration of the drawings.'[11] It is apparent that there were virtually no standing remains and that the wealth of artefacts described by Coxe only fifty years before had all but vanished. Lee talks of the quarrying of ruined buildings, fragments of Roman pottery, of a hypocaust 'not preserved because it stood in the way of improvements', and of another, 'turned into a garden tank'.[12] However it was still possible to see the shape of the ancient fortress, 'Partly by the remains of the actual walls and partly by an elevated ridge formed from their ruins'.[13] The remains of the amphitheatre were still discernible, although local people called it 'King Arthur's Round Table'. Alongside the theatre remains was a field called the Bear-house field, which, according to Lee, 'Probably derived its name from its having been the place appropriated to the animals destined for the sports of the theatre.'[14] Lee reports that outside the walls considerable remains of burial urns had been unearthed, particularly along the old road between Caerleon and Caerwent,

---

10 Coxe, *Monmouthshire*, 80.
11 Lee, *Delineations*, 1845, p. vi.
12 Ibid. 3–5.
13 Ibid. 3.
14 Ibid. 4.

the ancient Venta Silurum. But again, these tombs had been 'ransacked in a search for treasure' and 'broken up to mend the roads'.[15]

It is apparent that the remains were under threat from a number of directions: as a source of stone for building activity; because they posed an obstruction in the way of some proposed changes; or because of an assumed artistic or monetary value. Even superstition could be a problem, as the fate of one glass vessel illustrates. 'It contained a large quantity of charcoal and burnt bones. After having exhibited it to one or two persons, it was thrown with its contents into the bed of the river, the labourer being unwilling, for some superstitious feeling, to keep human bones in his house.'[16] Surviving artefacts were scattered about the locality in the private collections of individuals. In spite of all these difficulties, Lee's conclusion was quite positive: 'Caerleon is a place of unusual interest to the antiquarian and where the ground has been materially raised by the ruins of one series of buildings over those of another, no excavation can be made without the chance of adding something to the present collection of Roman antiquities.'[17]

The impression derived from Lee's description of the site and from a survey of the sources of information available at the time is that the Caerleon antiquarians were presented with a range of fragments, both material and textual. If they were to form any coherent picture of their town during the Roman period, they would have to find some way in which they could bring these fragments together in order to make sense of them. However, more immediately, they were confronted with the knowledge that even those fragments were being lost and this probably prompted Lee's determination to preserve what remained.

Social and economic Caerleon

Caerleon is on the river Usk, about four miles north of the estuary on the Severn where the river is still tidal. It therefore offered easy access to the sea to enable the provisioning of a large body of men in the Roman fortress. Presumably the benefits offered by the site were still appreciated in the medieval period as the various accounts, including those of Geoffrey and Giraldus, continue to emphasise the importance of the site after the Romans left. Apart from being the centre of Arthur's court, it was also claimed as the site of a bishopric and of a college of astronomy. It was mentioned in the Domesday Book and it is certain that the Normans built a castle there. However by the time Coxe visited the town in 1799 its significance had declined: 'The town of Caerleon is reduced from its ancient extent and grandeur, to an inconsid-

---

15 Ibid. 6.
16 Ibid. 22.
17 Ibid. 7.

erable place. Since the removal of the port to Newport, it is no longer the centre of trade and communication and was scarcely visited by travellers.'[18]

A small fishing port in 1801, Newport had become the hub of an extensive transport system, bringing coal and metal products to the port for export. The population of just over 1,000 in 1801 reported by Coxe, had been fed by an influx of migrants from the countryside and had risen to 19,323 according to the 1851 census. By contrast Caerleon's population rose only slowly from the 763 reported by Coxe in 1801 to 1,539 in 1851. The relative decline of Caerleon is highlighted by travellers' accounts contrasting its poverty in the mid-nineteenth century with its glorious past. For instance, a Mr and Mrs Hall, who visited in 1855 ask, 'Is this poor village, an assemblage of ragged houses and mouldering walls, is it indeed that great city where the legion named "invincible" lived?'[19]

An alternative and perhaps more realistic description of the town in the nineteenth century is to be gathered from contemporary trade directories. For instance, Slater's royal, national and commercial directory (1858–9) reported that Caerleon was 'An ancient market town' which now consisted of 'two streets, indifferently paved and the houses, mostly old and irregularly built.'[20] The directory lists the businesses in the town including wheelwrights, maltsters, bakers, butchers, tailors, and a weekly provision and cattle market. All of which creates a picture of a small market town supplying the rural area around with goods and services. The only other employment was in two tinplate works 'in the vicinity'. These had been started in the eighteenth century and had been flourishing, but like the town generally, they were being overtaken by developments elsewhere. By the middle of the nineteenth century, the two works were declining and the local school logbook noted that, 'families are leaving because of the lack of orders for the tinplate works'.[21] In addition to the working-class population of Caerleon, there were sixty-three men listed in the 1854 electoral roll as eligible to vote, rather more than the number listed as 'ministers of religion and gentry' by Slater's directory in 1858. Many of these people were also committee members of the archaeological society, founded in 1847. They include the two proprietors of the tinplate works, the Anglican minister and Edward Lee.

[18] Coxe, Monmouthshire, 107.
[19] Art Journal, Apr. 1859, 117. Another tourist made a similar comment: 'How the mighty have fallen. Can this mean town scarcely rising above the rank of a village, be the place of which Giraldus speaks?': C. Cliffe, The book of south Wales, Bristol Channel, Monmouthshire and the Wye, London 1847.
[20] Slater's royal, national and commercial directory, 1858–9, Newport 1860, entry on Caerleon in Monmouthshire.
[21] P. Hockey, Caerleon past and present, Risca 1981.

The Caerleon Archaeological Association

On 28 October 1847 a group of people calling themselves, 'friends to the formation of a museum of antiquities at Caerleon' met in Lee's house. They decided to set up the Caerleon Archaeological Association. They had two objectives. The first was 'To build a museum to preserve the remains of the past which would otherwise be destroyed' and second, 'the furtherance of any antiquarian pursuit, whether by excavation or otherwise'.[22]

The meeting elected a chairman, secretary and six committee members; the bishop of Llandaff had already agreed to be the patron. The chairman was Sir Digby Mackworth, the local squire and a retired professional soldier, in which capacity he had been a part of the military force used to put down rioting in Bristol in 1831. He was a devout Christian, a pillar of the local church and a teacher in the Sunday school. Two of the committee, David Jenkins and William Powell, were Anglican ministers, the former the incumbent of Caerleon church. Henry Hawkins and Illtyd Nichol were local landowners and farmers. John Butler and John Jenkins were the proprietors of the two local tinplate works. Edward Lee was the secretary. Another prominent member was Octavius Morgan, who became the chairman in 1853 after Mackworth's death. He was the local MP and the brother of the wealthy local landowner, Lord Tredegar. He also played a prominent role in the national antiquarian bodies. Other active members were Thomas Wakeman, a landed gentleman whose main interest was in medieval charters, and Francis Fox, a railway surveyor.

With the exception of Fox, these men were all wealthy property owners, well educated and with time to pursue activities outside their work. In this respect they were similar to the typical groups which Philippa Levine identified in her study, although it is probable that there were a greater number of industrialists than might have been expected in a typical English county group. Reports in the local newspaper, the *Monmouthshire Merlin* make it clear that they had many interests in common. Their names appear again and again in the lists of those involved in groups and committees, whether to oversee the installation of new sewers in Caerleon or to pass judgement on their fellow citizens as JPs. These men were a part of the ruling elite in the area and this was emphasised by the roles they played in their local community.

The only individual who presents a more complicated picture is Edward Lee himself. Insofar as he was a wealthy man with a reasonable amount of leisure, he was quite typical, but he differed from his fellow antiquarians in several significant ways. He came from a wealthy merchant family in Hull

---

[22] CAA minutes, 27 Oct. 1847. The minutes are handwritten in a series of notebooks. They are unpublished and in the possession of the Monmouthshire Archaeological Association, the name adopted by the Caerleon group later in the century.

and had only moved to south Wales in 1841. He was therefore the only non-native in the group. More significantly, he was a dissenter and therefore denied access to the traditional centres of classical education at Oxford and Cambridge. In spite of this he appears to have had a good knowledge of the classical Latin texts, as his writings are full of classical references. He had been an early and enthusiastic member of the local literary and philosophical society in Hull, and had helped to set up its museum. It is probably through his association with the 'Lit and Phil' that he met John Phillips, a founding figure of the British Association of Science and later a professor of geology at Oxford. Under Phillips's influence Lee became fascinated with geology. Many years later he wrote that 'It was a common thing in the larger towns of the North of England for well known scientific men to deliver courses on natural philosophy and science. In general they were attended, not only by young learners, but by the older and wealthier classes, who at the time considered it essential to increase their store of knowledge.'[23]

Lee travelled widely, particularly in northern Europe. In Denmark he came into contact with the new archaeological ideas of Thomsen and Worsaae and their theories about the three-stage development of pre-history. As a result, Lee was familiar with the new ideas that were to completely recast the theories of pre-history later in the century. Crucially, his main interests lay in geology, the science that was at the forefront of new ideas concerning the age of the earth and how it had been formed. It is impossible to know to what extent Lee informed his fellow antiquarians in Caerleon about these new theories and, if he did so, how they were received. But it is clear from the minutes of the CAA that it was his interest and energy that drove the group forward.

It is possible to follow the activities of the association through the minute books and the very detailed reports in the *Monmouthshire Merlin*. The AGMs were the only regular meetings and there appears to have been little formal attempt to educate the members in the way that Lee had experienced in Hull. From the beginning the main focus was on the creation of a museum in which to preserve the threatened antiquities. Any other activity, whether it was the writing of learned papers or arranging an excavation, was done on an individual basis. For instance, in 1848, a local farmer, John James, arranged for a tessellated pavement discovered on his land to be uncovered. It was subsequently donated to the museum. The following year, during the course of laying a new lawn in his garden, the committee member, John Jenkins, discovered the foundations of a Roman building that he paid to have uncovered.[24] However it was not until 1855 that the society was able to fund its first official excavation at the Caerwent site.

[23] J. E. Lee, *Notebooks of an amateur geologist*, London 1881, 1.
[24] Idem, *Description of a Roman building and other remains lately discovered at Caerleon*, London 1850. Lee wrote, 'It is much to be regretted that it [the remains] cannot be preserved entire, consistently with alterations which Mr. Jenkins is making' (p. 6).

From 1847 the AGMs followed a similar pattern. They were held in Caerleon and after the reports and the election of officers a number of papers were read. These were almost exclusively written by members and were usually concerned with items of interest discovered during the previous year. The objects were laid out on a table for the members to examine. After the formalities, the meeting would visit a Roman site of interest in the town, which had been uncovered for that purpose by the landowner concerned.

The newspaper accounts of these meetings suggest they were very sociable affairs with as many as eighty people sitting down to the meal that always rounded off the proceedings. The dinner involved speeches and general congratulations all round. The sense of a small group in which everyone knew everyone else comes over clearly, but it is difficult to judge how much the wider membership was involved in any activities other than the formal dinner. At the 1860 AGM Lee asked members to take a more active part, remarking that 'to be useful, a society ought to include a number of working members'.[25] This would seem to suggest that most of the work had fallen on just a few shoulders and that it was the officers and committee who wrote the papers and arranged for site activity.[26]

Lee and Wakeman were the county representatives for the BAA and Morgan was an active member of the Society of Antiquaries in London and acted as vice-chairman for a number of years. All three men contributed articles to national archaeological journals.[27] The national archaeological bodies were entertained and shown the sights in Caerleon in 1851 and 1855. Charles Roach Smith visited on several occasions and reported the findings in the *JBAA*. Lee's books were reviewed and praised in all the national journals and he in turn subscribed to most of the archaeological books published during this period. Finally Lee corresponded with many leading figures in the field, whom he lists in the front of his books. Apart from Roach Smith these included Albert Way, the secretary of the AI; Professor Theodor Mommsen the Roman historian and world authority on Latin inscriptions in Berlin and the Revd C. W. King, a Cambridge don and authority on Roman coins. It was through this network of letters and reports that the work of the Caerleon archaeologists became familiar to a wider British audience.

In the beginning the over-riding concern of the group had been the preservation of the Roman remains and the construction of a museum. However

---

25 Anon., 'Caerleon Archaeological Society', MM, 25 Aug. 1860, 4.
26 This was a problem experienced by several societies. For instance, the failure of the Wiltshire Topographical Society in 1850 was attributed by its founder, John Britton, to 'So little assistance and co-operation from other gentlemen of the county. He must own that he feels his zeal much abated, and that he must relinquish his efforts in despair': C. W. Pugh (ed.), *The Wiltshire Archaeological and Natural History Society, 1853–1953*, Devizes 1953, 6.
27 J. Lee, 'Inscriptions and antiquities discovered at Caerleon', *AJ* viii (1851), 157; O. Morgan, 'Excavations made within the walls of Caerwent', *Arch.* xxxvi (1855), 423; Anon, 'Caerleon Archaeological Association', *GM* xxxiv (1850), 415, all contained a detailed report of the CAA AGM which was presumably sent in by Lee.

once that objective had been achieved, exclusive concentration on matters Roman ceased and members' varied interests become more apparent: Octavius Morgan and Thomas Wakeman were concerned with the medieval history of the area and Lee was more interested in its pre-history. These topics probably reflected the interests of the wider archaeological world as a whole, where, on the one hand there was an enormous interest in all things Gothic, while on the other the discoveries in Abbeville, in France, excited an interest in the newly realised ancient history of humankind. After 1855 the annual meetings were no longer held exclusively in Caerleon nor did they always visit Roman sites. For the next few years the meetings were held at a variety of castles and in 1860 the annual meeting took part in an excavation of a Bronze Age barrow and Lee read a paper on the flint implements found on the site.[28]

The only major excavation undertaken by the society was at a Roman site, Venta Silures (Caerwent), five miles away. This was believed to have been the main settlement of the Silurian tribe which had been taken over and used as the administrative centre by the Romans. Roach Smith visited the village of Caerwent in 1847 and observed that there was still considerable evidence of Roman walls and masonry but that three tessellated pavements which had been reported to the Society of Antiquaries in the previous century had all disappeared. His report concluded that

> The entire place offers a tempting field for a systematic investigation; it may, indeed, be considered almost as unbroken ground, for the discoveries of tessellated pavements, shafts and capitals of pillars, with other remains of buildings, such as are upon record, appear to have been the result of accident, and were never followed up by any regular researches.[29]

It was probably as a result of such enthusiastic reports that it was decided to excavate the site in 1855. The dig was carried out under the direction of John Akerman, although Octavius Morgan wrote all the reports.[30] The remains of many buildings, including what appeared to be a bathhouse, were uncovered but the picture they revealed was confusing: 'The arrangement of all the Romano British villas and houses which I have seen is, I must confess, to me very unintelligible and seems to bear no relation to the plans of Roman villas in Italy.'[31] It was clear that Morgan was using his knowledge of the remains in Italy to guide him in deciphering the problems presented by the Caerwent site. He cited Pompeii and the classical texts to construct a model of what he thought should be on the site and concluded, 'All these apartments I think

---

[28] For instance, Usk in 1856, Raglan in 1857 and White in 1859.

[29] Roach Smith, 'Notes on Caerwent and Caerleon', 255.

[30] The original intention had been that the excavation was to be carried out by the BAA whose members had visited the site in 1854, but these plans had fallen through because of indiscreet letters written by the association's secretary, Thomas Hugo, to Octavius Morgan and the Revd Frank Lewis, the owner of the Caerwent site.

[31] O. Morgan, *Excavations prosecuted by the Caerleon Antiquarian Association within the walls of Caerwent in the summer of 1855*, London 1856.

our baths exhibit, arranged in the most compact manner.'[32] After a detailed plan and a model had been constructed for display in the museum, directions were given for the site to be filled in carefully, 'so as not to injure or destroy what is curious and thus to preserve its existence for the gratification and information of future antiquaries'.[33]

A museum for Caerleon

Lee had been prompted to write his book, *Delineations of Roman antiquities*, to draw attention to the fact that the material Roman remains of the town were being lost and destroyed. Once the level of destruction had been described the provision of a building had become the primary objective for the newly formed society in 1847. This was a very ambitious project: most museums founded during this period made use of rooms in already existing buildings and finance was to be a continuing anxiety.[34] The 1845 Museums Act enabled local authorities to raise a halfpenny rate for the creation of museums to instruct and amuse the public and Lee had hoped that there might have been some funding from this source, but he was to be disappointed.

The museum site in the centre of Caerleon, next to the church, was on land donated by Digby Mackworth. In view of their concern to save remains, it is perhaps rather surprising that committee members do not appear to have questioned whether their choice of site might actually be obscuring some of the remains they were seeking to protect. It is clear from their written papers that the committee was aware that the site stood almost exactly over the point at which the two main roads through the fortress would have crossed and, therefore, that this would have been the location of several important legionary buildings. But there was no suggestion that excavation was considered prior to the start of the building work.[35]

The committee decided that they wanted a building in the Doric style with 'dimensions to be twenty foot by forty foot and sixteen foot high inside. It was to be lighted from above by a roof light, the floor to be raised three foot above the road, with four pillars in front and five pilasters on each side'.[36]

[32] Ibid. 16.
[33] Ibid. 28.
[34] A brand-new, purpose-built museum was usually only provided where there was a wealthy patron to foot the bill, as in Cirencester.
[35] The Revd David Jones delivered a paper in which he related the site of the Roman fortress to the configuration of the contemporary town: 'If we look at these roads pointing inwards, we shall find they all meet in the open square by the church, which stands as nearly as possible in the intersection of the lines drawn diagonally from the angles of the camp. Here was the forum': MM, 14 July 1849. The museum was therefore built directly on the top of the spot that Jones had correctly identified as important.
[36] E. I. P. Bowen, 'Presidential address', AC (1971), 3. Bowen's notes say that he got this information from the society's minute book. I did not see such an entry when I read the minutes, although the actual building did accord with this description. Bowen's source is

The structure was to incorporate four columns of freestone which, according to Coxe, had probably belonged to some Roman structure. Like the recently completed British Museum, the choice of the Doric style was in keeping with the Greek revival, which had been fashionable earlier in the century and was still considered appropriate for museums of classical art and artefacts.[37] Whatever the reasons for the choice of style, the minutes merely record that the Doric was chosen and that an architect friend of Lee's from Hull had agreed to prepare the designs without charge. What is clear is that the building was expected to be 'handsome' and 'an ornament to the town'. *The Monmouthshire Merlin* described it as being erected, 'with such classical taste to serve as a museum'.[38] Evidently the style was seen as important in conveying the seriousness of the endeavour.

From the beginning there were all kinds of problems. First, not all the members appear to have understood the need for a museum or why its contents should be restricted purely to the archaeological remains. Lee had to explain why the committee was collecting both subscriptions and donations:

> Questions have been asked as to the intended appropriation of both, which would seem to argue that our circulars have not been as widely circulated, or at least so generally read as we had imagined. Our first object is to establish a museum solely for antiquities. However desirable it might be to have a general philosophical museum within the neighbourhood, this does not fall within our province.[39]

He went on to explain that once the museum was built, the committee would be willing to undertake further excavations, but that in the meantime the building work was a priority.

The work itself was also presenting difficulties. The original builder was found to have cut corners and some of the work had to be redone. But the main problem was a lack of money. At every AGM there were appeals to the members to contribute more funds and advertisements were placed in all the local papers asking for contributions. The 1850 *Archaeological Journal* carried a review of Lee's latest book, *Description of a Roman building and other remains lately found at Caerleon* and ended with the observation that all these remains

therefore unclear. However, the minutes are brief and give the impression that the main discussions and decisions were not made at the formal committee meetings.

[37] William Wilkins had been responsible for the Greek Revival style of the Yorkshire Philosophical Society's museum, which Lee would have been familiar with because of his close friendship with the museum's curator John Phillips.

[38] Anon., 'Caerleon Archaeological Association', MM, 28 July 1849, 4.

[39] Anon., 'Caerleon Archaeological Association', MM, 14 July 1849, 3: 'If only the building was once finished and the antiquities displayed, there would be an end for ever to the perpetual questions; what is it intended for? And what is there that can be put in it? If those who asked these questions, and there are many that do, want to devote an hour or two to an examination of all our treasures; the wonder would probably be not that Caerleon is now building a museum, but that so long a time has elapsed before a museum has been built.'

were to be housed in 'the museum actually in the course of construction ... but the contributions have not proved wholly adequate to the completion'.[40] There was a footnote explaining that Lee had written the book to raise funds and that any contributions would be acknowledged. There is no record as to the response to this appeal.[41]

Despite these problems, Lee was able to report to the 1850 AGM that the lower floor was already being used to house the heavier sculptures. The smaller items however needed to be displayed in glass cabinets, for which, as yet, they did not have the finances. After the meeting, the whole company went to inspect the new building, which had been decorated with flowers and where a large number of antiquities were temporarily displayed on tables with explanatory tickets. According to the *Monmouthshire Merlin*, 'The room is decidedly handsome and is well adapted for the purposes of a museum.'[42]

The building was finally opened to the public on 2 August 1850. In view of the publicity given to all the previous events, such as the annual meetings and fund-raising events, it was a surprisingly low-key occasion. At a committee meeting later in the month it was decided that there should be a prominently placed box for donations and a visitors' book. It would appear from this that there was no entrance charge, although this was to change later in the century. The same committee meeting also decided to appoint a keeper at a fee of not more than three guineas a year. The minutes do not record when this appointment took place, but the membership list of the society in 1863 lists a keeper, a Mr Powell, living at the post office in Caerleon (presumably his main source of income). There are only rare reports of what was inside the museum in the early years. One was in the *Merlin* in 1851:

> The upper or main floor is devoted to a display of tessellated pavements and several decorated tombstones and a variety of other articles of the ponderous kind; while the more minute portions in glass cases, attract very particular attention for being articles in common use in the private house or the workshop of the artisan, such as were handled in the days when the Romans held sway in Britain.[43]

Later visitors to the museum described it as a dark, narrow room with the walls covered in stone inscriptions. The displays were in high, black-painted cabinets and consisted largely of coins and other small objects.

The best guide to the original collections is Lee's illustrated catalogue *Isca Silurum*, published in 1862. It is reasonable to suppose that the approach

---

[40] J. Lee, 'Roman building and other remains lately found at Caerleon', *AJ* vii (1850), 99.
[41] In 1854 it was reported that Lee was still trying to liquidate the remaining debts. 'He requests on the one hand the contribution of objects of art, books, pictures, prints etc and on the other proposes that the same shall be dispersed again by 100 tickets to be issued at ten shillings each': Anon., 'Notes of the month', *GM* xli (1854), 280.
[42] Anon., 'Caerleon Archaeological Association', *MM*, 20 July 1850, 4.
[43] Anon., 'Caerleon Archaeological Association', *MM*, 8 Aug. 1851, 4.

and layout of the guide reflects that of the museum itself. The contents are entirely archaeological, despite the offer of at least one collection of 'curiosities' turned down by the committee in 1851.[44] In the main the objects were Roman and from Caerleon. Those that were not were grouped together as either 'Medieval' (ranging from glazed tiles and impressions of an early seal to a badge of Charles I) or 'Celtic' (including the contents of the barrow excavated in 1860 and some fragments of stone crosses). The Roman contents were classed under the headings of stone, earthen, vegetable, animal and metallic materials. There was a separate section for the coins. Lee's descriptions are brief and refer to the objects in isolation, rather than to any possible context in which they might have been used; as he says: 'the drawings speak for themselves'.[45]

Before the CAA was set up Caerleon's status as a Roman site rested on a few scattered remains and obscure references. It was almost entirely due to the activities of the local antiquarians that the significance of the site was acknowledged and made known to the national antiquarian world. They quite literally put Isca Silures on the map. But if the Caerleon antiquarians were unusually proactive archaeologically, their attitude to the social implications of the Roman past was more typical of other local societies. The decision to build the museum in the Greek revival style and its prominent site in the middle of the town suggest the importance that they attached to the preservation of the Roman history of their town, but it was also a testament to their parochial interests. The fact that the site donated by Mackworth was directly on top of the archaeologically important centre of the fort did not deter them; the museum building was an imposing reminder of past greatness and symbolised the hopes of its founders that 'this building would be the first step in restoring the town to its ancient importance'.[46]

[44] CAA minutes, 31 Jan. 1851.
[45] Ibid.
[46] The hopes are those of the chairman (Mackworth) at the stone-laying ceremony for the new building: MM, 24 June 1848.

5

Corinium

In the summer of 1849 workmen digging a trench for a sewer in the main street of Cirencester uncovered two large and intricately patterned mosaic pavements. The discoveries attracted a great deal of interest and the finds were reported nationally in *The Times* and the *Gentleman's Magazine* and in the local paper, the *Wiltshire and Gloucestershire Standard*. The report in the *Illustrated London News* included a dramatic picture of a mosaic being lifted from the ground against the backdrop of the old town with its ancient church rising immediately behind the wooden lifting crane (*see* frontispiece).[1] The discoveries prompted renewed interest in the town's Roman past and a steady flow of visitors to the museum in which the mosaics were displayed.

Knowledge of Roman Cirencester before 1849

The Roman name, Corinium, had appeared in the *Antonine itinerary*, in which it was named as the meeting point of several major roads. It was also described as the capital of the province of the Dobunni (Corinium Dobunorum) in the eighth-century *Ravenna cosmography*.[2] It had therefore always been assumed that there had been a Roman centre somewhere in the vicinity. The fact that the contemporary town stood at the point at which the Fosse Way, Ermine Street and Akeman Street met, and the number of Roman remains discovered over the years, had led to a general assumption that the town of Cirencester was indeed the site of Roman Corinium. The nature of the settlement however remained uncertain, with some arguing that there had been a military presence in the form of a fort and others suggesting a purely administrative function. In the medieval period the town was mentioned in some of the early chronicles, but these accounts were often fanciful and very misleading. For instance, John Buckman wrote that 'Richard of Monmouth concludes that Corium was built by a Roman general in the time of Claudius, probably by Plautius ... and that it had walls and a castle in the time of Constantine and was strongly fortified.'[3] Apart from the lack of any evidence to substantiate these claims, it is unclear whether Buckman is referring to

---

1 *ILN*, 8 Sept. 1849.
2 See A. L. F. Rivet, 'The British section of the *Antonine itinerary*', *Britannia* i (1970), 34, and I. A. Richmond, 'British section of the *Ravenna cosmography*', *Arch.* lxxxxiii (1949), 1–50.
3 J. Buckman and C. Newmarch, *Remains of Roman art in ancient Corinium*, London 1850, 9.

Geoffrey of Monmouth or Richard of Cirencester.[4] What is clear is that the town's Roman past remained confused.

More reliable reporters were those sixteenth-century travellers, John Leland and William Camden, whose accounts of visits to the town were frequently quoted. Leland observed that 'a man may yet, evidently perceyve the cumpace of foundation of towers sumtyme standing in the waul'.[5] A few years later, in 1586, Camden wrote 'that this was a considerable place is evident from the Roman coins, chequered pavements, and inscriptions in marble dug up here'.[6]

The first antiquarian account was by William Stukeley in *Itinerarium curiosum* (1721). He said that 'Here they dig up antiquities every day and in the plain fields, the tracks of foundations of houses and streets are evident enough. Here are found many mosaic pavements, rings, intaglios and coins in abundance and all bear testimony to the ancient grandeur of this place.'[7] Stukeley also reported a vault supported by pillars of Roman brick, which he thought were the remains of a temple. Sixty years later, in 1780, when Samuel Rudder wrote *History and antiquities of Cirencester*, he relied heavily on Stukeley's account and quoted whole passages from the *Itinerarium*. However he disagreed with Stukeley's opinion that the town had been created by the Britons before the Roman invasion. In spite of the fact that neither Caesar nor Strabo mentions Corinium, Rudder uses them to justify his belief that the town was built early in the Roman occupation and became an important station for the Roman army: 'These authorities will stand their ground against the fond conceits and loose conjectures of later writers.'[8] Rudder speculated on the origins of the oval earthworks on waste ground to the west of the town, just outside the supposed lines of the Roman walls which was known locally as the Bull Ring: 'Probably a Roman theatre, but history is silent to the use of it. Mr. Camden mentions one something like it in Westmoreland called King Arthur's Round Table, which he thinks might possibly be a jousting place.'[9] Other writers had suggested that the mound was either a quarry or a burial ground.[10]

It is interesting to observe the way in which each new account of the town's past builds upon and uses information contained within the earlier texts. Comments from past authors are introduced, presumably to add extra weight to the contemporary author's views; but this is done with very little attempt to question the sources of the original. So, as Rudder had relied upon Stukeley, so Beecham relied on Rudder as a source of information for his

---

4   See chapter 1 n. 23 above.
5   This is cited in S. Rudder, *History and antiquities of Cirencester*, Cirencester 1780, 6.
6   Ibid. 28.
7   Ibid. 12.
8   Ibid. 7.
9   Ibid. 28.
10 It is in fact the Roman amphitheatre. The inhabitants of the town have used it for centuries as a site for various entertainments.

History and antiquities of the town of Cirencester (1842). Beecham's account gives a picture of the town and the way in which its past was perceived just prior to the discoveries of 1849. He also makes use of Giraldus' twelfth-century description of Roman remains at Caerleon:

> This description by Gerald of Wales, which so graphically sets forth the elegancies and the conveniences introduced by the Roman settlers, may serve as the model by which to imagine ancient Corinium, surrounded by the lofty walls, of great width and strength and the centre of different roads connecting it to remote parts of the country ... It is no wonder that it became a favourite station for the troops and that much labour and expense was lavished to render it a fitting residence for the luxurious and wealthy colonialist. The remains must prove that the Anglo Roman city was at least one of the richest and best populated settlements in the island.[11]

Beecham's description is an example of the way in which local historians in the mid-nineteenth century created coherent images of the Roman past in their locality. The vividness of the account relies to a considerable extent on a twelfth-century description of another Roman site, written many centuries after the Roman departure in the fifth century. Taken together with the luxurious nature of the remains and mosaics, Giraldus' descriptions enabled Beecham to create a picture of Cirencester that confirmed his imaginative view of life in a Roman town. It was a picture that was not only based on the physical remains, but also on a range of pictorial and literary associations suggested by the words 'Rome' and 'Roman'. The effect was heightened by the contrast provided by Beecham's portrayal of the British settlement replaced by the Roman town: 'Domestic architecture consisting of rude huts formed of stakes, wattled together and placed like the wigwams of American Indians amidst impervious forests and swamps.'[12]

The view that Cirencester was an important and wealthy centre was reinforced by the discovery of several beautifully decorated mosaic pavements in the eighteenth century.[13] Their influence is to be seen in Thomas Wright's observation that 'Corinium, a town filled with magnificent houses and public buildings ... Some of the richest and most elegant mosaic pavements in this island show its ancient splendour.'[14] Most of them had been found in the surrounding countryside and their discovery suggested that there had been a whole series of large and prosperous villas in the vicinity of the town. Between 1789 and 1817 Samuel Lysons had excavated villa sites at Woodchester, Withington and Great Witcombe and all had revealed mosaics and were reported in the *Archaeologia*.[15] A particularly fine pavement had been discov-

---

11 W. K. Beecham, *The history and antiquities of the town of Cirencester*, London 1842, 196. For Giraldus' original description see chapter 4 above.
12 Ibid. 3.
13 Buckman and Newmarch, *Remains of Roman art*, 25–34.
14 Wright, *Celt, Roman and Saxon*, 135.
15 S. Lysons, 'Roman antiquities discovered at Combe End farm', *Arch.* ix (1789), 319–23;

ered on land belonging to Lord Bathurst. He had it removed and displayed in his garden for his visitors to admire. Other examples had been found in the centre of town, lying beneath shops and houses in the cellars. A reviewer in the *Gentleman's Magazine* thought that 'the pavements of Cirencester are much the same as Rome itself'.[16]

By the mid-1840s the antiquarians were convinced of the importance of the town in the Roman period. Although there were no standing remains, the outline of the old city could still be made out from the shape of the contemporary town. The mosaic on Lord Bathurst's estate was comparatively familiar to the townspeople and other impressive fragments were displayed prominently round the town. For instance, the Corinthian capital unearthed in Mr Gregory's nursery garden in 1808 had been re-erected near the abbey grounds and several of the prosperous townspeople had accumulated small collections of artefacts.

But if these old accounts had made people familiar with their Roman past, they had also drawn attention to the steady loss and destruction of the remains. Many of the features noted by Stukeley and Rudder had already disappeared. Their books were both a record of new discoveries and a reminder of what had been lost due to development and neglect. In the 1820s and 1830s a large area to the south of the town, including the medieval Shambles, had been pulled down. This had been regarded as the poorest part of the town and its removal and the construction of a culverted water supply were seen as an improve-ment. But no regard had been given to what might have lain underneath and been destroyed as a result of this activity. No complaints were heard and no one individual put himself forward to keep an eye on any possible antiquities, as had been the case in other parts of the country.[17] As Beecham remarked, 'The taste for preserving remains of bygone taste and genius is of such recent date. Little has been preserved, but mutilated parts, which like the bones of the mastodon leave to the imagination alone the magnitude and configura-tion of the whole.'[18] Roach Smith was more optimistic. After visiting the town in 1846, his opinion was that 'it would take a volume to do justice to the vestiges of ancient Corinium which are still in existence and we are now convinced that many interesting discoveries are likely to be made'.[19]

'Roman antiquities discovered in the county of Gloucester', *Arch.* x (1790), 131–6; and 'Remains of several Roman buildings and other Roman antiquities', *Arch.* xviii (1817), 112–25.

[16] Anon., 'Roman pavements Cirencester', GM xxxiv (1850), 24. The same review compared some murals found in London with those in the villa attributed to Cicero at Mola di Gaeta. Comparisons of Romano-British artefacts with those found in Italy were common.

[17] For instance, Roach Smith in London and Lee in Caerleon.

[18] Beecham, *History and antiquities*, 196. It could be argued that the absence of remains left greater scope for the imagination.

[19] WGS, 11 Aug. 1846.

Social and economic Cirencester

In the medieval period Cirencester had been a centre of cloth production and the size and beauty of the abbey was a reminder of those prosperous times. In fact Daniel Defoe, who visited the town in the early 1700s, considered that 'Cirencester is still a very good town, populous, rich, full of clothiers and doing a good trade in wool.'[20] But by 1849 the French wars and mechanisation had finally put an end to the wool trade and the town had become reliant on the agriculture carried out in the surrounding countryside. This left the town vulnerable to the fluctuating fortunes of that one industry and the local newspaper made frequent references to the 'distressed state of agriculture'.[21] The possible negative effects of the repeal of the corn laws in 1846 caused particular apprehension, as can be seen from a remark of the president of the Cotteswold Naturalist Field Club, who described the head of Ceres on the newly uncovered mosaic as 'Starting in horror at the advance of free trade'.[22]

Although there was continuing concern about social unrest and the effects of free trade, Cirencester started to flourish again largely as a result of the general improvement in agricultural prosperity that began around 1850.[23] In 1849 a trade directory described the town as having 'A pleasing and highly respectable appearance and its inhabitants – many of who are opulent, seem to enjoy a large share of domestic comfort and prosperity. It is lighted by gas, well paved and effectively supplied with good water.'[24] There was a steady increase in population from 4,130 in 1801 to 6,096 in 1851. In 1843 the Great Western railway opened a new line which linked Cirencester to the main line to London and this facilitated the flow of visitors, anxious to see the Roman mosaics. But in spite of these changes the structure of local government remained archaic. Local affairs were administered through the court of the lord of the manor, Lord Bathurst, and town officials, such as the poor law guardians, were all appointed by him. It was not until 1876 that the town was finally incorporated and thus able to elect a council.

Bathurst played a pivotal role in the life of the town. The first Lord Bathurst had inherited the family estates in 1704 and, unlike the Whig landed aristocracy who often moved their estates away from centres of popu-

[20] D. Defoe, *A tour through the whole island of Great Britain* (1724–6), London 1971, 359.
[21] For instance, 'The depression which weighs down the energies of the peoples of this kingdom residing in the agricultural districts is apparent at every assemblage of those dependent upon trade and commerce for their support': WGS, 24 Sept. 1849.
[22] Anon., 'Account of meeting 27th Sept. 1849', PCNFC i (1853), 48.
[23] The social concerns were fairly typical. For instance, the paper described a lecture by the Chartist leader in the Temperance Hall in 1849 as 'sewing seeds of social discord and discontent': WGS, 7 May 1849. The same edition reported that it had received a letter suggesting that the farmers of the Cotswolds should 'Unite for mutual defence in a political crisis. They should bear in mind the emblem of the bundle of sticks, union is strength.'
[24] Hunt and Co., *Directory of Gloucestershire and Bristol*, Bristol 1849, 81.

lation in order to achieve an uncluttered rural aspect, chose to emphasise his ties with the local community. His house, Cirencester Park, was situated in the town, only separated from the street by a large stone wall: a position which seemed to symbolise his dominant place in local society. The 4th Lord Bathurst continued this close association with the town and its activities. As lord of the manor he was the automatic choice as figurehead for any activity. It was entirely typical that he should provide the land for the new agricultural college built in 1845 and that when the mosaics were uncovered in 1849, he should offer to build a museum to house them, on his land.

There were a number of professional men in the town whose names, Brown, Bowley, Brewin, Mullings, Newmarch and Cripps, occur again and again in the membership lists of groups and committees. They were solicitors, surveyors and merchants and, like many middle-class men in a similar position in the nineteenth century, they devoted much of their spare time to organising and running societies and charitable affairs. But Bathurst's dominant position and the archaic method of local government ensured that no potential rival was either able or willing to put himself forward as a leader or possible source of influence. Another factor could have been that several of these families were Quakers of long standing, which put them somewhat outside the normal elite group.[25] The only remaining source of possible influence within the town was the agricultural college, which attracted lecturers from outside, several of whom were to take a leading role in the archaeological activity following the 1849 discoveries.

The 1849 discoveries and archaeological activities

When the workmen uncovered the mosaics in August 1849 the professor of geology and botany at the agricultural college, John Buckman, cleared away the debris, assisted by a group of students. He described the flurry of activity to save the mosaics:

> Tracings of the floors, as they were gradually explored, were made by Mr. Cox of Cirencester, assisted by the vicar and some of the professors of the Royal Agricultural College, and even a few students shared in the work. A busy scene it was to see all these volunteers kneeling and patiently tracing, stone by stone the complicated details, of which the colours were carefully matched by Mr. Cox.[26]

It was clear that if the pavements were to be saved then they would have to be moved and Buckman devised an ingenious system to raise them and the brick structure on which they stood. It was at this point that Lord Bathurst offered

[25] The Bowns, the Bowleys and the Brewins were all Quakers. It was reported that the Friends Meeting House could seat up to 700 people.
[26] J. Buckman, 'The removal and relaying of Roman tessellated floors', AJ xiii (1856), 215.

to pay the cost of removal and storage and to build a museum to house them on estate land. They were stored, part in the local church and the rest on the lawn in front of Bathurst's mansion, until a museum was finally completed in 1856.

John Buckman was a self-made man. He was born in Cheltenham in 1814 and after a private education became a pupil of a surgeon-apothecary, before going to London to study botany, geology and chemistry.[27] He was actively involved in the Cheltenham Philosophical Institute, founded in 1823, and wrote regular articles on geology and the natural sciences for the local Cheltenham newspaper.[28] In 1846 he was appointed a professor and curator at the Birmingham Philosophical Institute. In the same year he was one of the founding members of the Cotteswold Naturalists' Field Club, a group whose interests were mainly in the natural history of the area.[29] In 1848 he was appointed professor of geology and botany at the Agricultural College in Cirencester. The wide range of topics covered in his books would suggest that he was a man of many interests, as a comment from the CNFC would seem to confirm: 'Mr. Buckman ... is extremely wanted, though were he to present himself wherever he is wished for; he must divide himself into as many parts as he has friends.'[30]

The discovery of the pavements, and the proposed museum, generated a great deal of interest and considerable press coverage, so it is perhaps not surprising that Buckman should also write about the discoveries. In 1850 he and another Cirencester resident, Charles Newmarch, published *The remains of Roman art in ancient Corinium*. In it they say that their purpose was to collect together all the information about the scattered antiquities of Corinium: 'By means of accurate drawings and descriptions, to afford to the antiquary, and to the man of taste, an opportunity of forming conclusions as to the state of the people who occupied this interesting station at a period long prior to the one marked by modern civilisation.'[31] They hoped that the detailed review of the Cirencester remains would 'contribute something to the general history of the Roman occupation of Britain'.

Buckman described the Roman town: 'Corinium was a city of great impor-

[27] This lack of specialisation was quite typical of the period. In 1841 the scientist Thomas Huxley is reported as studying chemistry, history, Latin, Greek, algebra, geometry and physics whilst apprenticed to a doctor.

[28] These were published later and included *Our triangle: geology, archaeology and botany of the most picturesque and interesting spots of Cheltenham*, Cheltenham 1842, and *A guide to Pittville: containing an analysis of Pittville's saline waters*, Cheltenham 1842.

[29] Anon., 'Proceedings', *PCNFC* i (1853).

[30] Anon., 'Account of meeting on 5 Aug. 1851', *PCNFC* i (1853).

[31] Buckman and Newmarch, *Remains of Roman art*, p. vi. A twentieth-century archaeologist of Cirencester described the book as 'A well illustrated quarto with a useful list of coins; but it is somewhat one sided owing to the importance which its authors attached to the technique of mosaic floors and is hardly up to the level of archaeologists' knowledge of Roman things which was current at about 1850': F. Haverfield, 'Roman Cirencester', *Arch.* lxix (1920), 199.

tance under the Roman rule, notwithstanding that the ravages of time, and, still worse, the destructiveness of anti-conservative proprietors, have obliterated much valuable evidence.'[32] After giving a general description of the town, its roads, fortifications and architecture, there are several chapters devoted to detailed descriptions of the mosaics, their designs and their chemical and geological properties.

Two main themes ran through the descriptions. The first was a desire to demonstrate the utility of the finds and the way in which a detailed analysis of the production methods could assist contemporary manufacturers to improve their own methods. The second was a concern with the mosaics as art. They were not presented as examples of flooring in Roman houses, but as examples of beautiful objects completely detached from their original purpose.[33] Buckman compared the figures on the mosaics with 'the finest Greek schools' to be found in the British Museum's collections and quoted Richard Westmacott in justification for his views:

> Interesting as these pavements are, as monuments of past time, they have a further claim on our attention for the qualities of art exhibited in them ... Here is a grandeur of form, dignity of character, and great breadth of treatment, which strongly reminds me of the finest Greek schools ... Such works were produced after examples of the very highest reaches of art.[34]

To convey the beauty of the mosaics, Buckman used comparisons with Roman examples. For instance he quoted an article in the *AJ* in which the author compared the Cirencester mosaics with 'the gorgeous floors of the Vatican Museum rescued from the ruins of Hadrian's Villa and other decaying edifices of the Romans in Italy'.[35] Buckman concluded that 'under Roman rule, this colonial settlement possessed temples and dwellings of like magnificence, and evidencing the same principles of design as those which characterised the mother country'.[36] It would seem that it was only by comparing them with the very best that he could do justice to the Cirencester remains. There is even a sense that he regarded them as equal in artistic worth to mosaics found in Rome: a very different view from conventional thoughts about the relationship between Britain and Rome.

Buckman was anxious to continue with the excavations. He wrote that 'It is to be regretted that no systematic plan of investigation about the places where

[32] Buckman and Newmarch, *Remains of Roman art*, 9.
[33] This was noted by another Cirencester archaeologist, Wilfred Cripps, in 1898: 'Even in modern times competent archaeologists have been content with the discovery of fine tessellated pavements and other objects now preserved in the local museum, and seem to have directed too little attention to the plan and structure of the buildings containing them, or the relation of these buildings to the town itself': *Proceedings of the London Society of Antiquaries*, 2nd ser. xvii (1897–9), 201.
[34] Buckman and Newmarch, *Remains of Roman art*, 46.
[35] He is quoting C. Tucker, 'Collections illustrative of Roman occupation in Britain: no. 1 Corinium', *AJ* vi (1849), 330.
[36] Buckman and Newmarch, *Remains of Roman art*, 18.

stone work has been found has yet been undertaken.'[37] It is even possible that he wrote the book to raise funds to further the work, but if that is the case, he did not say so and therefore we can only speculate about his motivation.[38] In the preface he acknowledges the support he had received from the public, a fact that is emphasised by the very long list of subscribers which follows.[39] But lack of funds continued to be a problem. In March 1851 he reported to the Archaeological Institute the results of a recent dig in the Watermoor district of the town and noted that these would be continued when funds became available.[40] His next report to the institute, in the autumn, explained that a local antiquary, Mr Thomas Brown, had paid the costs of the summer's activities, but he was now appealing for 'the friendly aid of archaeologists' to add to local resources which were not 'fully adequate'.[41] In October 1851 Buckman and Newmarch placed an advertisement in *The Times* appealing for funds to carry out the first systematic excavation at Cirencester.[42]

The difficulties that they were experiencing in raising funds would suggest that Lord Bathurst was unwilling to donate money for further excavations. It is difficult to imagine that, had he been willing to do so, there would not have been effusive thanks and comments on his generosity, as was the case when he paid for building the museum. In the absence of any evidence, it is only possible to speculate as to the reasons why this might have been the case. One possible explanation could be that he was not interested in the archaeological finds themselves, particularly the more mundane domestic artefacts, which were the main finds in these later digs. The mosaic pavements had attracted attention precisely because they were dramatic and seemed to create a powerful link with the Roman past, with all its associations of wealth and opulence. Bathurst might have wished to be seen to be involved with those associations, particularly with the museum, whose central position in the town emphasised his authority. His comparative lack of interest in archaeology generally can be inferred from the remarks he made when welcoming the annual meeting of the BAA in Cirencester in 1868: 'Although archaeology cannot vie with the cheery excitement of the chase, nor possess the all absorbing interest of the turf, yet it tends not to extravagance and ruin. Surely the student who

---

[37] Ibid. 19.

[38] In a court case in 1858 the Cirencester publisher, Bailey, alleged that a third person was infringing his copyright to the book. In his testimony Buckman stated that, with the exception of the chapter on coins, he was the only author and had sold the copyright to Bailey prior to the original publication in 1850.

[39] The list includes 749 in all, including that of Prince Albert.

[40] J. Buckman, 'Proceedings', *AJ* viii (1851), 186–90.

[41] Ibid. 415.

[42] *The Times*, 18 Oct. 1851.These appeals for funds were being made at the same time as the British government was helping to fund large-scale excavations in the Middle East such as Layard's at Nineveh. The irony was not lost on Roach Smith, commenting on the lack of research on Hadrian's Wall: 'It is commendable to institute societies for researches at Nineveh and Babylon; but it is inconsistent to leave the no less wondrous monuments of our own country unexplored': *Collectanea antiqua*, iii. 155.

pores over the ancient remains of Greece and Rome ... cannot be said to have passed a flat, unprofitable day.'[43]

The Cotteswold Naturalists' Field Club

What stands out from the description of archaeological activity in Cirencester is the absence of any attempt to form a local group to excavate and preserve the remains. In other parts of the country the energy and enthusiasm generated by new discoveries had led to the formation of local archaeological associations and societies.[44] Such a group could have served as a focus for raising interest in conservation and funds for excavation. One possible reason for this not happening in Cirencester could have been the existence of the Cotteswold Naturalists' Field Club, which might have been seen as a potential focus for archaeological activity in the area.

The first meeting of the club was held on 7 July 1846 at the Black Horse Inn near Cheltenham. It was formed to 'investigate the natural history, antiquities, agriculture and other objects worthy of interest in the Cheltenham district'.[45] Among its members were several Oxford professors, the principal of the agricultural college in Cirencester, several members of the Cheltenham Literary and Philosophical Society and a number of professional men, including solicitors, surveyors and doctors, many of them from Cirencester. John Buckman, then still at the 'Lit and Phil' in Birmingham was at the inaugural meeting and remained an active member after he moved to the agricultural college in 1848. Although the group visited Roman sites on their summer walks, were shown the museum at Cirencester and were lectured by Buckman on the excavations, the primary interest of most of the members was the natural sciences, especially botany and geology. These were seen as 'A healthy and most fascinating, far more than either, a most holy study; for what is the study of Natural History, but an approach to the Creator and all his works?'[46]

The format of the meetings was to have breakfast together in a local inn, followed by a walk to some point of interest in the area and then a return to the inn for dinner. The impression given by the journal is that these meetings were a pleasant social gathering, providing a group of like-minded 'gentlemen of science' with a congenial forum in which they could learn a little and enjoy

[43] Anon., 'Proceedings', JBAA xxv (1869), 25.
[44] An architect, John Clarke, wrote about this lack of interest in archaeological remains in Gloucestershire: 'One would imagine that some public interest would be excited at the discovery of interesting relics of the Roman sway in Britain; that corporate bodies or local institutions would gladly avail themselves of the opportunity afforded of forming the nucleus of a local museum; that the citizens would feel a pride and pleasure in surveying the exhumated [sic] remains of Roman grandeur ... Alas! We relate with shame and sorrow that no such interest was excited': 'Proceedings', GM xli (1854), 248.
[45] Anon., 'An account of a meeting on 2nd July 1847', PCNFC i (1853), 12.
[46] Ibid. 14.

themselves at the same time.[47] Buckman gave papers on the archaeological activities in Cirencester as well as on geology, botany and agriculture. In 1854 he became the secretary, a post he held until 1860. Thus his time and energy were devoted to the CNFC rather than to the formation of a specifically archaeological group in Cirencester. It could be argued that it was the very diversity of his activities and interests that prevented him from being more effective in Cirencester.

The museum

The first museum in the town had been started as an addition to the Cirencester public library and reading room, which had been established in 1835. The minutes record the beginnings of a general collection of minerals, fossils and antiquities with a volunteer curator.[48] The variety of objects resembled a 'cabinet of curiosities' rather than a systematic collection. The exhibits ranged from 'the musk pod from the musk deer' through 'fossils unearthed during the construction of the railway' to a 'charred beam from Herculaneum'. The lending library did not flourish, and in 1847 it was taken over and amalgamated with the lending library in the local bookshop, Baily's. In 1856 a letter from Canon Powell to Buckman asks him to put the Roman remains from the reading room museum into the new Bathurst Museum that had just opened.[49]

The new museum was built on the Bathurst estate in the centre of the town, opposite the railway station. Lord Bathurst paid for the building, the display cabinets and the caretaker's wages. Buckman was the first curator. Pictures in the *ILN* show a rather nondescript, barn-like building with large arched windows, the floor area covered by the pavements and apparently with no other contents at all.[50] However, Buckman's list of the contents and plan of the layout of the museum show a number of cabinets around the walls, containing artefacts arranged according to their material, such as iron, bronzes and pottery. In a talk to the CNFC in 1857, Buckman said that he felt that the main value of the exhibits lay not in their artistic value, but in 'explaining to us some facts connected with the inner life of this interesting people'.[51] The intention had always been that it should be a museum of 'Roman Corinium' and in the main this intention was followed. An 1858

[47] I use the term 'gentlemen of science' advisedly as the term seems accurately to describe the CNFC and its activities.
[48] Minute book of library committee, 1838–47, 3 Nov. 1836, Cirencester Public Library, box L2–1 (9).
[49] The letter, dated 5 July 1856, is in a box marked 'early museum' in the present Cirencester museum. The box also contained Buckman's' plan of the layout of the museum, a list of the contents in 1856 and the visitors book. The box was one of many in a storeroom and the contents were un-catalogued.
[50] *ILN*, 2 Aug. 1856.
[51] J. Buckman, 'Annual address', *PCNFC* ii (1857).

newspaper report notes the addition of Etruscan pottery, 'mainly for the sake of comparison ... as nothing can be more serviceable to the student of antiquities than having seen examples of work from far different countries'.[52] The list of contents notes the names of donors, but there is no mention of the dates when the exhibits were found or the locations. A few objects are drawn rather crudely. There is no indication that this list was for anything other than Buckman's private use. A visitors' comment book during the early years contains many complaints about the lack of a printed guide or catalogue. It was not until 1867 that Arthur Church, professor of chemistry at the agricultural college and one of Buckman's successors as museum curator, compiled a proper catalogue.

The visitors' book records a steady stream of visitors from all over the country, including an official visit from the BAAS meeting in Cheltenham in 1856. In the same year there was also an excursion train from London to Lord Bathurst's park and fifty-three of the excursionists visited the Roman Museum. Altogether Buckman estimated that there were around 2,000 visitors in the first year. The number of visitors from London and the south-east are an indication both of the national interest generated by the mosaics, and a demonstration of just how easy travel had become as a result of the railway.

Later activity

After the burst of activity following the discovery of the mosaics and the building of the museum, the level of interest in archaeological work in Cirencester died down considerably. Small-scale excavation continued and Buckman reported the results in the *AJ*. The finds were deposited in the museum, which continued to attract a number of visitors.[53] Buckman himself left the town after a major disagreement with the college authorities in 1863. The dispute concerned his supposed neglect of his college duties and it is possible that his interest in matters archaeological and Roman had diverted him from his work.[54] He retired to farm in Dorset. His interest in the Roman past continued, however, and he reappeared at the Chedworth villa site in 1865, when he helped the owner, Lord Eldon, arrange his museum.[55]

Bathurst chose a soldier, Captain Charles Abbott, to replace Buckman, and then Arthur Church. In the preface to his catalogue Church remarks that 'The absence of labels and a catalogue has been felt as a drawback to

[52] WGS, 11 Sept. 1858. The article was probably written by Buckman.
[53] There had been nearly 4,000 visitors between 1856 and 1858: ibid.
[54] Buckman, *Address to E. Holland*. See also Sayce, *Royal Agricultural College*, 59–60.
[55] Chedworth is a few miles north of Cirencester. The villa site was discovered in 1864 on land owned by Lord Eldon. James Farrer excavated it and Eldon paid for roofing to protect the site and for a museum to display the finds, which Buckman helped to set up. In view of his failure to produce a catalogue for the Cirencester museum, it is ironic that that he did so for the Chedworth site. His co-author was Robert Hall, a member of the CNFC: J. Buckman, *Notes on the Roman villa at Chedworth*, Cirencester 1872.

the value and usefulness of the collection. The present arrangement of the objects in the museum is not satisfactory.'[56] By 1912 when the fifth curator, Edward Sewell, was appointed, the museum was in a very dirty and neglected condition and the exhibits were in 'a hopeless muddle'.[57] The state of the collection is rather surprising in view of the fact that material continued to be added throughout the later years of the century. Work on a proper supply of water and a sewerage system during the 1870s had led to extensive tunnelling through the foundations of the older buildings of the town.[58] The surveyors responsible for much of the work were John and Thomas Bravander who recorded the Roman remains as they were found. The artefacts they collected were donated to the Bathurst Museum in 1881.

In 1890 Wilfred Cripps, a wealthy local property-dealer, began to create another museum in the town. In an attempt to locate the Roman basilica, he and his wife, Helena, had paid for a series of excavations in 1897–8.[59] They were assisted by the country's leading Romano-British archaeologist, Professor Francis Haverfield.[60] In order to display their collection, the Cripps built an extension to their house in Cirencester that became known as the Cripps Museum. It would appear that during the last decades of the century, both Bathurst and Cripps were intent on extending their collections regardless both of each other and of the wider interests of the community as a whole. This situation was only finally resolved when the two collections were amalgamated in 1937 under the direction of the local authority.

The use of their owners' names to identify the museums in Cirencester is a testament to the personalised character of antiquarian activity in the town. With the exception of Haverfield's work on the basilica site at the end of the century, the approach to the Roman past in Cirencester bore a greater resemblance to excavations in the eighteenth century than it did to the tentative attempts at a more modern approach to be found elsewhere, such as at Caerleon. It was not only the style of local government, which was still

---

[56] A. H. Church A guide to the Roman remains at Cirencester, Cirencester 1867. He does not give his reasons for this remark and nor does he appear to have rearranged the contents as his catalogue follows Buckman's plan closely.

[57] The note is in Sewell's handwriting in the box of early museum papers (see n. 49 above): E. C. Sewell, 'The Corinium museum Cirencester and its curators', TBGAS lv (1933), 317–21.

[58] When Wilfred Cripps reported on his excavations on the basilica site later in the century, he explained that he had been unable to follow the curving wall of the apse because 'The public street under which it then runs, with its sewer, gas and water pipes, cannot easily be disturbed. It seems certain that in placing the sewer the very foundations of the Roman walling were removed by blasting': 'Roman basilica of Corinium at Cirencester', Proceedings of the London Society of Antiquaries 2nd ser. xvii (1897–9), 204.

[59] Cripps had determined the site of the basilica by studying the configuration of roads through the town in order to determine the centre of the Roman settlement, where he believed both the basilica and the forum would have stood. He said he used as a guide the excavations carried out a few years before at the Roman site at Silchester: ibid. 202.

[60] Haverfield reported the excavations in the national journals: 'Roman Cirencester', 161–200.

feudal, but attitudes to the past and associated artefacts was also backward-looking and very traditional. It should be no more of a surprise that Buckman quotes Richard Westmacott's opinions of the mosaics, based as they were firmly in the eighteenth century, than that Lord Bathurst should appropriate the mosaics as his personal property. Both are indicative of an old-fashioned response to the Roman past that in other parts of the country was slowly giving way to new techniques and knowledge. Rather than seeking to use the discoveries to extend understanding of the Roman period in Britain, concentration on the mosaics confirmed the superiority of beautiful classical art and largely ignored the relevance of more mundane objects.

6

Camoludonum

In 1846 a group of leading members of the British Archaeological Association went on a two-day excursion to the Essex town of Colchester: a destination probably chosen because it was the one British town that figured unequivocally in the Roman texts. The intention was to encourage local members to 'make researches' and 'afford the members residing in London an opportunity of offering suggestions and co-operation'.[1] On the first day they were shown the castle, the walls, several churches and the ruins of a monastery. In the evening there was a dinner, after which local antiquities were exhibited and the day's findings discussed. The following day was spent viewing local collections. These included a museum to which 'the corporation has devoted a room in the town hall',[2] a collection of Roman bronzes and coins owned by a local businessman, a Mr Vint, and the collections of two other members of the local gentry, in which they saw antique marbles and mosaics.

Sources of knowledge

The Claudian invasion of 43 CE, in which Roman troops defeated the British tribes, is described in both Suetonius' account of the reign of Claudius (17–24) and in Dio Cassius (LX.19–24). They describe the capture of Camolodunum, the major settlement of the British Catuvellauni tribe, whose ruler, Cunobeline, was described by Suetonius as 'king of the Britons'. After the success of the initial invasion, Claudius returned in triumph to Rome and the victorious Roman troops used the Catuvellaunian capital as the site for their first fortress, which within a short time was transformed into a *colonia civitas* for retired legionary soldiers.

Tacitus tells how Camulodunum (Colchester) became the provincial capital and was the site of a temple to the God Claudius built soon after the invasion. He describes the temple as 'Like the citadel of an eternal tyranny, while the priests, chosen for its service, were bound under the pretext of religion to pour out their fortunes like water.'[3] Tacitus then gives an account of the revolt of the British tribes led by the Iceni queen, Boudica, in 61 CE. He describes the undefended Roman citizens of Colchester fleeing into the temple, which was taken by storm and the defenders put to death. Once

1 A. White and C. Baily, 'Report of an archaeological visit to Colchester', *JBAA* ii (1846), 364.
2 Ibid. 367.
3 Tacitus, *Annals*, ed. J. Jackson, London 1969, xiv, xxx.

the revolt was put down, Tacitus describes how the British were eventually reconciled to Roman rule: 'Little by little the British went astray into alluring vices: to the promenade, the bath, the well appointed dinner table. The simple natives gave the name of culture to this factor of their slavery.'[4] However once Colchester had ceased to play a role in the wider world, the town is not mentioned again in the Roman histories. There is no account of the Romano-British town itself, which, judging from the buildings that remained standing and the wealth of artefacts found, must have been quite extensive. It is no wonder that the Revd Edward Cutts, secretary of the Essex Archaeological Society, remarked that 'These great writers have given us but the merest skeleton of the Roman history in Britain.'[5]

The first antiquarian account of the Roman remains in Colchester appeared in Camden's *Britannia* (1586) in which he noted the evidence of Roman occupation in the town, but did not think it was the site of the original *colonia civitas*. The 1720 edition of the *Britannia* placed Camulodunum, 'the chief quarter of the Romans', at Maldon and such was Camden's stature in the eyes of all subsequent antiquarians that this statement led to endless controversies and disagreements. In 1748 the local historian Philip Morant studied the *Antonine itinerary* and surveyed the remaining earthworks. He concluded that 'by laying all circumstances together, it may appear to any unprejudiced person, that Colchester hath a better right to reclaim Camulodunum as its own than any other place where it had been fixed by writers ancient and modern'.[6] He thought it probable that the town walls were Roman, but that the castle had been built later using 'broken Roman bricks taken from the ruins of more ancient edifices'.[7] William Stukeley visited the town in 1759 when he 'survey'd the wonderful works of Cunobeline', and produced drawings of the earthworks around the town.[8]

The antiquarians also retold the story of the Roman conquest of the town and the revolt under Boudica. Some idea of the extent to which their work was influenced by the Roman texts can be gained by comparing their version of events with that of Tacitus. For instance, in descriptions of the significance of the temple of Claudius, it is clear that Tacitus was both the source of their information and provided a model for how the events should be described. Thus, in 1825, a local historian, Thomas Cromwell, wrote that the temple was 'A fortress built to ensure their perpetual bondage, whose rapacious priests would not abate their demands for its support.'[9] The Revd H. Jenkins in 1853 described the temple as 'A symbol of Rome's eternal domination over the conquered Britons', and 'the exactions of the college of priests exhausted

4 Ibid. xxix–xxxvii.
5 Cutts, 'Roman remains at Coggeshall', 100.
6 Morant, *Colchester*, 12.
7 Ibid.
8 See Piggott, *William Stukeley*, 147 n. 401.
9 T. Cromwell, *History of Colchester in Essex*, London 1825, 29.

the wealth of a rich and populous province'.[10] In 1858 another local anti-quarian, Dr P. M. Duncan wrote that 'In the eyes of the Britons, it seemed the citadel of eternal slavery. The priests ... devoured the whole substance of the country.'[11] It is clear that the nineteenth-century image of the British revolt was formed through reading Tacitus. They are a testament, both to the power of his description and to the hold that the classical texts still had on the thoughts and imagination of the nineteenth-century antiquarians.[12]

Roman remains in 1846

Following his visit in 1846, Roach Smith wrote a description of the remains for the *JBAA*. He noted the rapid rate at which they were being destroyed due to 'the increase of population, in the demands of luxury, and in necessary alterations and improvements'.[13] But in spite of these changes there was still a considerable amount to be seen. He described the wall which, 'although levelled in parts, can be traced distinctly almost throughout its course of a mile and three quarters'.[14] He included a plan of the remains of the town's western gate, the Balkerne Gate, with its one arch and a room still intact. But Roach Smith thought that the most striking feature was the preponderance of Roman bricks and tiles in all the buildings and the confusion to which this could lead. For instance, the Norman castle at the centre of the town 'presents many points of similarity to the Roman style ... and the tiles have been so plentifully used, and disposed so perfectly in the Roman style, as to impress upon the spectator a notion of much earlier antiquity'.[15] In spite of this, he did not consider that any part of the castle could be Roman, although he thought it likely that it stood on the site of an important Roman building and had been built using Roman materials. Finally, Roach Smith described some of the more remarkable artefacts, such as the statue of a sphinx found on the building site of a new hospital in 1820, and the antique bronzes in Vint's collection.[16] Roach Smith noted that a large number of objects had been unearthed to the west of the town, outside the Balkerne Gate on the main

10 H. Jenkins, *A lecture on Colchester castle*, Colchester 1853, 9–10.
11 Duncan, 'Walls at Colchester', 29.
12 General histories of Roman Britain were just as reliant on Tacitus' descriptions. See, for example, H. M. Scarth, *Roman Britain*, London 1883, 48.
13 C. Roach Smith, 'Notes on Roman remains at Colchester', *JBAA* ii (1846), 29–30.
14 Ibid. 30.
15 Ibid.
16 Mr Hay had donated the sphinx to the hospital. When he died most of his large collec-tion of antiquities was bequeathed to the Museum of the Scottish Antiquaries in Edin-burgh and so lost to Colchester. Modern archaeologists think that Vint's bronzes were probably forgeries. They are of a quantity and type which makes it unlikely that they were a part of a store of grave goods. It is possible that they were manufactured in Italy in the eighteenth century, in one of the many workshops that were turning out 'antiquities' for the unwary tourists.

road between Colchester and London, where, according to Roman tradition, would have been the site of the main cemetery. During the nineteenth century it had been the site for both the new hospital and the union workhouse and had yielded 'a vast quantity of remains, such as were commonly deposited with the dead'.[17]

Roach Smith's article suggests that there was still considerable evidence of the Roman past to be seen in Colchester, although the re-use of Roman building materials was creating difficulties in distinguishing Roman from later constructions.[18] It was also clear that a great deal more evidence was to be discovered underground. The digging and excavating involved in the construction of the railway system, sewers and major public enterprises such as the hospital, workhouse, a corn exchange and a new town hall, were revealing quantities of small artefacts and extensive evidence of foundations. Some small-scale excavations were being organised, such as that in Mr Round's garden next to the castle in 1850, but most of the evidence for the Roman town remained buried beneath Victorian Colchester.

Thus Colchester presented a rather confusing picture to the archaeologists. On the one hand, they had more written evidence of the early Roman period than was the case for any other Roman site in the country. But these written accounts ceased once Colchester no longer played a part on the national stage. Furthermore, unlike some of the other Roman sites, no inscriptions or tombstones had been unearthed which might have thrown light on the life of the city later in the Roman period. As Duncan remarked, 'No inscriptions have been found either in Colchester or on the wall, indicating the Emperor, legions and cohorts, by whom this grand memorial of Roman design and perseverance was erected; yet no other city contains such evidence of continuous occupation.'[19] Failing inscriptions, Duncan was forced to rely upon coins, but this evidence was rarely specific: 'Very little can be gleaned from them of the date of the erection of the walls of Colchester, but they proved that the Romans occupied the town, during the whole of their stay in Britain.'[20] The Romano-British town of Colchester and its inhabitants, both native and Roman, remained obscure. The quantity and variety of artefacts suggested that this had continued to be an important and populous site throughout the Roman period, but how and in what manner it had declined remained a mystery and the re-use of Roman building materials served merely to add another layer of confusion.

[17] Roach Smith', 'Roman remains at Colchester', 43.
[18] The preponderance of Roman materials is still a characteristic feature of Colchester today.
[19] Duncan, 'Walls at Colchester', 33.
[20] Ibid. 35.

Social and economic Colchester

During the medieval period Colchester had been important for cloth production but by the beginning of the nineteenth century the cloth trade had
declined due to technological changes in production. As a result, the town
had become depressed and run down, reliant on providing goods and services
for the surrounding rural areas. Local affairs were in the hands of a corporation dominated by a ruling oligarchy of business and commercial men, which
attracted accusations of mismanagement and corruption.[21] Throughout the
century public life in Colchester was split between the Anglican Tories on
one side and Liberal dissenters on the other, a split which was reflected in all
aspects of the town's life, including education, institutions and even archaeology.[22]

Colchester's economic position began to revive in the 1840s largely due
to two developments. The first was the construction of the rail link between
London on one side and the east coast ports on the other. The resultant boom
in trade led to the erection of a corn exchange and a flourishing brewery
business. The second factor was the construction of a permanent barracks in
1856 to replace the temporary staging-post set up for troops on the way to the
Crimea. The addition of another 3.000 people proved to be a welcome boost
to local producers and providers of services. As a result of these changes,
the population began to increase steadily, from 17,790 in 1841 to 23,815 in
1861.

William Wire and archaeological activity

The number of artefacts and remains of buildings discovered in Colchester
had risen as building activity in the town increased. But neither the chief
citizens nor the council appeared to be interested in conservation. As was so
often the case in the mid-nineteenth century the necessary drive for a more
organised response to preservation was brought about through the energy and
enthusiasm of one individual: in Colchester that was William Wire.

Wire was a native of Colchester. He had trained as a watchmaker in
London and had returned to the town in 1828 to set up his own business. His
journal and surviving letters describe the purchase of a vast range of artefacts,
maps and typographical books over a fifteen-year period between 1842 and his
death in 1857.[23] His journal records his almost daily tour of the building sites to
enquire about the possible discovery of artefacts. He paid particular attention
to the construction site of a new bridge, possibly prompted by the knowledge

[21] VCH, *Essex*, IX: *Borough of Colchester*, ed. J. Cooper, Oxford 1994.
[22] There were, for instance, two elementary schools, the National attached to the
Anglican Church and the British attached to the Dissenters.
[23] For Wire's journal and correspondence see chapter 3 n. 22.

that river sites elsewhere had proved to be fruitful sources for archaeological finds.[24] He tried to create a museum for the town, but failed because he had to sell his collection to pay off debts in 1840.[25] Despite financial problems, it was not long before he started buying again. The evidence of his letters and journals suggest that he regarded the study of the past as more than the collection of odd facts and curiosities. He distinguished between collecting objects to learn from them, and collecting antiquities for a cabinet of curiosities, which he termed 'unconsidered trifles'. He described the collecting habits of John Taylor, town councillor and leading citizen, and others, as 'purchasing antiquities for a museum without either judgement or discretion'.[26] However there is a certain inconsistency between these scathing comments on the collecting habits of others and his apparent willingness to include all 'articles of interest or curiosity' in his own museum. Possibly the interests of a museum proprietor and those of a 'man of archaeological science' did not always coincide.

Wire was largely responsible for making contact with antiquarians in other parts of the country. He corresponded for many years with Roach Smith in London, exchanging information and artefacts. It was probably due to this connection that Wire was appointed the Colchester representative for the BAA when it was formed in 1843. He took the position seriously and there are several reports from him in the association's proceedings. For instance in 1846 Wire forwarded Roman bracelets, and in 1849 he sent a plan and notes of some recently discovered Roman foundations.[27] He visited London to see some recent discoveries and met the antiquarians and antique dealers, William Chaffers and Edward Price. He went to the British Museum and was 'struck by the paucity of antiquities found in this country'.[28] Back in Colchester he showed the sites of the town to the veteran antiquary John Britton and was a part of the group that entertained the BAA in 1846.

Wire not only collected artefacts for his own collection, but also dealt in antiquities commercially, and his journal and letters provide an insight into the antiquities market in the 1840s and 1850s. His letters indicate that he had customers all over the country, including Joseph Clarke in Saffron Walden, Professor John Henslow in Cambridge and Henry Ecroyd Smith, in

---

[24] For instance, Roach Smith described discoveries made on the presumed site of a Roman bridge in the Thames at London. These included bronzes and a 'colossal head of Hadrian': 'Roman remains recently found in London', *Arch.* xxix (1842), 165.

[25] The flyer he had printed to advertise this project proclaimed that 'William Wire, watch maker and dealer in antiquities, begs to announce that he has fitted up a room for the express reception of articles of interest or curiosity, to form a nucleus for a museum to be called the Colchester Museum. Terms of admission, either pecuniary or something of interest that will not only enhance but add to the value of such an establishment. All articles deposited are to be considered the property of the museum': see E. J. Rudsdale, 'Colchester Museum, 1846–1946', *Essex Review* lvi (1946), 1–8, 57–63, 141–7, 189–93.

[26] WWJ, entry for 30 May 1843.

[27] Anon., 'Proceedings', *JBAA* ii (1846), 101; W. Wire, 'Proceedings', *JBAA* v (1849), 85.

[28] WWJ, 19 Aug. 1843.

Yorkshire, and that he sold coins to both Richard Neville and Roach Smith. His main customer was Edward Acton of Grundisburgh, a wealthy local landowner.[29] When financial pressures again forced Wire to sell his collections in 1851, he wrote letters to old customers with a list of objects for sale and their prices, which throw some light on the value attached to these artefacts.[30] The increased demand for antiquities contributed to the problem of forgeries, a subject that figures prominently in the correspondence between Wire and Roach Smith.[31]

The market for artefacts also caused problems within the town, as the arguments about the town hall site illustrate. In 1843 it had been decided to replace the mediaeval moot hall with a new building. John Taylor told Wire that the contractors could keep all the building materials, but that any antiquities were to be considered the property of the town council. When Wire visited the site, the contractor told him that he would like to imprison any man who sold Wire antiquities and to transport Wire himself for buying them. When Wire complained, Taylor and Marsden, denied that he had been excluded from the site. However Marsden and Vint both threatened to ensure that any man selling antiquities was sacked.[32] None of the participants in this drama was disinterested: Vint and Taylor were councillors and private collectors, Marsden was in charge of the Disney collection at Cambridge and Wire himself was both a collector and a dealer. It is also more than likely that the workmen involved would have been only too keen to trade if they thought they could get away with it.[33]

Finally, it was Wire who was the moving force behind the meeting, held on 14 August 1850, to set up an archaeological association in Colchester. The minutes record the group's aims: '[To] obtain and record faithfully accounts of antiquities; to collect and preserve any heraldic or genealogical notices; to

[29] When Wire died in 1857, Acton bought his remaining collection. When Acton died three years later, Mr Round of the EAS bought those parts of the collection connected with Colchester and Essex and offered to sell them to the society. According to the society's minutes, £40 8s. were received in response to a circular requesting funds to buy the collection from Round: EAS minutes, Colchester Museum, 13 Feb. 1862. Wire's journal and letter book were with the collection and hence have survived.

[30] See chapter 8 below.

[31] For instance Wire's journal records the discovery of a large cache of artefacts on the new poorhouse site. They included daggers with Greek names on the handles, a Roman urn, impressed intaglios with Egyptian hieroglyphics and busts in an Egyptian style. 'It is said by some antiquarians that the whole of the above, excepting the urn, are of modern fabrication': WWJ, entry for 19 Mar. 1844.

[32] Marsden had bought an antiquity from a workman and got the man sacked for selling it: ibid. entry for 16 Sept. 1843.

[33] Wire's journal describes several incidents that demonstrate the workmens' awareness of the market: 'A labouring man showed me a small brass figure of Jupiter he had ploughed up in a field. I offered him money, but having previously offered it to Mr. Vint, he would not sell it to me. It is engraved in *Arch.* xxxi': ibid. entry for 11 May 1843. Further, 'A labouring man digging up a tree, found an earthen urn containing 951 silver coins, which he took up to London and sold for ten pounds. Kept very secret': ibid. entry for 9 May 1854.

investigate the ecclesiastical, castellated and domestic architecture and to act to preserve from threatened destruction any interesting monuments of past times; [and finally] to collect coins and antiquities of any country, but most particularly of this town.'[34] The membership of the new society consisted of local businessmen, such as John Laing and John Taylor, and a number of local ministers. It is noticeable that there are no members of the local gentry in the list. At the first meeting in September, Wire was made secretary, but in November it was resolved that 'Revd. Medley be requested to act as Hon Secretary.' The following year it was decided to hold the meetings during the day, a move which necessarily excluded working men such as Wire. The minutes do not say who proposed either these changes or their reasons for doing so, but Wire believed that it was to exclude him:

> After all my efforts and expense, I find that they have approved as secretary someone who knows very little of antiquities ... Fancy a secretary of a successful body who is unacquainted with the subjects that may be brought under discussion. Autocracy of power usurps the place of autocracy of mind ... I was told it was impossible for me to know much of antiquity because I had not had a classical education.[35]

In fact, by the summer of 1851, Wire had stopped attending the meetings all together.

In September 1852 it was proposed that the Colchester group should be extended to include members from the whole county of Essex. A committee was set up to plan the new group, including the Revd H. Jenkins and Dr P. M. Duncan from Colchester, Charles Round from the castle and John Marsden as members. John Disney became president after Lord Braybrooke, Richard Neville's father, declined the post.[36] The bishop of the diocese and the lord-lieutenant of the county were invited to be patrons. The intention to include representatives of all the leading citizens of the county indicates that the Essex Archaeological Society was determined to be more socially 'upmarket' than the town-based society had been. As if to confirm this, the rules stipulated that the vice-presidents were to be either noblemen or MPs. Wire is not mentioned. As he told Roach Smith:

34 CAS minutes, Colchester Museum, 14 Aug. 1850.
35 Wire to Roach Smith, 6 Sept. 1850, Wire letter book. As to his replacement, the Revd G. R. Medley, he says 'But there is this in his favour, not one of the others can find fault with him or laugh at his ignorance. Besides which he has had a classical education'. In another letter he complained that 'I have been obliged to resign the secretaryship, they made it too hot for me. It is assumed that no one can understand archaeology, but had a classical education backed by a long purse': 12 Feb. 1851, ibid.
36 EAS minutes, 1 Sept. 1852. Disney, a wealthy local barrister, had inherited his father's collection of classical antiquities formed in Italy in the previous century. He had added artefacts from Pompeii and written a catalogue, *Museum Disneianum* (1846–9). John Disney founded the chair of archaeology at Cambridge in 1851 and bequeathed his collection to the university.

1. Zohan Zoffany (1733–1810), 'Charles Townley and his
friends in the Townley Gallery'. © Townley Hall Art
Gallery and Museum, Burnley, Lancashire/
The Bridgeman Art Library

2. (left) James Havard Thomas, 'Boadicea' (1902), Cardiff City Hall.

3. (below) 'The liberation of Caractacus' (from an original by C. Panormo): H. Roberts, *Chester guide*, 2nd edn, Chester 1858.

4. 'Mr Charles Roach Smith's collection of London
antiquities, lately added to the British Museum':
ILN, 8 Sept. 1856.

5. William Daniels, 'Joseph Mayer in Clarence Terrace,
c. 1840', Liverpool Museum.

Are you aware that there will be a public meeting to form an Essex Archaeological Association and after a feed of seven shillings and sixpence including a pint of wine? The meeting I may attend, but the dinner is beyond my reach. In the formation of this society I have been kept quite in the dark, because I am not rich enough to join the aristocrats.[37]

The manner in which the Essex Archaeological Society took over the original Colchester group and in so doing marginalised Wire can be seen as an example of the way in which a fractured community dealt with the aspirations of someone who was not a part of the recognised elite.

One area in which Wire considered himself most vulnerable was in his lack of education, most particularly in the classics. He refers repeatedly to his anger that he was ridiculed for his supposed failings. Although it is clear from his journal and letters that Wire was a prickly individual, who was quick to take offence at any supposed slight, it is probable that his lack of a formal classical education was used as an excuse to exclude him. Most of his detractors will have had at least some acquaintance with the classics, as they formed an important part of the curriculum in schools of the period.[38] Wire rarely makes references to the classical texts that appear so regularly in most contemporary archaeological reports. He stressed that his opinions had been formed 'from the study, experience and reflection of twenty years, although they may seem contrary to the opinion of a BA or MA'.[39]

In 1854 the Essex Archaeological Society and the Colchester Corporation started to discuss the amalgamation of the town museum with that of the association. Wire was keen to be the curator of the extended museum and wrote letters and lobbied all the leading figures in the town, but he was unsuccessful:

When it was known I was a candidate for the situation, some parties who have influence set another person in front ... Had I been a conservative, no objection would have been made, but having advanced liberal principles and not being inclined to abandon them now, is the chief obstacle in the way of my election.[40]

The final irony in Wire's position appears in the last minutes of the Colchester Archaeological Society when thanks were given to Jenkins for 'his kindness

---

[37] This is cited in Rudsdale, 'Colchester Museum', 6, in which he says that it is taken from a letter from Wire to Roach Smith, dated 8 Dec. 1852. It is not clear where Rudsdale found this letter, as it does not appear in the Wire letter book where the last letter is dated April 1852.

[38] Wire, whose son was the only non fee-paying pupil in the local grammar school, was in favour of a wider curriculum. He wrote to the bishop of London, the official controller of the curriculum, to complain about the limited range of subjects taught in the school: *Essex Standard*, 10 Nov. 1843; 10 Apr. 1845; 21 June 1850. These are cited in A. F. J. Brown, *Colchester, 1815–1914* (Essex Record Office lxxiv, 1980), 64–5.

[39] Wire to Roach Smith, 3 June 1851, Wire letter book.

[40] Wire to Roach Smith, 8 July 1851, ibid.

in having formed the Association'.[41] Wire had officially been written out of the historical record.

Wire's disappointment and frustration led him to withdraw from archaeological activity in the town. He started to sell off his collection and even suggested to Roach Smith that he might start a small printing press 'in order to publish his views to the world'.[42] In another letter he says that a guide to the town would not be a bad speculation, but 'I have the material, but not the ability to put them into a nice readable shape.'[43] He told Ecroyd Smith that 'my love for antiquarian pursuits have abated in great measure because of the coldness shown to me by those who at one time proffered the greatest respect, because my circumstances will not allow me to feed them well'.[44] Wire had been forced to give up his business because of debt and failing health, which he attributed to stress caused by the unkindness of his fellow antiquarians. In the last letter in his letter book, in April 1852, he claimed that he had given up a good trade to rescue the town from oblivion. The final words on his archaeological importance can be left to his friend Roach Smith: 'He had great perseverance and intelligence, but failed to find favour with the leading town's people and in consequence, masses of choice antiquarian material was lost to science.'[45] William Wire died in 1857 after catching a cold in his new job as a postman.

A museum for Colchester

The need for a place of safe-keeping for the archaeological finds was becoming increasingly pressing. Apart from the private collections of individual residents, the only other museum in the town had been set up as a part of the Colchester Philosophical Society in 1820. The contents were the usual eclectic mixture to be found in museums of the period. In addition to shells, fossils, rock and mineral samples, there were numerous Roman artefacts, including coins, earthenware vessels, tiles and a piece of Roman tessellated pavement. The building suffered fire damage in 1835 when many of the contents were lost.

In 1846 the Colchester Corporation designated one room in the town hall to be used as a town museum and it was this room which was seen by the BAA visitors.[46] The museum contributions book, in which all donations were recorded, shows that for the first four years there was a steady flow of gifts,

41 CAS minutes, 11 May 1852.
42 Wire to Roach Smith, 7 July 1851, Wire letter book.
43 Wire to Frederick Fairholt, 18 July 1851, ibid. Fairholt was an illustrator and engraver who was responsible for many of the illustrations in contemporary archaeological books and articles. He was a close friend of Roach Smith.
44 Wire to H. E. Smith, 20 Feb. 1852, ibid.
45 Roach Smith, *Retrospections*, ii. 36.
46 Cf. the provisions of the 1844 Museum Act. Wire remarked that Charles Round had

including grave goods found in John Taylor's garden in 1848. But there are no entries after 1850. The decline in the Town Hall Museum appears to have started at the same time as Charles Round offered the Essex Archaeological Society a room in the castle for use as a museum. But the society's minutes do not make it clear how the decision to merge the two collections was made. It is possible that a Tory-dominated local authority felt that the provision of a museum was more appropriately provided by a private body. Between 1852 and 1860 the minutes make frequent references to meetings between representatives of the Corporation and the society to discuss finance, the curator and respective rights of ownership. It was in this museum that Wire aspired to be the curator. But Wire was already dead by the time the museum finally opened to the public, on 27 September 1860.

The decision to move the museum from the town hall to the castle can be seen as significant in several ways. In the first place, the contents brought together the collection owned by the public representatives, in the form of the corporation, and the collection owned by private citizens, in the guise of the Essex Archaeological Society. As such it was an example of public and private interests coming together to express local pride in Colchester's role in British national history. The joint ownership of the museum emphasised that this great past belonged to both the town and its private citizens. The fact that it was finally realised as a public museum in the private arena at the castle, rather than in the public space at the town hall, emphasises the importance of private activity in most contemporary archaeological spheres.

Controversies

The nature of the evidence for Colchester's past presented problems to antiquarians. On the one hand the textual accounts gave vivid descriptions of two events, the invasion and the revolt, which allowed and indeed encouraged antiquarians to use their imagination in order to fill in the gaps between these ancient fragments. On the other hand, the continual reuse of old building materials rendered the physical remains confusing and ambiguous and had led to conflicting theories and heated debate.

The actual location of the original town continued to be argued. Camden's assertion that the site of Camulodunum was at Maldon and not Colchester had led to confusion. Unsurprisingly, most of the local antiquarians believed that their town was the site of the ancient city. For instance Thomas Cromwell, in 1825, was convinced that such were the ruins at Colchester that 'on them alone might rest its claim to be considered the Camulodunum of Latin authors'.[47] Roach Smith was of the same opinion but gave a more reasoned justification for his views: 'We have Colonia in the fifth Itinerary of

refused to join discussions about a town museum because 'he thinks it will detract from his attempts to build a new church': WWJ, entry for 18 Dec. 1844.
[47] Cromwell, *Colchester*, 41.

Antonius at fifty two Roman miles from London. Colchester is, I believe fifty-one. Gruter gives an inscription of a person styled assessor of the Roman citizens of Colonia Victriconius in Britain at Camulodunum.'[48] But, as Jenkins pointed out, the dispute had been revived as recently as 1853 in Dr Smith's *Dictionary of classical geography*, in which this popular authority claimed that Camden had been correct.[49]

An associated debate arose over the question of whether the Roman town had been built on the same site as the capital of the defeated British tribe, as claimed by Suetonius and Dio Cassius, or about three miles away. Duncan maintained that the abundance of coins inscribed with images of their king, Cunobelin, which had been found around the remains, confirmed Colchester as the site of the capital.[50] Wire was unconvinced and felt that the subject was obscure: 'I am aware that realised wisdom is against me, but I cannot conceive of a place to have been the chief town and residence of royalty and to have left no vestiges of its former occupancy.'[51] He even disputed Duncan's claims that many British coins had been found: 'That is not a fact, as after thirty years experience in visiting excavations made for drainage and other purposes, what coins of Cunobeline have been found (and they are very rare) are either on the level of Roman remains or associated with them.'[52]

But the most contentious issue was the origin of the castle. This stands in the centre of the town and resembles a large Norman keep but is clearly constructed with Roman bricks and tiles. By the 1840s there had been many changes to the original structure, including a shallow style roof and a rather Byzantine shaped tower. It had also completely lost one floor. The *Colchester Chronicle* records that in 1076 William the Conqueror granted Colchester to a Norman baron, Eudo Dapifer, who 'Built the castle on the foundation of the palace of Coel, once king.'[53] If nothing else this indicates that the site had always been identified with an important building. For the next five hundred years it was used as a prison and as a garrison during the Civil War. By 1683 the castle stood empty and was bought by a local builder for use as building materials. He had already dismantled the top floor before he went bankrupt.

48 Roach Smith to Wire, 8 Dec. 1852.
49 Jenkins, A *lecture on Colchester castle*, 5.
50 Duncan, 'Walls at Colchester', 26.
51 Wire to Roach Smith, 1, 30 Dec. 1851, Wire letter book. The latter contains Wire's only classical reference: 'Just look at Tacitus Book 12, section 31 and Book 14, section 31 and see if there is not room to doubt the existence of the colony having been planted in this part of the country.'
52 WWJ, entry for 1 Sept. 1855. Previously Wire had described Duncan as 'a young hand who only started with antiquities five months ago': Wire to Roach Smith, 10 Nov. 1851, Wire letter book. The name Camulodunum was the Roman version of fortified place (dunum) of Camulos, the Celtic god of war. The original Roman fort was built within the enclosure and the Roman site spread westwards from the fort: P. Crummy, *City of victory: the story of Colchester, Britain's first Roman town*, Colchester 1997, 34–5.
53 Crummy, *City of victory*, 144. According to Crummy, 'the identification of the temple as the palace of Coel should not put us off since this could have been what the Norman builders believed'.

It then stood empty again until a wealthy local man, Charles Gray, bought it and added it to the grounds of his elegant eighteenth-century house where it featured as a romantic ruin in the landscape. It was Gray who had the new roof and tower added in 1760, in the belief that they enhanced its 'Roman' appearance.

To the antiquarians, two aspects of the castle building were beyond dispute. One was its position, which had obviously been chosen to dominate the town, and the second was that it incorporated Roman building materials. The major disagreement was over who had built it? The most popular view was that it had been the site of a major Roman building that was still largely intact when the Normans arrived in 1066. Like the Romans before them, the Normans wanted a building which would emphasise their power and authority over the conquered local population. They had therefore dismantled the Roman edifice and used the materials to construct a large keep on the same site. According to this popular version, the castle was Norman, although built with Roman materials. The other view was that the original Roman temple had been reconstructed after the revolt in CE 61 and that the Normans had merely re-modelled the existing building and converted into a fortress. According to this point of view, the castle was the Temple of Claudius with Norman modifications.

Edward Cutts was the main advocate for the Norman castle theory. He was supported by most of the rest of the society and by Roach Smith and William Wire, although Jenkins continued to believe that the castle was Roman. Limited excavations were carried out in an attempt to discover more about the foundations of the castle, but they proved inconclusive. In 1850 Wire wrote that 'Revd. Jenkins is at war to prove that the castle stands on the same site as the Temple of Claudius.' And in 1851 that 'there will be some of the most out of the way and absurd opinions that ever emanated from any man suspecting the antiquity of a place'.[54] The 'war' was carried on in print. In 1852 Jenkins produced *Colchester castle built as a temple of Claudius Caesar*, to which Cutts replied with *Colchester castle not a Roman temple* in 1853.[55] The author of an 1855 review of the two publications in the *Quarterly Review*, described Jenkins as

> A man of genius ... But when his enthusiasm leads him on to declare that the castle of Colchester is nothing less than the actual temple of Claudius with certain transmutations, which the British took, but failed from its

---

54 Wire to Roach Smith, 6 Sept. 1850; 15 Feb. 1851, Wire letter book.

55 Jenkins's reply to Cutts had a postscript: 'It remains for me to inform the dictator that fragments of Roman stucco – i.e., of lime mixed with pounded tile, still adhere to the walls of the first storey of Colchester Castle; and if he will stoop from his assumed pre-eminence to explain to men of common sense how the Normans could possibly build walls on which the Romans laid the stucco, he will then be the most extraordinary, as he is indisputably the least civil, of architects and archaeologists in the present year A.D. 1853': Jenkins, *Lecture on Colchester castle*, 47.

vastness and solidity to destroy; we can no more accept his ingenious and eloquent arguments than the vague surmise of General Roy.[56]

However, in spite of this conclusion, the author was aware that Colchester remained a 'centre round which the legends and traditions of the island were grouped'.[57]

Sense of place

As the article in the *Quarterly Review* had pointed out, Colchester had continued to provide a rich source of associations and stories through which contemporary commentators could both visualise the past, and their own identity in relation to that past. Colchester's history offered a particularly rich source of such stories. There is the British king Cunobelin, whose ancestor Cassivellaunus was defeated by Julius Caesar. The belief that Colchester had been the site of a tribal capital before the Roman occupation had led antiquarians to speculate that the tribe concerned was that of Cunobelin and Cassivellaunus. Cunobelin achieved further prominence as Cymbeline in Shakespeare's play. In his article about the town walls, Duncan quoted lines from the play and claimed that 'Cunobelin, the Cymbeline [sic] of the heroic British traditions, does not exist in the verse of the bard alone ... his coinage in pure gold and in bronze, [is] so familiar to the collectors at Colchester.'[58] Another popular character was Helena, mother of the Emperor Constantine the Great. According to the *Colchester Chronicle*, Helena was the daughter of a local king, born in Colchester. She is supposed to have married the Roman general, Constantius, in order to persuade him to lift his siege of the town. After the birth of their son in Colchester, she is reputed to have founded the St Helen's chapel. Her association with the town is underlined by her portrait on the Colchester borough charter of 1413 and her statue on the top of the 1899 town hall.[59] Many antiquarians relished that part of their work that enabled them to feel closer to the past and to bring it to life; if it also enhanced the importance of their locality, so much the better. What is important is not the truth or otherwise of the stories, but their availability

---

56 C. Merrivale, 'Review of books on Colchester castle', *QR* cxciii (1855), 89, 98. Charles Merrivale was a historian and author of *A history of the Romans under the empire* (London 1850–64). Modern archaeologists believe that the castle was built around and over the podium of the Temple to Claudius. The size of the keep, the largest Norman keep in the country, was dictated by the Roman foundations. This was not finally proved until Mortimer Wheeler's excavation in 1920: Crummy, *City of victory*, 142–8.
57 Merrivale, 'Books on Colchester castle', 98.
58 Duncan, 'Walls of Colchester', 26. He is quoting act III, scene v.
59 Cromwell, *Colchester*, 41, acknowledges that neither Camden nor Gibbon believed in Helen's connection with Colchester, but he still concludes: 'not withstanding these learned opinions, we really conceive the balance of argument to be in favour of the truth and consistency of the facts cited in our chronicle'.

to be used in emphasising the importance of the town in national history. In Colchester this had actually been the case during the revolt and the firing of the temple, when, in Duncan's words, Boudica 'stands forth on the stage of history'.[60]

Boudica (or Boadicea as she was called by the Victorians) has been an important symbolic figure in national British history, literature and art for many centuries. But she was a particularly potent figure in the history of Colchester because of the descriptions given of the sacking of the town by her and her troops during the CE 61 revolt against Roman rule. In 1748 Morant described her as a 'brave virago, who when provoked by the brutish and unnatural usage of the Romans, made a vigorous attempt to shake off their galling yoke'.[61] In contrast Cromwell, in 1825, described her troops as 'putting to the sword, burning, hanging, crucifying and by every other method destroying every Roman who fell into their hands'.[62] These two views are further evidence of the local antiquarians' reliance on the classical texts, where they are available. Morant used the description in Tacitus and Cromwell the much harsher description in Dio Cassius.[63] The two texts provided the raw material for different interpretations of the British queen and the revolt and therefore later historians could make use of the version that best suited their interpretation of the past.

Colchester's ability to bring the past to life seems to have been a potent force arising from the fertile mixture of vivid text and suggestive architecture. This resonance is evident in Duncan's article about a plot of land close to the Roman wall, which he described as 'The quietest corner in old Colchester, replete with antiquarian interest ... and alive with the memories of the past.'[64] He lists the succession of different inhabitants from 'Celtic barbarism, then of the golden reign of Cunobelin, [to] part of the grounds of wealthy Roman proprietors'.[65] He continues 'It does not require much fancy, to conjure up the villa, and its gardens, and its cool baths.'[66] In the Middle Ages it was the site of a friary, which was abolished during the dissolution of the monasteries, and in the eighteenth century it was used as a botanical garden. But in 1858 'The quiet nook, loved by Celt, Roman and solitary friar ... now belongs to a freehold building society, redolent of shares and £10 voters; the quietest part of the quiet corner being used as a burial place for Quakers.'[67] This small area seemed to demonstrate continuity with the past, each period leaving characteristic remains by which it could be identified.

Boudica's dramatic appearance in the classical texts meant that the

---

[60] Duncan, 'Walls of Colchester', 28.
[61] Morant, *Colchester*, 13.
[62] Cromwell, *Colchester*, 30.
[63] See Tacitus, *Annals* XIV.xxx.159, and Dio Cassius, *Epitome* LXII.1–2, 3–6, 7–12.
[64] P. M. Duncan, 'The Roman cloaca at Colchester', *TEAS* i (1858), 210.
[65] Ibid. 212.
[66] Ibid.
[67] Ibid. 215.

Colchester antiquarians were in a unique position because nowhere else had such detailed and colourful accounts of the Roman presence in its area. The combination of vivid text and suggestive architecture proved to be a heady mix, inspiring them to imagine stories linking their town with major national events. The problem for the antiquarians in Colchester was not to create something out of very little, as was the case in Caerleon and Cirencester, but rather to avoid hyperbole taking over. It was a trap that several local anti-quarians fell into and led to frequent disagreements particularly between the most active members of the county association and William Wire. However it is hard to read Wire's comments without becoming aware of the social differences flowing beneath the antiquarian disputes. To over-emphasise his words is to run the same risk as Colchester's historians when faced with the Roman texts, but there are enough comments from other people, particu-larly concerning the 1843 split in the BAA to confirm that he had some justification for his sense of rejection. All the social and economic evidence describing Colchester in the mid-Victorian period suggests that it was indeed a divided community and that antiquarian activity, like everything else in the town, presented another opportunity for the divisions to be played out.

7

Deva

On 16 March 1849 a meeting was held at the rectory of St Mary on the Hill, Chester, in order to form a society for the study of the history, archaeology and architecture of the area.[1] In the same year the delegates to the annual conference of the BAA were told that Chester 'afforded rich and plentiful remains of antiquity'.[2] The numerous nineteenth-century guides all stress the city's importance as a fortress and administrative centre during the Roman occupation. The visitor might assume from these descriptions that they would be able to see significant Roman remains. But, as in most of Britain, evidence of Chester's Roman occupation had largely disappeared. What made Chester different from the other towns in this study was that, rather than being destroyed, old buildings had been adapted and reused. The effect had been to draw attention to their antiquity, while at the same time confusing their origins, thus rendering their age and period problematic.

It certainly made the task of locating Roman Chester more difficult for the antiquarians. In an article about Chester's Roman remains, Roach Smith remarked on the difficulty of detecting 'the original Roman work among the anomalous and perplexing styles of different periods, by which it was surrounded and embedded'.[3] He was referring to the walls, but his comment could as easily be applied to most aspects of the town's Roman past. When the American Nathaniel Hawthorne visited the city in 1853, he remarked on the same paradox: 'It is all very strange, very quaint, very curious to see how the town has overflowed its barriers, and how, like many institutions here, the ancient wall still exists, but is turned to quite another purpose than what it was made for, so far as it serves any purpose at all.'[4] A tourist guide in 1856 also commented on the mixed messages presented by the city's buildings: 'What is this Elizabethan building? Surely this has no tale to tell, no musty connections with mediaeval times. No truly: here we have a creation of the modern age.'[5] There is an irony at the heart of 'ancient' Chester that in fact much of it is a Victorian city.

1   Its full name was the Chester Architectural, Archaeological and Historical Society.
2   C. Roach Smith, 'Roman remains at Chester', *JBAA* v (1849), 232.
3   Ibid. 212.
4   N. Hawthorne, *English notebooks*, Boston 1884, 453, entry for 1 Oct. 1853.
5   Hughes, *Stranger's guide*, 103.

Tracing the past

The evidence of Chester's Roman past was scattered and consisted of a range of small clues, which had to be drawn together to recreate a coherent picture. The classical texts, old antiquarian reports, foundations of buildings and arte-facts and even the geology of the site all contributed to the final picture. The controversies and differing interpretations that resulted are indicative of just how difficult it was to trace the Roman past. And the complexity of the evidence is such that it is sometimes difficult for a present-day historian to understand the nineteenth-century antiquarians' interpretation of their Roman history.

All the commentators were agreed that the modern city was built upon the site of the Roman legionary fortress of Deva. The classical accounts of the Roman army's activities in north Wales and Cheshire were the basis for this belief. In the *Annals* Tacitus describes the campaigns of Ostorius Scapula and of Suetonius Paulinus, who fought the British on the island of Mona (Anglesey).[6] And in the *Agricola* Tacitus describes the eventual conquest of Mona before Agricola went into winter quarters, from which, in the next year, CE 79 he proceeded to march north into modern Lancashire.[7] The histo-rians assumed that the base for these campaigns was the legionary fortress of Deva. In his geography, written in CE 140, Ptolemy refers to the site of Deva as the headquarters of the Twentieth Legion, as does the *Antonine itinerary* written a few years later. According to Dio Cassius, when Severus divided the island into two parts in CE 197, both the Second and the Twentieth Legions were stationed in Upper Britain.[8] But between the death of Severus in CE 211 and the final departure of the Roman forces in the fifth century, there are no further references to Deva. The only clue is offered by the lists of military and civil dignitaries in the *Notitia dignitatum*, compiled in CE 408, where no mention is made of the Twentieth Legion, which had presumably already left Britain.

An example of the way in which an early nineteenth-century historian viewed the classical texts as evidence is to be found in Joseph Hemingway's *History of the city of Chester* (1831). He refers to the lack of information prior to the invasion, which had led to 'vague conjecture and curious speculation'. But for the Roman period itself 'the lights of history are as clear and distinct as they are numerous and authentic'.[9] He quotes Caesar, Tacitus, Pliny and Ptolemy for general information and Dio, Ptolemy and the *Antonine itinerary* as sources for his belief that Chester was the headquarters of the Twentieth

6   Tacitus, *Annals* XIV.xxix.155, 157.
7   Idem, *Agricola* xviii. 61.
8   Dio Cassius, IV.xxiii. In Upper Britain the Twentieth Legion was at Chester and the second legion was at Caerleon.
9   J. Hemingway, *History of the city of Chester from its foundation to the present time*, Chester 1831, 2, 11.

Legion. However, despite these references to the light thrown by the classical texts, he says that the last three were 'very defective' as they 'don't count non-Roman soldiers'.

The seventeenth- and eighteenth-century accounts of the Roman remains presented a confusing picture, as can be seen in the various descriptions of the city gates. The old medieval Northgate had been pulled down and replaced by another in the neo-classical style designed by Thomas Harrison, who had spent much of his early life in Rome. He stated that when he pulled down the old gate to make room for the new one, he found the old substructure to be Roman.[10] The history of the Eastgate, which had been pulled down in 1768, was more problematic as there were a number of varying descriptions and sketches made before its demolition. When Stukeley visited Chester in 1725, he wrote, 'I observed immediately two arches of Roman work. I was over-joyed at the site of so noble an antiquity.'[11] However, his illustration shows three arches rather than two. The antiquarian Thomas Pennant, writing shortly after the gate's demolition wrote, 'On taking down the modern case of Norman masonry, the Roman appeared in full view. It consisted of two arches formed of vast stones.'[12] Again, both the sketch illustrating Pennant's description and the one which accompanied another description by Broster, which he claimed to have done while it was still standing, diverge from the written descriptions. Roach Smith merely drew attention to the discrepancies, but concentrated on the figure which, it had been claimed, had stood on the pillar between the two arches. He thought the drawings showed more resemblance to work of the sixteenth or seventeenth century 'than Roman; but the original drawing may have been inaccurate'.[13]

In the light of these differing accounts, it is not surprising that Hemingway preferred to rely on the evidence of material remains in Chester: 'The shape is that of a Roman fort and her advanced architectural science is clear from the walls and arches. The remains of her ancient ramparts are distinctly visible in our present castle and we recognise her Praetorium where St Peters church now stands.'[14] The numerous tiles and bricks embossed with the legionary

10 Thomas Harrison studied architecture in Rome. He designed a house for Lord Elgin and when Elgin was appointed ambassador to the Porte, Harrison urged him to procure casts of all the remaining sculptures in Athens. A guide described the new bridge as 'unequalled in many points by any which Greece or Rome had built': Hughes, *Stranger's guide*, 76.

11 W. Stukeley, *Iter Boreale*, London 1727, 31, cited in Watkin, *Roman Cheshire*, 107.

12 T. Pennant, *Tour in Wales*, i, London 1810, 150–1, cited in Watkin, *Roman Cheshire*, 107. Hemingway attempted to clarify the confusion by using comparisons with Roman examples: 'This species of double gate was not infrequent. The Porte Erquilina and Porte Portesi at Rome were of this kind': *City of Chester*, 339.

13 Roach Smith. 'Roman remains at Chester', 215. Roach Smith had discussed the unre-liability of illustrations as evidence when he examined a Roman sepulchral monument found by Christopher Wren in London: 'In Gale and Handen the figure is represented with short hair and a short sword held across the body; while in Horsley and Pennant it is represented with long hair in ringlets hanging over the shoulders like a judge's wig and a great sword like a Highland claymore': *Collectanea antiqua*, i. 127.

14 Hemingway, *City of Chester*, 26.

symbols of the boar and initials VV (Valeria Victrix) had lent weight to the antiquarians' conviction that Chester was the site of Roman Deva. The discovery of Roman artefacts and remains of Roman buildings had given some depth and a sense of reality to a Roman past which appeared to have been smothered by later development.

In 1849 Roach Smith wrote an article about the Chester remains. He described the walls with their series of gates, which completely enclosed the city; a figure of the goddess Minerva in a shrine;[15] the remains of a hypocaust; various altars with inscriptions; inscribed tiles, stones and pigs of lead; some sepulchral urns and a variety of other small objects. In fact, with the exception of the walls, there was a typical selection of the remains that were to be anticipated from most sites with a Roman past. But, unlike most former Roman sites in Britain where new development had obliterated the Roman remains, in Chester the city's strategic importance as a base for campaigns into Wales had ensured that the Roman walls had been used and extended by later builders. It was, in effect, a frontier town on the boundary with hostile territory.

Another factor adding to the confusion was the building materials. Chester stands on red sandstone rock and this characteristic stone was used by the Romans for the construction of the walls, as well as by later builders of the cathedral and the churches. The result is that there are no examples of Roman brick and tiles being re-used later as building material, as can be seen in other towns built on Roman sites such as Colchester. Roach Smith refers to the uniformity in style and arrangement commonly found in Roman buildings throughout the Roman empire and the confusion that arises when this familiar style is not found: 'Here, the construction to which we alluded, has been deviated from so thoroughly, that it has been questioned whether any vestiges of the original Roman walls are yet extant.'[16] If Roach Smith, the leading British archaeologist of his day, found Chester confusing, it is hardly surprising that others should do so as well.

It was the walls that excited the most controversy. Aethflaeda, the daughter of Alfred the Great, was believed to have extended them in the Saxon period. The first antiquarian to describe Chester's walls was William Stukeley, in 1725. He suggested that 'between Eastgate and the river, the Roman wall is pretty perfect for one hundred yards together'.[17] Thomas Pennant disagreed, arguing that 'no part of the old walls exist but they stood, like the modern, on the soft freestone rock', a view echoed by Lysons a few years later.[18] In the mid-nineteenth century the local antiquarian, William Massie, conceded that the south and west walls had been extended, but he still believed that a

---

[15] Roach Smith attributed the preservation of the figure to 'early Christians adopting the image as a statue of the Virgin': *Collectanea antiqua*, vi. 30.
[16] Roach Smith, 'Roman remains at Chester', 211.
[17] Stukeley, *Iter Boreale*, 33, cited in Watkin, *Roman Cheshire*, 95.
[18] Pennant, *Tour in Wales*, 147, and S. Lysons, *Magna Britannia*, ii, London 1810, 427, cited in Watkin, *Roman Cheshire*, 95.

large part of the north wall above the foundations was Roman. Roach Smith reported Massie's belief that 'particular parts which he had noticed varied so remarkably from the general construction, and at the same time harmonised so strikingly with each other, as to incline him to believe that he had detected the original Roman work among the anomalous and perplexing styles of different periods'.[19] When Thomas Hughes researched the 1771 construction of the Nantwich canal, he found that 'the line actually took the course of the ancient Roman fosse, excavated some 1,500 years before'.[20] The controversy was to rumble on and be the subject of conferences and books in the 1880s.[21]

Another subject for debate was the so-called 'Roman bath' discovered in Bridge Street some time between 1720 and 1730. All the antiquarians who had visited the town mentioned it, including Horsley (1732), Pennant (1810) and Lysons (1806–22). In fact it was the hypocaust for a large building as became apparent when an adjoining site was demolished in 1863 enabling further excavation. In a report, the local antiquarian Dr T. Brushfield compared the findings with the recent excavations at Wroxeter and with Bath: 'I am strongly of the opinion that they formed a portion of the Public Baths, that they joined the Basilica, and that both opened into the space on the North and West sides which formed the Forum of the Roman Deva.'[22] The London archaeologist, William Tite, disagreed. He thought that the site was that of a temple, built about a century before the Romans left Britain. He based his opinion on the discovery of a series of column bases, 'an arrangement which gives the appearance of a small temple ... The whole of this part of the building might, therefore have constituted a four-columned Corinthian portico, about the size of the Maison Carree at Nimes'.[23] He also cited the remains at Bath and, using information from both sites, he drew a detailed plan of the 'probable state of the Roman Temple and baths at Chester, with a comparison of the columns and entablatures found in a similar structure at Bath'.[24] Tite claimed that 'there is but little which can be attributed to fancy. The screen of columns fronting the street is imaginary, but the foundation wall of it is really there. The appropriation of the apartments is also conjectural, but it is, nevertheless, reasonable and consistent with ancient authorities'. In spite of his protestations to the contrary, Tite's opinion owed as much to the classical texts and his imagination as it did to the few fragmentary remains. And he was not alone. Antiquarians' knowledge of other sites, such as the Maison Carrée and the monuments in Rome, moulded their expecta-

19 Roach Smith, 'Roman Remains at Chester', 212.
20 *Cheshire Sheaf*, iv. 176, cited in Watkin, *Roman Cheshire*, 105.
21 Restoration work carried out in the 1880s discovered Roman gravestones built into the fabric of the northern wall. This reawakened the debates about the wall's origins.
22 T. N. Brushfield, 'Remains of Roman buildings discovered in Bridge Street Chester', *JCAAHS* iii (1869), 72.
23 W. Tite, 'Roman architectural remains found in the city of Chester in 1863', *Arch.* xl (1863–5), 288.
24 Ibid. 290.

tions and fired their imaginations, with the result that their conclusions often tell us more about the antiquarians than they do about the remains.

Tite was at pains to stress that his motive for producing the plan of the Chester remains was the need for an accurate survey of the findings before they were hidden again beneath a new building. He says that although he knows such a plan should have been done by 'a professional local antiquary', he did not think this had happened. Tite seems to be unaware of the Chester Archaeological Society and this would suggest that the society was no longer very active. But before examining the history of the society it is necessary to outline the social context in which it was founded.

Social and economic Chester

In the sixteenth and seventeenth centuries Chester was a prosperous trading centre, using the Dee for the import and export of goods and to supply water for the production of cloth. In 1701, when Defoe visited the town, he deplored the darkness of the Rows, but described the streets as 'very broad and fair and run through the whole city in straight lines, crossing in the middle'.[25] This would seem to indicate that the city streets still followed the basic outline laid down in the Roman fortress. Several characteristic black-and-white timbered buildings, such as Stanley Place and Bishop Lloyd's House, were built during this prosperous period. However, by the beginning of the nineteenth century, the Dee had silted up and Stockport had become the industrial centre of the county, linked directly to the port of Liverpool by canals.[26]

There can be little doubt that the impact of these changes led to hardship in the town, particularly among working people. But there were those who saw the decline of manufacturing as a positive development. In 1831 Joseph Hemingway described the advantages of the town as an excellent situation, good air and 'an absence of manufactories and the crowds of the lowest rabble they engender render it a desirable residence for the higher classes and there are few places where the gentry form so great a proportion of the community as here'.[27] He describes the sort of people who were attracted to live in the town as 'junior branches of good families dependent on moderately competent incomes, retired military officers, resident clergy ... who enjoy all the advantages of polished society. A state of things which naturally induces numbers of similarly circumstanced to take up their domicile amongst us'.[28] He lists the city's facilities as a theatre, an assembly room, music and choral societies and reading rooms and libraries which 'afford ample means for the

---

[25] Defoe, *Tour*, 392. In 1872 Henry James described them as an 'architectural idiosyncrasy. They are a sort of Gothic edition of the blessed arcades and porticoes of Italy': *English hours* (1905), ed. L. Edel, London 1981, 59.
[26] Swift, *Victorian Chester*.
[27] Hemingway, *City of Chester*, ii. 341.
[28] Ibid.

indulgence of the lazy lounger and the gratification of the man of literary or scientific research'.[29] Hemingway considered the tradesmen and shopkeepers to be respectable, less flashy and less concerned to make a good impression than the tradesmen in Liverpool. His analysis finishes with the workers: 'They are well instructed in lower branches of education, but there is much less taste in this class for reading and the requirements of useful knowledge, than among the weavers and other mechanics of Lancashire.'[30] He deplores the lack of libraries and facilities for the poor and says that in this respect Chester is 'behind hand with most of the provincial towns of equal importance'. He suggests that the public-spirited should provide 'useful books at a cheap price and thus stop working people wandering about the city, where they contact habits of profligacy'.[31]

This is an interesting, if rather unsubtle, analysis of a provincial town in 1830. It suggests that Chester was more likely to attract a conservative middle-class population precisely because it was seen as remote from the sort of industrial and social unrest occurring elsewhere. It is possible that the appearance of the city, with its ancient buildings and cathedral, suggested a continuity and stability that stood in stark contrast to the industrial centres across the Mersey. It also ignored the social problems that did exist, for behind the main streets, courts were being subdivided into housing for the poor which has been described as 'appalling slum courts which, in relative terms, was as bad as that in the region's industrial towns'.[32] It is estimated that by the 1860s about 17 per cent of the population was living in such conditions which probably played a part in causing two major outbreaks of cholera in the town, between 1831and 1848–9.[33]

Chester's economic prospects were dramatically improved by the arrival of the railway in 1840. The town became a centre for routes all over the country including London, Liverpool and north Wales. By 1856 ninety-eight passenger trains were passing through Chester every day, carrying an average of 3,500 people: more than 1.25m. per year. What had started out as a staging-post to other destinations quickly became a tourist attraction in its own right, a development in which the city's ancient buildings played a significant part. The effect on the town was to halt the economic decline of the previous decades. The visitors stimulated trade in Chester's shops and service industries and between 1840 and 1875 the number of businesses rose by 46 per cent. Browns, the 'Harrods of the north', was rebuilt in the black-and-white style in 1858.[34]

29 Ibid. ii. 344.
30 Ibid. ii. 346.
31 Ibid. ii. 347.
32 Herson, 'Victorian Chester', 17.
33 Ibid. 29.
34 William Tite wrote that 'I found Chester to be gradually changing its character, in consequence of the overpowering influence of the railroad system, which makes it the great centre of the lines of commerce in that district ... Many new and magnificent houses and shops are now occupying the places of the picturesque old wooden buildings of earlier

The tourist boom heightened awareness of the commercial advantages offered by the town's picturesque appearance and the realisation that it had to be protected. In a speech praising the restoration work done on the cathedral, Raikes pointed out the advantage of such work in attracting visitors.[35] Where the preservation and restoration of the city's ancient buildings proved impossible, new houses were built in the style of the old, as it was the overall effect of age that needed to be achieved, rather than purity of detail. When Henry James visited the city in 1872, he recognised that many elements of the ancient appearance were in fact modern and represented a sanitised version of the past that its former inhabitants would hardly recognise: 'These elaborate and ingenious repairs attest a highly informed consciousness of the pictorial value of the city. I indeed suspect that much of this revived innocence of having recovered a freshness that never can have been, of having been restored with usurious interest.'[36] It is probable, although never overtly stated, that an increased awareness of the economic value of the city's ancient appearance, and the need to protect it, was a part of the motivation for the creation of the Chester Architectural, Archaeological and Historical Society, in 1849.

The Chester Architectural, Archaeological and Historical Society

It was William Massie who invited 'a few individuals representing clergy, laity and professional architects' to form an antiquarian society in Chester.[37] The group's objectives were included in the prospectus sent to potential members. They were the improvement of architectural taste, science and construction; the illustration and preservation of the remains of antiquity and other objects of interest in the city; the recommending of design for the restoration, construction and improvement of building and other works; the collection of historic, archaeological and architectural information, documents, relics, books etc.; and finally, the mutual suggestion and interchange of knowledge on these subjects.[38]

The prospectus lists the names of those who had agreed to be involved, and this gives some indication of the sort of membership the committee was hoping to attract. The dean, the chancellor, Raikes and the canon in residence, the Revd J. Eaton, represented the bishopric. There were also two vicars, Frederick Ford and William Massie. The lay members were J. Hicklin, editor of the *Chester Courant* and two architects, M. Penson and James Harrison. The bishop of Chester and the lord-lieutenant, the duke of West-

times': 'Roman architectural remains found in the city of Chester in 1864', *Arch.* xl (1866), 285.
[35] A. Raikes, 'Inaugural address', *JCAAHS* i (1849–55), 26.
[36] James, *English hours*, 35–43.
[37] CAAHS minutes, 16 Mar. 1849, Cheshire Record Office.
[38] Prospectus published in the *Courant*, 13 Mar. 1849.

minster, had agreed to be patrons. The prospectus stated that 'They will be a sufficient guarantee to you as to the character of the undertaking.'[39] The most striking feature of this list is the number of clergymen, which is probably an indication of the pre-eminent position of the cathedral and the bishop within Chester's society.

The society was to be governed by a council, composed of equal numbers of clergy and laity, and it was stipulated that the latter had to include working architects. There would be a regular series of meetings at which lectures would be given and it was proposed that these should be published in a journal. It was envisaged that a library and a collection of artefacts, drawings and plans would be made available to members. This outline of the administration and anticipated activities is significantly more detailed than in the other groups. It is a rather top-heavy organisation, which suggests that the intention was to include all the most prominent and important people in Chester society.

Four classes of membership were suggested: full members, who would pay £1 per year and be eligible to stand for the council; associate members, who would be unable to stand for the council or invite visitors, but who would otherwise be able to use all the society's facilities (for 10s. a year); 'a third class for persons of enquiring minds among our artisans, admission to the lectures and exhibitions at one shilling per quarter'; and lastly ladies, who could join for 5s., but could not stand for office.[40]

The minute book gives some membership details. In June 1849 there were thirty-four full members, two associate members, five ladies and one lone quarterly member. Among the new recruits were Mr Potts (the chairman of the Corporation's Improvement Committee), the Revd A. Rigg, principal of the training college, and B. Bayliss, inspector of works for the town council.[41] By December 1852 there were ninety full members, twenty associate members, twenty-one ladies and eight quarterly members.[42]

William Massie was the secretary and moving force behind the society until his death in 1856. He was a member of the local gentry, educated at the free grammar school until he was sixteen. He then joined the army and was sent to India, where he was impressed by the temples and other relics of ancient religion. After his return to Britain in 1830 he decided to join the church and went to Trinity College, Dublin, where he won the prize for classics. Another leading figure in the society was Raikes. He had followed a more conventional path into the Church: Eton and Cambridge, and then spending some time travelling in Greece.

The society's journal reports and the minute book give an impression of a group of middle-class men, most of whom knew each other through a variety of other roles that they played in the town. The new society offered another arena in which they could meet and share common concerns. Social meet-

[39] Ibid.
[40] Ibid.
[41] CAAHS minutes, 1 June 1849.
[42] Ibid. 31 Dec. 1852.

ings and enjoyment played an important part in the group's success, as the journal explained: 'Good will and social feeling have been promoted between parties who would otherwise rarely meet except on business.'[43]

The annual outings were popular events and offered the chance to meet like-minded people in other societies. The society entertained the Liverpool group on their annual outing to Chester in July 1850, and in 1853 groups from Warrington, Liverpool and Manchester joined the Chester Society for a visit to the museum in Warrington. The rest of the day was taken up with visits to local churches and the remains of a Roman road and the day ended with a *conversazione* at the house of a local historian, a Mr Marsh.[44] The decision to hold the committee meetings during the day effectively excluded working men from the ruling body. But despite this, the CAAHS was unique among archaeological societies of the period in its attempts to attract a working-class or artisan membership via the quarterly fee. It could be argued that only a really confident body, in a city where social and religious differences were relatively non-contentious, had the assurance to encourage membership among working men.

Group activities

As its name suggests, the members' interests were wide-ranging. This was reflected in the subject matter of the lectures, which ranged from Roman artefacts through to the elected knights for the shire in the seventeenth century and from obsolete punishments to all aspects of architecture. The medieval period and ecclesiastical architecture were of particular interest and there were field visits to draw plans and make sketches of local churches and to survey headstones in churchyards.[45] Massie was interested in the Roman period. He presented several papers on some waterlogged wood which had been found buried in river silt at Birkenhead. He was convinced that the wood was part of a Roman bridge, constructed to allow troop movements across the estuary: 'This log of oak may serve as a peg on which to hang a discussion about the ancient geography of this country.'[46] His evidence included passages from Herodian and Dio Cassius about troop movements in Britain during the Roman occupation. He also referred to 'the well known description of Caesar's passage over the Rhine in which he had said that it would not be in accordance with the dignity and greatness of the Roman nation to have recourse to ferries'.[47] Massie felt that the Birkenhead bridge would

---

[43] Ibid. preface.
[44] The museum was owned by the Warrington Natural History Society. According to the *JCAAHS* i (1849–55), 338, it contained 'a rare collection of curiosities, illustrative of archaeology, geology, entomology, ornithology and all the other scientific ologies'.
[45] CAAHS minutes, 21 Dec. 1849, 2 June 1851.
[46] W. H. Massie, 'On a wooden bridge found buried under the silt at Birkenhead', *JCAAHS* i (1849–55), 55.
[47] Ibid. 71.

have been exactly the same as that on the Rhine, only on a smaller scale. Finally he quoted General Roy's *Military antiquities of the Romans in north Britain* (1793) on the size of timbers required to build a bridge and Leland's sixteenth-century account, in which it was suggested that the sea had flooded the area on which the bridge would have stood. The whole article is an interesting example of the way in which one small object could be used to build up a picture of the Roman past.

Examples of more substantial Roman remains in Italy were used to explain and illustrate the meagre British remains. For instance, a paper on Roman domestic architecture was illustrated with drawings of the house of Sallust at Pompeii. Similarly, Massie compared a number of tombstones and urns with more complete examples in the museum at Tivoli, and produced pictures to emphasise his point. It is possible that Massie was thinking of Pompeii and Tivoli when he used a Corinthian column, the bases of further columns and a silver coin of Trajan, discovered during building work, to infer the existence of 'a city of no mean character'.[48] But this impression was at least partially based on comparisons with major Roman remains in Italy, rather than the evidence from Chester. It was almost as though Roman Chester was seen as an extension of Rome itself.

The society did not carry out any excavations. The remains that were discovered were unearthed as a result of building activity, as in the case of another Roman hypocaust that came to light in 1852. Although described by some members as a 'Roman bath', Massie pointed out that it was more likely to be part of an extensive system of hot air flues to heat a building. Other discoveries led to arguments, for instance an altar with a Greek inscription, found in 1850. The inscription referred to Hermogenes, a physician, who had erected it in thanks to the deities who had preserved him from trouble. Massie used pictures of altars from Pompeii and coins of Vespasian to throw more light on the find. He speculated that this Hermogenes could be the man described by Dio Cassius as physician to the Emperor Hadrian. But he concluded that 'It would be building a large inference on somewhat bare evidence to conclude that this was the Hermogenes who set up the altar.'[49] Raikes, however, was determined that the altar should demonstrate the importance of Chester in Roman Britain. He remarked that the use of Greek was relatively uncommon in Britain and that it was possible that the physician had been with Agricola during the conquest of north Wales: 'The mere fact of his residence here and the use of the Greek language are sufficient to show that Chester must at that time, have been a place of some importance and advanced civilisation.'[50] But Raikes did not want to draw too close a parallel, since Hermogenes was a pagan and therefore to be pitied because of 'the blindness which led him

---

48 Ibid. 199.
49 Ibid. 200.
50 A. Raikes, 'On a fragment of a votive altar, *JCAAHS* i (1849–55), 361.

to honour those ideal beings who deserved it not'. Like antiquarians in other parts of Britain at the same time, the Chester society was eager to emphasise the importance and prominence of their locality in the great events of the past, but there were some aspects of the classical world with which they did not wish to be identified.

More unusual was that, unlike many other societies, a museum was not a major objective. In July 1849 the society agreed to rent two rooms in the county court building but these were mainly to act as a meeting place and reading room.[51] By 1855 the meeting rooms had moved to the Chester library building and discussions began with the library about the joint appointment of a librarian and curator.[52] A librarian was appointed and glass display cases were fitted round the room. The contents consisted largely of objects donated to the society by the members, although a few things were bought such as a gold torque, found in a drain in 1852, and books for the society library.[53] But it was not until 1857 that the minutes actually used the word 'museum' and many more years before the society finally had a proper museum building.[54]

The reasons for the Chester society's lack of interest in forming a museum collection are not obvious. The two local landed families, the Grosvenors and the Egertons, both had collections and therefore it is possible that a town museum was seen as unnecessary.[55] But, more important, the emphasis on the preservation of the city's ancient building façade was undoubtedly the society's main priority. The commercial value of the ancient appearance was not lost on those members who were also some of the town's leading businessmen. Finally, while some members saw the advantage of a museum to the tourist trade, no individual with the time, money and enthusiasm put himself forward for the task of putting one together.[56]

[51] CAAHS minutes, 25 July 1849.The same note records that Mr Catheral had offered the society the use of rooms over his bookshop and printing works and that his offer was declined. Would it be too fanciful to suggest that this could have been because the society did not want to be so closely associated with 'trade'?
[52] Ibid. 10 May 1855.
[53] The CAAHS accessions book records the books. They included *Vitruvius Britannicus* (Colen Campbell), Smith's *Dictionary of antiquities*, *Pompeiana* (Gell), *Ancient coins* (Akerman), *Collectanea antiqua* and *Excavations at Lymne* (Roach Smith), *Delineations of Roman antiquities* (E. Lee) and miscellaneous papers by, amongst others, Thomas Wright and John Collingwood Bruce. The society also subscribed to the national archaeological journals.
[54] In 1865 three society members bought Stanley Place, an original black-and-white house in a poor state of repair, for £750. The intention was to restore the building and use it as a museum. The project failed to get off the ground before the society itself became moribund.
[55] The head of the Grosvenor family was the duke of Westminster, whose country house, Eaton Hall, was just outside Chester. According to Hughes's *Stranger's guide* the collection included a golden torque, 'An ornament worn around the neck of illustrious British warriors. Queen Boadicea and Llewellyn are both recorded to have been so decorated.'
[56] Museums were regarded as likely tourist attractions, particularly when they contained large and attractive remains such as mosaics. Cirencester's museum had over 4,000 visitors in the two years after its opening, many of them from other parts of the country and the

The society and architecture

A significant difference between the CAAHS and other societies was the importance attached to the study of architecture. There were regular lectures on architectural topics. For instance, Penson talked about half-timbered houses and T. Ayrton about Norman architecture and there was a day outing to Crewe to look at the proposed restoration of the church by Gilbert Scott. But their chief preoccupation was to influence the designs for new and restored buildings in the town centre. In fact, reading the minutes it is clear that they were operating as a watchdog over council and private building plans, in much the same way as a civic society would do today. At a meeting in December 1851 the Corporation asked their opinion on the design of new gas lamps, to which Mr Ayrton remarked that they were 'like a gallows placed there to scare away visitors'.[57] Penson exhibited his plans for a new building to replace Platt's chemist shop on Eastgate and was thanked for the 'tasteful style, in keeping with the older properties around'.[58] And when W. Brown, a member of the society, decided to rebuild and extend his shop on Eastgate in 1858, he showed his plans to the society for their approval, which was duly given.[59] The society was less happy about some other plans, and their concerns illustrate the continual battle to balance commercial interests and the preservation of the city's ancient façade: 'Unfortunately, it could not be expected that he [Mr. Gregory, the owner] would all together sacrifice his business views, but it was hoped that at least the carved timbers of the old house and, as far as possible, its external character, should be in some measure preserved.'[60] The society was involved in contemporary debates about church restoration. Members of the Liverpool Society were shown St John's Priory which called forth almost unbounded admiration, apart from 'the present style of pewing and wood work, which so sadly disfigures a building worthy of a different fate'. They were told that the duke of Westminster was going to pay for the remodelling of the interior in order that it should harmonise with the rest of the building.[61]

However, while the society as a whole displayed a rather conservative, antiquarian interest in Chester's ancient facade, several of its most promi-nent members were actively involved in the commercial and economic life of the city and had a financial interest in its development. F. Potts was devel-

British Museum attracted 37,260 visitors in one week when it displayed a mosaic from Athens: Anon., 'Mosaic at British Museum', *ILN*, 6 Jan. 1849, 6.
[57] Anon., 'Report of meeting on 1st Dec. 1850', *JCAAHS* i (1849–55), 204.
[58] CAAHS minutes, 1 Dec. 1851; 23 Apr. 1852. This is the building referred to by Thomas Hughes. Hughes wrote that the new building was 'a most successful and elegant illustration of the manner [in] which the antique character of our domestic architecture can be preserved, with every regard for modern requirements and comforts': *Stranger's guide*, 46–7.
[59] CAAHS minutes, 17 June 1858.
[60] Anon., 'Proceedings of meeting on 18th Nov. 1861', *JCAAHS* ii (1856–62).
[61] CAAHS minutes, 3 July 1850.

oping industrial land in the Chester suburb of Saltney, a possible Roman site; Charles Brown was creating a large department store on Eastgate, and Penson and Harrison were designing new hotels to cater for the tourists attracted to the town by its picturesque appearance. The minutes and journal do not give any indication that these diverse activities were seen as representing possible conflicts of interests, but none the less there was an anomaly at the heart of the society's attitude to the preservation of the old city. On the one hand, the members were anxious to protect the old buildings against the demands made by new development, but on the other they were equally anxious that Chester should exploit the economic prosperity which success as a tourist attraction offered. So, there was a need for both old historic sights and all the advantages and conveniences of modern life – what Henry James was to call 'antiquity with all mod. cons'.[62] The challenge was to find a balance between these two, potentially conflicting, objectives, and the society appears to have managed this reasonably successfully. It did help to preserve old buildings and played an important role in raising the Corporation's awareness of the need for new developments to be in sympathy with the old. At the same time the society was aware of the part that the city's ancient remains could play in attracting tourists. It expressed regret that the town council had not chosen to establish a museum, as had been done in 'Manchester, Warrington and other places less prolific in local remains, which after all, bring more visitors and travellers to Chester, for the benefits of the city, than almost anything else'.[63]

By the end of the 1850s the society appears to have gone into a decline. It could be that the diversion caused by architectural debates and concerns had meant that there was less energy available for archaeological pursuits. More likely is that the deaths of Massie in 1856 and Raikes in 1857 left the society without a leader.[64] Whatever the cause, there are several signs that the society had lost its vitality. As early as January 1852 the entries in the minute book become shorter and were mainly concerned with the meeting room and library, and there were no more newspaper reports. It was also more difficult to find lecturers, as the report in the journal of a meeting in November 1853 illustrated: 'The entertainment of the evening, though desultory and not possessed of much knowledge, was on the whole extremely agreeable;

---

[62] This is cited by Chris Miele in 'Conservation and the enemies of progress', paper given at a conference on 'The idea of heritage: past, present and future', London Guildhall University, September 1999.

[63] Anon., 'Proceedings', *JCAAHS* i (1849–55), 452. The speaker regretted that the town council had not used the provision in the 1845 Museum Act to raise money for such a purpose through the rates.

[64] Massie's obituary hinted at the difficulties he had faced. 'Those only who know what a task it really is to hold together such a society, to provide the necessary matter for the monthly meetings, and to keep alive the sympathies of often lukewarm friends, can fully appreciate either the extent or the value of Mr. Massie's services': 'The late Rev. W. H. Massie', 401.

the table talk being after all, less formidable and more acceptable generally than the delivery of a dry and abstruse paper.' The report continued, 'Mere diversion is not the principal object of these meetings and solid information cannot always be dressed in the garb of amusement.'[65] It appears that the society had become a successful part of the Chester social scene as the membership figures continued to rise, to more than two hundred by 1863. But at the same time the administration seems to have collapsed. No minutes appear in the minute book between December 1859 and December 1864 and no acquisitions were recorded between 1855 and 1883.[66] A description of a meeting in 1860 as 'large and fashionable' would suggest that the society had been successful in its desire to recruit the town's leading citizens, but that the members' objectives in joining were not necessarily to inform themselves of matters archaeological and historical.[67]

Tourism in Chester

One effect of the increased tourist trade was to stimulate the production of tourist guides to the town's main attractions. These guides provide another perspective on the way in which the people of the period visualised both the present and the past in Chester. They range from *Broster's guide* (1782) to Thomas Hughes's *Stranger's guide* (1st edn 1856). In themselves, these books provide a challenging jigsaw of attribution and relationship, which is almost as complicated as the challenges posed by the buildings they describe.

The town's mayor wrote the first edition of *Broster's guide*. By the sixth edition, in 1822, it appeared as *A walk around the walls and city of Chester*. Broster's book appears to have served as an example to the many others published in the early years of the nineteenth century.[68] When John Seacome published his *Chester guide* in 1836, he says in his preface that he had bought the copyright of *Broster*. If Broster was the exemplar for the early nineteenth-century guides, then Joseph Hemingway's *History of the city of Chester* (1831) was the main source for those guides written in the 1850s. A *Chester guide*, by Hugh Roberts (1851), and Pritchard's guide of the same name, published in 1852, are remarkably similar and they both follow Hemingway's words closely. This proliferation of guides, published by local booksellers, often in competition with one another, was characteristic of the period. A common feature and no doubt related to the competition between the publications, was the authors' disparagement of all the other guides. Thus, Hemingway

---

65 Ibid. 436.
66 It was during this low point that Tite visited the city and seemed unaware of any archaeological activity.
67 Anon., 'Proceedings', *JCAAHS* ii (1856–62), 374.
68 Examples are G. Bateman, *A stranger's companion in Chester*, Chester n.d; [?] Fletcher, *A stranger in Chester*, Chester 1816; and James Hansell, *A stranger in Chester*, Chester 1816.

in *Panorama of the city of Chester* (1836) refers to 'numerous small publica-tions which have been issued from the Chester Press' and describes them as 'bagatelles'.[69] However, Hemingway realised that there was a need for more popular accounts of Chester's past, since much of the information was either 'inaccessible or very expensive' and the original documents were 'concealed in the barbarism of an obsolete tongue'.[70] Other potential new customers were the railway passengers and several guides were produced specifically for their use.[71]

The guides all follow a similar format: a brief outline of Chester's history followed by a guided walk around the town to visit the main attractions, an account of the walls, the Rows and the cathedral. They all attribute its foun-dation to the Roman occupation and emphasise its importance as a Roman centre. Hughes manages this very effectively by contrasting the Celtic settle-ment with the Roman city that succeeded it:

> The rude huts of the Britons, the temples and altars of the ancient Druid, the mud walls and other defences, all vanished like a dream, while in their place arose the proud Praetorium, the pagan temples, the stately columns, the peerless masonry, the noble statues, the massive walls and all the other elements of civilisation which usually followed in the wake of grand old Rome.[72]

The image he evokes is as unrelated to the fragmented Roman remains in contemporary Chester as were the antiquarians' views discussed earlier. But, like the antiquarians, Hughes calls upon all the rhetoric associated with 'grand old Rome' to suggest Roman Chester. The two could almost be synon-ymous.[73]

Hughes's description of the city in 1856 is, in some ways, the most inter-esting because of the way he contrasts the old city and the changes brought about by modern developments. He is no cultural Luddite, mourning the loss of the past. Instead, he relishes the signs of change and modern devel-opment. For instance, in describing the railway he states that 'The Roman walls that resisted so successfully the Roundhead batteries have in our own time succumbed to the engines of peace. The railway trains, with their living freight, now career merrily through two neighbouring apertures in these ancient fortifications.'[74] Hughes believes that many of the changes had been

[69] J. Hemingway, *Panorama of the city of Chester*, Chester 1836, preface.
[70] Ibid. This was presumably what prompted him to write *Panorama*, which was intended as a pocket dictionary for the inquisitive traveller and curious tourist.
[71] Examples are Edward Parry's *The railway companion from Chester to Holyhead*, Chester 1848, and *The railway companion from Chester to Shrewsbury*, Chester 1849. There were also foreign visitors to be catered for and Thomas Pullin, a member of the CAAHS, produced a French/English guide in 1851.
[72] Hughes, *Stranger's guide*, 4.
[73] The clash of cultures suggested by this rhetoric was emphasised in the second edition of Robert's guide by the use of the illustrations of 'native Britons' discussed earlier.
[74] Hughes, *Stranger's guide*, 26.

beneficial. For instance, he praises the industrial development at Saltney and the new diocesan training college, 'a noble institution and a creation of the present age'. Above all, he points out the greater tolerance of the present as compared to the past when 'peace loving Quakers endured the rod of persecution for conscience sake. And yet, these were your oft vaunted days of civil and religious liberty'.[75]

Although Chester had been a major Roman centre, antiquarian activity had not put the city on the Romano-British map as had happened in Caerleon. This is not to suggest that Chester's antiquarians sought to play down the town's Roman inheritance; quite the contrary. They were as eager to point it out and associate themselves with past glory as was the case in other areas. However the city fathers were at least as concerned with the present day as they were with the past and the boom in tourism had sharpened their realisation that preservation and restoration were necessary; but in what style? Visitors to Roman Chester might have expected to find grand buildings in the classical style, with pillars and sculptured entablature, but instead they found a town centre dominated by vernacular wood and plaster buildings that were as historically evocative and corresponded more with current ideas of 'Old England' than did the Roman past. It is possible that the use of the classical style for many public buildings had meant that the vernacular style was now regarded as more 'truly old' than the classical. It certainly appeared more directly related to an English heritage than did the controlled marble buildings of classical Rome.[76] It had always been intended that the society would concern itself with more than the preservation of the past, be it Roman or any other and in practice its main focus was on the architectural heritage of the city. Above all else the covert aim of maintaining the *status quo* appears to have been most important. This was not a society founded to protect ancient remains or build a museum. Rather 'to facilitate the mutual suggestion and interchange of knowledge', a useful catch-all phrase which allowed social aims to be respectably hidden within an antiquarian exterior. Like so much else in Chester external appearance did not necessarily reflect what was inside.

75 Ibid. 99, 103.
76 J. M. Crook, *The dilemma of style*, London 1987; P. Mandler, *The fall and rise of the stately home*, New Haven 1997.

8

Finding the Past in the Ground

Whether members of a local society, working in a national institution or labouring alone to excavate an historical site, all antiquarians faced the same problem: how to read and interpret the myriad small and frequently broken objects that were appearing in the ground under their feet. In one guise or another it was a dilemma that demanded attention because without it their labours made little sense and they would be left with a pile of meaningless rubbish.

At the inaugural meeting of the Essex Archaeological Society in 1852 John Marsden attempted to explain how the objects could be used in a number of ways. He defined archaeology as the study of all the 'visible and tangible' relics of man's work in the past. He pointed out that while these material remains could be 'collected, analysed, classified and preserved' they also had an imaginative appeal that could be used by poets to evoke the sympathy of their readers. As both approaches utilised the same relics, Marsden thought that 'there is a close connection between the antiquary and the poet; between him who presents to us the airy and unsubstantial creations of his own mind, and him whose occupation is among objects, which he can touch and handle, and pry into, and weigh and measure'.[1]

For the antiquarians, the prime use of the objects was the information they could offer concerning Roman Britain. In 1855 Professor Marsden remarked that, even in the case of ancient Greece, more was known of their politics and religion as a result of archaeological advances than had been gained through the accounts of poets and historians. He compared this with the even scantier textual evidence about Roman Britain: 'The state of Britain under the Romans is now tolerably familiar to us: but we have learned it not from books, but from an investigation of their works, their roads, their houses, their hypocausts, their earthworks, their coins, their ornaments and utensils, their weapons, and the vast multitude of other miscellaneous relics which they have left behind.'[2]

Where there are no textual accounts, objects are often the only available source of information. But as Marsden's comments make clear, historical objects can be used in a number of ways. They can be studied as evidence in their own right, or they can be the means through which previously invisible periods and events can be brought into view. The ambiguity created by this apparent 'dual nature' arises from the fact that the objects are both a material

---

[1] J. Marsden, 'Inaugural lecture on archaeology', TEAS i (1858), 22.
[2] Idem, 'Introductory address', AJ xii (1855), 2.

reality in the present, while at the same time they represent an aspect of the past. They can be described purely in terms of their physical properties: their material and production, their size, shape and measurement, and usage. Conversely they can also be seen as symbols, their physical presence constituting only one part of their meaning. The interpretation of objects used in this way will be dependent not only on their location and relation to other objects, but upon the complex mixture of associations they evoke. As a result objects can be given a range of possible meanings and interpretations and their symbolic value can be used in historical narratives and to aid interpretation of contemporary events.[3]

This is reflected in the two approaches to studying the past discussed earlier. The various classification systems of Johann Winckelmann, Anne Claude Caylus and the Danish archaeologists all used the physical characteristics of the objects as a means whereby the past could be known and better understood. On the other hand, topographical accounts of a specific area used objects to evoke the past and to help in the creation of a narrative with which local people could identify.

The discussion about objects will therefore be in two parts: first, objects as evidence of the past; and second, their symbolic value in the present. In the first section the physical characteristics of objects, the kind of information they offered, how they were classified and used for comparisons with other examples from Italy (and in particular from Pompeii) will be discussed. Different museum collections, ownership, their layout and accessibility and the market that was created as a result of the interest in antiquities will also be analysed. The second section will consider the symbolic significance of artefacts and collections, both for their owners personally and for their influence upon their owner's social standing. It will examine the particular impact of human remains such as skeletons, skulls and footprints in enabling individuals to relate to the past and the narrative value of objects in imaginative reconstruction and identification. However, although the discussion is in two parts, it needs to be stressed that the different aspects of objects and collecting were in fact intimately connected at many points.

The object

It would appear from some of their comments that it was the very solidity of objects that had such an appeal for the antiquarians. Charles Roach Smith commented that in the void left by the lack of textual evidence objects represented 'something tangible, something which the eye can dissect, appropriate and comprehend'.[4] The same desire for hard evidence is apparent in Albert Way's assertion in 1844 that the main focus of interest of the newly-

[3]   These problems still concern modern archaeologists: see M. Shanks, *Classical archaeology of Greece: experiences of the discipline*, London 1996.
[4]   Roach Smith, 'Notes on Caerwent and Caerleon', 246.

created BAA would be to 'address itself to the illustration of tangible things'.[5] Another journal article talked of 'The silence of history ... where there is an eloquence in the sculptured fragment or the crumbling walls, the ornaments or appliances of everyday life.'[6] All these comments suggest a common desire to make contact with the past in a concrete and palpable way in order to fill the gaps left by the lack of texts. That is precisely what the physical objects offered. Indeed their very ordinariness could obscure their age, as was the case with a Roman shield that had been used as a pot lid and scoured weekly, or the piece of Samian ware used as a soap dish.[7]

Once in a collection, the objects became available for physical analysis. Edward Lee talked about the difficulty of preserving ivory objects and advocated the use of isinglass, as employed by Sir Austen Layard in the excavations at Nineveh. He used a local surgeon to identify the burned remains of bones in a jar, and modern tools to demonstrate the way in which marks on some pottery could have been produced by the tools available to the Romans.[8] But probably the most extreme example of the way in which the physical properties of artefacts could be divorced from their context and associations and studied purely as pieces of matter is to be found in the very detailed analysis that John Buckman made of the Cirencester mosaics. He produced a series of articles in which he examined the geological and chemical make-up of the tesserae and their colouring. His book, *Remains of Roman art*, includes chapters on the materials and construction of the pavements, including an analysis of the ruby glass.[9] Significantly, the only discussion of the subject matter of the paintings is in the form of quotations from Richard Westmacott.

The desire on the part of some antiquarians to present their subject as a science and their activities as scientific encouraged them to view the artefacts simply as individual physical objects rather than as one part of a wider whole. The very act of transferring them from a site to a collection or to a museum changed their meaning. On the site they remained in context as a part of Romano-British society. Once in a museum they became available for use as examples within a number of different classification systems. Thus, the removal of the Cirencester mosaics to a museum allowed Buckman to approach them as artefacts quite separate from their context, a villa in Romano-British Corinium. As local collections proliferated, some voices were heard questioning the automatic removal of objects from their sites. The historian Edward Freeman pointed out to the Archaeological Institute in 1851 that 'The deep interest associated with the monuments was wholly,

5 Way, 'Introduction', 6.
6 Lee, 'Roman building at Caerleon', 97.
7 The shield was described by Augustus Franks, 'Bosses of Roman shields found in Northumberland and Lancashire', AJ xv (1858), 55; the soap dish by Edward Lee in *Isca Silurum: an illustrated catalogue of the museum of antiquities at Caerleon*, London 1862, 29.
8 Lee, *Isca Silurum*, 46.
9 Buckman and Newmarch, *Remains of Roman art*, 55. Buckman's articles were 'On the substances employed in forming the tessellate of the Cirencester pavements', AJ vii (1850), 347–54, and 'On the removal of Roman tessellated floors', AJ xiii (1856), 215–25.

and in some instances, wantonly sacrificed by the dispersal of their most precious accessories.'[10] But in the ensuing discussion, Lord Talbot described the removal of the Elgin Marbles as 'perfectly justifiable and expedient'.[11]

The study of artefacts as single objects could be useful in a number of ways. They could offer technological solutions to contemporary manufacturers. After providing a chemical analysis of the ruby glass John Buckman concluded that 'A correct analytical knowledge might have saved former experimenters much time and trouble and an analysis of Roman ruby glass might have led again to the recovery of the art.'[12] Buckman had commented on possible cross-fertilisation between modern science and archaeology and ancient and modern production in an article in the AJ: 'My conviction is that the history of the past may provide much elucidation from modern science and that the science and art of the present may in their turn be greatly advanced by a correct examination and a due appreciation of what has been achieved in ancient times ... and may prove of no trifling practical advantage.'[13] A review of a new book that illustrated the artefacts found in Pompeii and Herculaneum pointed out that the information it contained would be useful to 'the artificer, the student in the school of design, to all, engaged in the study or the practice of decorative art'.[14] This view was supported by the comments of a locksmith who examined the keys in Roach Smith's museum: 'He observed that the principle of his patent keys had evidently been well understood by the Romans. He had, in fact, simply recovered what had long since been known and forgotten, like very many other supposed modern inventions.'[15]

Coins and their inscriptions were particularly valuable as they could be used to date the artefacts found with them. The potential information offered by coins and medals had long been recognised.[16] In 1839 John Akerman

10 E. Freeman, 'Proceedings', AJ viii (1851), 326. Freeman's views echoed those of William Gell in his book about the artefacts from Pompeii. Thus, 'It is much to be regretted that means could not be devised for their preservation on the precise spot at which they were originally found and where locality would have thrown around them an interest which they entirely loose when crowded with other curiosities in the Museum of Portici': *Pompeiana: the topography, edifices and ornaments of Pompeii*, London 1819, 14.

11 J. Talbot. 'Proceedings', AJ viii (1851), 327. Talbot's words draw attention to the highly political nature of archaeological conservation, then and now.

12 Buckman and Newmarch, *Remains of Roman art*, 60.

13 Buckman, 'Substances', 353. The use of the mosaics as models for modern manufacture was also pointed out in a review of Buckman's book in the GM xxxiv (1850), 243. (The author was probably Roach Smith who wrote most of the archaeological articles in the GM.)

14 Anonymous review of E. Trollope, *Illustrations of ancient art, selected from objects discovered at Pompeii and Herculanaem: AJ xi (1854), 89. The writer emphasises that, unlike other books on Pompeii, this one dealt only with objects and not architecture.

15 Roach Smith, *Catalogue of Roman antiquities*, 71.

16 Lord Bathurst quoted Joseph Addison's Dialogue on medals (1700) to the Congress of the BAA in 1869: 'Presidential address', JBAA xxv (1869), 23. However the evidence from coins could be misinterpreted. In a lecture on the Faussett collection, Wright pointed out that Faussett had wrongly attributed the graves to the Roman period because of the coins found in the graves: 'He concluded very hastily that the date of their deposit must

founded the Numismatic Society. He also wrote several guides to collecting coins, including *Ancient and modern coins* (1848) and *Coins of the Romans relating to Britain* (2nd edn 1848). Roach Smith became secretary of the society in 1853 and many other local antiquarians were also members. Most books about Romano-British sites contained lists of the coins found in the vicinity. Charles Newton, who had spent several years classifying the coin collection in the British Museum, pointed out their value as evidence: 'Roman coins are not Fasti, nor are Greek coins a treatise on ancient geography, yet the labour of numismatists has made the one almost the best authority for the chronology of the Roman empire, and has found in the other an inestimable commentary on Strabo and Ptolemy.'[17] John Buckman used coins of the Emperor Trajan and the Emperor Hadrian as evidence to date the Cirencester pavements, the design of which he compared with those from Hadrian's villa at Tivoli.[18] The images on coins could also be used to yield information. For instance, the Revd Charles King cited the similarity between a carved pillar found at Lydney Park with the Temple of Minerva on the reverse of a Marcus Aurelius coin as evidence that the carving was Roman rather than a seventeenth-century copy.[19]

In other instances it was the very 'blandness' of some artefacts that lent itself to any number of interpretations. Roach Smith could enthuse about the significance of a humble pot: 'I read upon this relic, whose insignificance had preserved it, a record of its humble history, brief and single, but eloquent from its simplicity and suggestiveness where all else was silence.'[20] But its 'suggestiveness' sometimes conveyed more of the observer than of the observed, as was the case with the large iron nails frequently found in Roman graves. These had prompted Wykeham Martin MP to suggest that they had been used for the purposes of crucifixion because this was a well known Roman punishment. Roach Smith disputed these ideas and used the evidence from other graves where nails had also been discovered in a vertical arrangement around the bodies, to suggest that the most likely explanation was that the wooden coffins had decomposed, leaving only the nails that had held them together: 'Modern antiquarians explain these relics in a more simple manner and more in conformity with the spirit of ancient customs.'[21]

But whereas this might have been the case with Roach Smith and his friends, other antiquarians continued to attribute meanings congruent with

have been the reign in which they were struck': 'On the Anglo-Saxon antiquities with a special reference to the Faussett collection', *Transactions of the Historical Society of Lancashire and Cheshire* vii (1855), 4.
[17] Newton, 'On the study of archaeology', 11.
[18] Buckman and Newmarch, *Remains of Roman art*, 121.
[19] W. H. Bathurst, 'Roman antiquities at Lydney Park', *Proceedings of the London Society of Antiquaries* 4th ser. (1871), 96–101. C. W. King was an expert on coins whom Edward Lee consulted frequently. He wrote the chapter on coins for *Isca Silurum*, Lee's Caerleon Museum catalogue.
[20] Roach Smith, 'Discoveries at Ickelton and Chesterford', 364.
[21] Idem, *Collectanea antiqua*, iii. 19.

their beliefs. One common mistake was to interpret classical objects as evidence of early Christian beliefs and practices. For instance, the well-worn statue of Minerva, carved on a rock beside the crossing point of the Dee at Chester, probably owed its survival to the medieval belief that it was an image of the Virgin Mary. And Roach Smith complained that classical pagan images on coins and medals continued to be given Christian interpretations, as in the case of a ring carved with the heads of Germanicus and Agrippina that was taken to be the ring given to Mary by Joseph on their betrothal.[22] In all these instances, the interpretation of an ancient object had been influenced by the belief systems of the observer. As a result, the object's supposed meaning often bore little relation to its original purpose.

Comparisons

A common way of reading more information into isolated objects was to compare them with others of the same type. The journals contain many examples of the way in which the archaeologists sought understanding by comparing objects with others found in different parts of the country. Perhaps unsurprisingly, detailed comparisons with Italian artefacts were regarded as particularly useful; for example the figures on Trajan's column were a good source of information on military matters. Some archaeologists had travelled to Italy to see these sights for themselves, but for those who had not, there was an increasing number of books that described and illustrated the monuments and artefacts. [23] One that was widely used was William Gell's *Pompeiana*, published in 1819, but there were many others.[24]

Roman texts and monuments tended to deal with public life such as religious and military ceremonial and, therefore, as a great number of the artefacts from Roman Britain were domestic, the findings at Pompeii were particularly

---

[22] Ibid. iv. 71.

[23] Frederick Fairholt kept a journal of his visit to Italy in 1856: Roach Smith, *Collectanea antiqua*, v. 1–64. Both Edward Lee and Roach Smith travelled to Italy later in the century. A review of the fourth edition of *Murray's handbook for southern Italy*, probably written by Layard, remarked that 'There are few persons of education who are not familiar with these things, and in these days of travel many have examined for themselves the unrivalled collection of antiquities gathered together from the buried town, which has given a wide renown to the Museum of Naples': QR (1864), 315.

[24] Amongst other books were Trollope, *Roman art*, pamphlets issued by the Society for the Diffusion of Useful Knowledge and more general travel accounts such as C. Dickens, *Pictures from Italy* (1846) and Willis, *Pencillings by the way*, 1st edn, London 1844. In 1854 the *Gentleman's Magazine* announced that Professor Zahn 'who has investigated Pompeii and Herculaneum for fifteen years is preparing to publish the twenty seventh and last part of his work on the monuments': Anon., 'Notice of publication', GM xliii (1854), 597. At £45 it would have been too costly for all but the well off. John Parker, the publisher and archaeologist, had thousands of photographs taken of ancient sites published between 1867 and 1869.

helpful and relevant.[25] The Cirencester historian W. K. Beecham underlined the importance of the domestic nature of the findings at Pompeii: 'Since 1800 ... the disinterment of the numerous specimens of the domestic economy of the Romans at Pompeii has explained the use of many of their remains, which was before only guessed at.'[26] Some of the comparisons were very specific and detailed, such as that made by a reviewer in the *AJ* who compared the carvings on the Colchester vase with the bas-reliefs on the tomb of Scaurus at Pompeii.[27] And, again in the first catalogue of the Cirencester museum, Arthur Church compared some scratches on a piece of Roman wall plaster with some similar graffiti found in Pompeii and Rome. He declared that 'It is very desirable that persons familiar with similar relics in Italy should examine this specimen since its genuineness has been called into question.'[28]

Apart from being a particularly rich source of domestic artefacts for comparative purposes, the excavations at Pompeii appear to have acted as a potent force on the British antiquarians' imaginations and most of the new sites excavated during the 1850s were compared with that city. Octavius Morgan described Caerwent as the 'Monmouthshire Pompeii' and his reports make it quite clear that he was using the Italian site as a guide to what he might expect to find there.[29] Like Morgan, Thomas Wright used the layout of the foundations at Pompeii to inform his excavations at Wroxeter: 'It is rather remarkable that the basilica held here exactly the same place in regard to the forum as at Pompeii.'[30] A report in the *ILN* gives an indication of the excitement and expectations aroused by Wright's excavations: 'It is the first time we have had the opportunity of ascertaining the character and condition of a Roman town in Britain and the discovery has a similar interest for the history of Roman Britain as that of Pompeii had for Italy.'[31]

The widespread use of the word 'Pompeii' was almost akin to shorthand for a whole complex of associations suggesting wealth and luxury as opposed to military organisation and war. This is not to suggest conscious intent on the part of the authors, rather that the word was so redolent with images and symbolism, that, for certain audiences, further words were unnecessary. For example, when Wright described some fragments of coloured wall

[25] For instance Richard Neville used an example from Gell's book to illuminate the use of a glass ampulla found at Great Chesterford: 'Recent discoveries of Roman remains at Great Chesterford', *AJ* xvii (1860), 118.

[26] Beecham, *History and antiquities of Cirencester*, 208.

[27] Anon., 'Book review', *AJ* xviii (1861), 96.

[28] Church, *Roman remains*, 21.

[29] O. Morgan, 'Proceedings', *AJ* xii (1855), 79. Morgan described the baths at Caerwent as as 'small and as perfect as any I have seen apart from Pompeii': *Excavations within the walls of Caerwent*, 18.

[30] T. Wright, *Ruins of the city of Uriconium*, Shrewsbury 1860, 69.

[31] 'Excavation of a Roman town at Wroxeter', *ILN*, 4 Sept. 1859, 386. This was probably written by Wright himself. Although it is possible that this could be an example of imperial Victorian Britain 'talking up' its important past in relation to imperial Rome, it is also indicative of changing ideas about the nature of Roman Britain.

plaster found at Wroxeter he first evoked the image of walls covered with 'fine historical subjects as in the walls of Pompeii'. Having created the image, only then does he acknowledge that 'nothing of this kind has yet been found at Uriconium'.[32] There is a similar juxtaposition in a newspaper report of the Cirencester mosaics, in which the author (probably Buckman) compares them with those at Pompeii and then adds that 'of course they were made by inferior workmen'.[33] The many references to Pompeii, and the importance attached to the findings there, are indicative of a major shift in the way in which Roman Britain was conceptualised in the 1850s and 1860s.

Collecting and museums

The 1853 *JBAA* contains a detailed description of a collection in the Maidstone house of the antiquary Thomas Charles. The house itself was suitably ancient and appears to have been, either intentionally or otherwise, a setting in which the antiquities could be realistically displayed. The description begins at the entrance: 'A venerable porch with a massive door still furnished with its ancient knocker and studded with medieval nails.' Among the objects inside the article mentions 'antique chairs, each of which has a history; large Indian vessels inlaid with silver cases, cases of Australian birds, the staff head of the colours of his regiment, borne by Mr. Charles' brother at the battle of Salamanca, a collection of fossil fish and a diptych that had been found at St Peter's church founded by St Boniface, uncle to the queen of Henry III'.[34] It is only after this lengthy description that the article turns to the Roman antiquities that were displayed in glass cases running the length of the room. The detail of the description and the manner in which objects, such as the diptych and the banner, were linked to named individuals recall the methods of Scott or the Musée Cluny in Paris.[35] It was a setting that emphasised age rather than specific periods and thus decontextualised the individual objects. They no longer represented either their date or function; but had become instead props in an idealised and unspecific past.[36]

[32] Wright, *Uriconium*, 49.
[33] *WGS*, 24 Sept. 1849.
[34] Anon., 'Proceedings of the congress', *JBAA* ix (1853), 413–14.
[35] The Musée Cluny had been created in 1843 as a result of bringing together the medieval collections of two Frenchmen, Albert Lenoir and Alexandre Du Sommerard. They were housed in Du Sommerard's medieval house in Paris: S. Bann, *The clothing of Cleo: a study of the representation of history in nineteenth-century Britain and France*, Cambridge 1984, 77.
[36] Thomas Charles was a doctor. He took part in a number of excavations at Roman sites in Kent. After his death in 1855 he left his house and collection to the town of Maidstone. His friend, the illustrator Charles Pretty, became the curator of the museum that also housed the collections of the Kent Archaeological Society founded in 1858. Roach Smith criticised both Charles and Pretty for their failure to produce a catalogue: 'Every year now weakens the means of identification of many of the most interesting objects, and unfortunately Mr. Charles never even labelled them': *Collectanea antiqua*, vi. 313.

These general collections were severely criticised by those who sought to portray archaeology as a science. Predictably, Roach Smith led the attack. He described the collecting activities of the dilettante gentlemen of the past as 'the odious and still prevailing propensity to appropriate antiquities to gratify the childish feelings of retaining possession of things as merely old'.[37] He contrasted this with his own approach, describing how the whole tone and character of his future life had been influenced by the sight of Roman remains being destroyed in the city of London: 'I became at once a collector; and something more; I studied what I collected.'[38] Roach Smith was not alone in his views. In 1851, Lloyd Baker, the chairman of the Cotteswold Naturalists' Field Club, told his members that fifty years before collectors and museums were laughed at because their museums were too often 'A collection of heterogeneous objects, whose interest lay in their rarity and the only pleasure of the possessor was being able to say that he had got such and such things that others had not.'[39] He warned that although collecting was on the increase 'yet it is often to be regretted that the collection is commenced too vaguely, in which case much of the labour is wasted or misdirected'.

Some 'collections' hardly merited the title at all. A report in the JBAA in 1848 described the sorry state of the artefacts salvaged from the Roman centre of Bath. They were owned by the local Philosophical Society, but the author found they were housed in what could only be described as a lumber-room:

> A more chaotic scene I never beheld. Heaps of books, manuscripts, bills of parcels, plaster casts, fragments of sculpture, boxes of Samian ware, encaustic tiles, pieces of Roman amphorae and mortaria, were all thrown together ... A huge heap of encaustic church tiles lay half smothered in dust, presenting a quiet leaning post for the ponderous cast of a gigantic head and shoulders of a Hercules or Jupiter, who seemed to the imagination to recline his head as if dismayed at the surrounding chaos – looking like Caius Marius mourning over the ruins of Carthage.[40]

This was an extreme example and would have been criticised in any age. But many of the collections do appear to have consisted of a somewhat motley selection of different objects put together without any real purpose. The contents of some of the early museums do not appear to have differed substan-

---

[37] Roach Smith, 'Roman remains at Chester', 232. Roach Smith's friend, Charles Warne, was even more disparaging. He talked of those who dug in burial mounds for no better reason than the: 'indulgence of a craving acquisitiveness, and the adornment of glass cases with ill-understood relics, to be paraded for the empty admiration of those who may descend to flatter the equally vain and ignorant collectors': Roach Smith, *Retrospections*, iii.178.

[38] Idem, *Retrospections*, i. 114.

[39] Lloyd Baker, 'Address', PCNFC i (1853), p. vii.

[40] Anon., 'Proceedings', JBAA iv (1848), 148–9. The author was probably Roach Smith.

tially from the Charles collection in Maidstone.[41] And even quite serious collectors showed decidedly squirrel-like tendencies. In spite of his keen interest in Roman artefacts, and the fact that he obviously took his archaeological activities seriously, Wire's museum in Colchester also contained a mixture of objects more reminiscent of a cabinet of curiosities than a serious collection. Indeed he called it his old curiosity shop.[42] And Joseph Mayer's Egyptian Museum in Liverpool has been described as 'trembling on the verge of chaos'.[43]

Clearly there was some way to go before antiquarian collections could be regarded as a serious aid to study. There was agreement that collections should enable detailed comparisons and thus allow the development of a system of categorisation, similar to those developed in other sciences such as botany. Indeed, Charles Newton told the Archaeological Institute that 'A museum of antiquities is to the Archaeologist what a botanical garden is to the Botanist. It presents his subject compendiously, synoptically, suggestively, not in the desultory and accidental order in which he would otherwise be brought into contact with its details.'[44] The difficulties arose when they tried to decide how best to go about achieving this aim. There were disagreements about what should be collected, how objects should be described and displayed and even who should own them.

The first requirement was to be able to correctly attribute artefacts to particular periods, but lack of knowledge frequently made this difficult. The availability of a framework offered by an accepted chronology in the classical texts, meant that issues of attribution were more straightforward in those collections that were primarily Roman. For instance, as its name suggests, the 'Museum of Roman Antiquities' in Caerleon was set up to house the Roman artefacts from the fortress site. The catalogue confirms that the majority of the contents were both Roman and local. It also illustrates the way in which common assumptions about Roman Britain influenced the way in which the objects were described. The tendency to use the generic label 'Roman' obscured the fact that Britain had been a part of the empire for four hundred years with the result that Roman Britain was presented as a static and unchanging society. Another assumption, that Romano-British products were inferior, meant that any well-made artefacts were automatically presumed to be imported. For instance, in the section on Samian ware, Lee pointed out how abundant such ware was on Roman sites in Britain, but concluded that 'There are very sound reasons for believing that the superior

[41] For instance Neville's museum at Audley End and early museums in Colchester and Cirencester.

[42] Wire to anon., 2 Feb. 1852, Wire letter book. Charles Dickens's book of the same name was published in 1840–1.

[43] This is quoted in Gibson and Wright, *Joseph Mayer*, 43.

[44] Newton, 'Study of archaeology', 26. It is worth remembering that many antiquarians were also interested in natural history. For instance Buckman was a professor of botany and Lee was an experienced geologist. Both men were therefore used to working with systems of classification.

kinds of this ware were chiefly imported from Gaul and Germany. But there can be no doubt that an inferior description was manufactured in England.'[45] Such assumptions, and the resulting museum displays, perpetuated the notion that Roman Britain itself was inferior and that the really important developments were those that took place in Rome.[46]

But these were matters of interpretation within a known framework. Artefacts from Celtic and Saxon Britain were significantly less well documented and therefore presented greater problems. As John Akerman remarked in his *Archaeological index*, 'How much such a work has been needed will be seen by reference to many volumes of very imposing size and great pretensions, where Celtic, Roman and Anglo Saxon objects are confounded with each other in a manner calculated in every way to embarrass and perplex the archaeological student.'[47]

Graves were a particularly important source for artefacts, but antiquarians experienced difficulty in distinguishing between those created prior to the Roman occupation and those that had been made after their departure. Graves dating from the period of Roman occupation itself were easier to identify because of the greater familiarity of the artefacts found in them. A reviewer of Akerman's *Pagan Saxondom* highlighted the problem: 'It is no easy matter to detail distinguishing characteristics of an Anglo Saxon barrow from one of an earlier date.'[48] The attribution of artefacts from such graves was difficult and was made more so where artefacts of different periods were found on the same site. For instance, among the few Celtic objects in the Caerleon museum were some bronze 'celts'.[49] Roach Smith and Wright had argued that as they were probably of Roman manufacture, they should be classified as Roman or Romano-British. But Lee disagreed, arguing that although they had been discovered on a Roman site, they were manufactured for use by the Celts: 'It is almost certain that many celts were made in Roman times, and probably by Roman hands; but as they were not introduced by the conquerors,

---

[45] Lee, *Isca Silurum*, 27. The labourers on excavation sites shared the assumption as this comment, reported by Richard Neville suggests: 'Other relics are of earlier date and better workmanship, and to use an expression of my labourers, everything is "more regular Roman;" they term it, in consequence, significantly, "the best" ware': 'Remarks on Roman pottery chiefly discovered in Cambridgeshire and Essex', *AJ* x (1853), 225.

[46] In 1851, the year the British Room in the British Museum was opened, a guide to the museum's antiquities omits all references to British or Romano-British antiquities 'being as yet too insufficiently arranged to admit of classification or description': Vaux, *Handbook*, preface.

[47] Akerman, *Archaeological index*, preface.

[48] Anon., 'Archaeological notices and antiquarian intelligence', *JBAA* xii (1856), 102. This was probably written by the historian and Anglo-Saxon expert, John Kemble.

[49] This was the contemporary name for a bronze axe head or chisel. These objects had been described thus because earlier antiquaries had supposed them to be the instrument to which the Romans gave the name of Celts. Wright felt that it was 'not good as a technical term, because it is mistaken too generally as implying that things to which it is applied are Celtic and it would therefore be better to lay it aside': *Celt, Roman and Saxon*, 72.

and as they are chiefly associated with Celtic remains, it seems to me that they cannot well be classed as Roman antiquities.'[50] However the artefacts could offer guidance, for instance when Neville discovered two bodies in one grave in Essex: 'Here we have one tumulus containing two different modes of internment, which were customary at two different periods, one Roman, the other British.'[51] He used the artefacts as a guide to the age of the bodies: 'With the un-burnt skeleton we found flint weapons, acknowledged to be the earliest relics of the earliest inhabitants. Next came burnt bones, iron knife and bronze fibula fragments, Roman and covered in plating. Therefore this would lead us to suppose it belonged to a later period and would tend to confirm the two distinct burials.'[52]

The layout of the collections was also open to debate. The Danish 'three age' system, according to which objects were divided into three basic types, stone, bronze and iron was not used by the museums in this study, although its influence can be detected in Neville's analysis of grave artefacts. The failure to use the system was not a result of ignorance since the Danish archaeologist Jens Worsaae had visited Britain on several occasions and lectured to the national archaeological bodies; his books had been translated into English; and he maintained a long correspondence with Roach Smith. But it was heavily criticised by, amongst others, Thomas Wright who called it 'a vague system of metallic periods'.[53] He attacked the system again in a paper he delivered to the BAAS in 1854: 'The proper and the only correct arrangement of a museum of antiquities was the ethnological one.'[54]

It is possible that a system that had been devised to classify pre-historic objects did not appear relevant to collections that were mainly composed of Roman and later artefacts. But it is also possible that the notion of describing the Roman remains as 'Iron Age' presented difficulties to the antiquarians. The idea of the primacy and superiority of classical artefacts and the civilisations that had produced them was still very much a part of the antiquarians' mental map and was an assumption that underpinned much of their work. Their writings are scattered with references to the superiority of the Romans, what they taught their British subjects and what was still to be learned by emulating Roman methods. Viewed in this way, the Romans were almost ahistorical. To see them as a part of an 'Iron Age', lumped together with others

---

[50] Lee, *Isca Silurum*, 111. Lee commented that: 'it was perfectly natural that the new comers, with their increased facilities for casting metals, would like to carry on a lucrative trade by supplying the natives with them'.

[51] Neville, *Sepulchra exposita*, 28.

[52] Ibid. This is a good early example of techniques that would become more common later in the century.

[53] Wright, *Celt, Roman and Saxon*, p. viii.

[54] Idem, 'Early ethnology of Britain', GM xlii (1854), 604. He was still arguing his case with the pre-historian John Lubbock in 1866. He told Mayer that 'Sir John Lubbock had prepared a paper against me on the bronze dagger to read at the Ethnological Society by which I am to be annihilated': Wright to Mayer 1 Mar. 1866, BL, MS Add. 33347.

and seen as a phase of material culture, probably required a leap in conceptual thinking that many antiquarians, including Wright, were unwilling to make.

If there is little evidence to suggest that the Danish system was adopted in the museums, there was no common alternative. The original layout of the Caerleon museum is not known, but Edward Lee's catalogue is probably a reasonable guide to the way in which the artefacts were arranged. He chose to divide them into material categories of stone, earthen [ware] (that included tessellated pavements), vegetable, animal and metallic. He had a separate catalogue of coins and two further sections, Celtic remains and medieval antiquities. He stated that he had based his arrangement on that used by Mr William Wilde in the catalogue of the Museum of the Royal Irish Academy: 'This arrangement seems admirably adapted to objects of one period, though not at all proper to be carried out in a general catalogue comprising objects of various ages.'[55] It is significant that Wilde's system was designed to classify scientific collections of biological and geological objects with which Lee as a geologist would be familiar.[56] As Lee had travelled extensively in Scandinavia, it is more than likely, given his interests, that he had visited the museum in Copenhagen. His comments suggest that had his artefacts covered a longer period, he might have used the Danish system.

Roach Smith's catalogue of his Museum of London Antiquities (see plate 4) was also largely made up of Roman objects. He stressed that although the collection had been formed as a result of a series of accidents rather than through a coherent acquisitions policy, it was not a result of mere fancy or caprice. The objects are divided into even more sections than those in Lee's catalogue, namely sculptures, bronzes, pottery, red glazed pottery, potters' stamps, glass, tiles, pavements and wall paintings, sandals in leather, utensils and implements, coins and finally Roman and Romano-British artefacts. What is interesting about this arrangement is that, despite his familiarity with the Danish work, it is not based on any apparent system of classification and reads more like an inventory. Roach Smith may have been the Roman expert of his day, but the sections on 'Roman' and 'Romano-British' indicate that he too had trouble in attributing objects with any certainty. When he describes an enamelled bronze plate he says the workmanship and ornamentation are comparable to Roman enamels, but the details of the design suggest that it might be sixth century. Or, about a spear head in iron, 'I have placed these two spear heads under the head 'Roman', chiefly because the sockets for the stave are perfect, while the early Saxon heads, which, in other respects they resemble, are almost invariably split in the socket'.[57]

Of the four locations examined in this book only John Buckman's rough sketch for the museum in Cirencester still exists.[58] It shows a rectangular

---

[55] Lee, *Isca Silurum*, introduction.
[56] See W. Chapman, 'The organisational context in the history of archaeology: Pitt Rivers and other British archaeologists in the 1860s', *Antiquaries Journal* lxix (1989), 23–42.
[57] C. Roach Smith, *Catalogue of the Museum of London Antiquities*, London 1854, 84, 83.
[58] It is in a box labelled 'early museum' in a storeroom in Cirencester Museum.

space with seven cases around the walls in which were displayed bone and glass; pottery; tiles and wall paintings; potters' names and marks; bronzes; iron implements; and vases. Although the range of objects was less extensive, the Cirencester display seems to bear some resemblance to Roach Smith's arrangement of his collection. But what made the Cirencester collection unique was the prominent position given to the tessellated pavements that took up the whole of the floor space in the centre of the building. Indeed, readers of *ILN* could have been excused for thinking that the pavements were the only exhibits on display as nothing else is shown.[59] Buckman described the museum to the Cotteswold Club: 'You were struck with the one thousand exhibits not from their intrinsic value nor from their beauty of form, but from the many articles they contain of domestic use.'[60] However as in the *ILN* picture, the space given to the pavements in newspaper reports and Buckman's book, all suggest that the pavements were regarded as the 'stars' of the display. As the frequent comparisons to Pompeii indicate, the effect was to ensure that Romano-British Cirencester was pictured as more 'Roman' than 'British'. It is a good example of the way in which the view of the past could be influenced by a museum display emphasising certain objects rather than others.

Ownership was another contentious issue. Collections had traditionally been created by private individuals, either as an eclectic mixture of the strange and exotic, reflecting the personal interests of the individual collector; or as representative of artefacts of the great classical civilisations. The Charles Museum was an example of the former; the collection of ancient marbles and specimens of ancient art owned by John Disney was an example of the latter. Disney donated his collection to the University of Cambridge in 1850, the same year that he endowed the chair of classical archaeology first held by John Marsden. A catalogue to Disney's collection was published in 1846–8 and was reviewed in the *AJ*. The review praised Disney's actions in sharing knowledge of his treasures with the public, but drew attention to the number of artefacts that were not so available: 'Few persons are aware of the vast aggregate amount of the private collections in this country.'[61]

To the activists in the emerging science of archaeology, the Charles and Disney collections offended in several respects. What the new science required was orderly, systematic collections of all the artefacts from a particular period, not just those judged to be representative of 'great art' or a reflection of personal caprice. Once formed, the collections had to be in the public

---

[59] Anon., 'Roman tessellated pavement at Cirencester', *ILN*, 2 Aug. 1856, 123.
[60] J. Buckman, 'Annual address', *PCNFC* ii (1854), in a report of the meeting on 27 Jan. 1857.
[61] Anon., 'Notice of archaeological publications', *AJ* vi (1849), 83. It was still much the same later in the century, as an 1883 review of Professor Michaelis's *Ancient marbles in Great Britain* pointed out: 'The student naturally wants to know the whereabouts of all the remains of ancient art and as these are spread about the country in various private collections, he was left pretty much without a guide': *The Antiquary* viii (1883), 27.

domain, either physically in a museum, or alternatively in a well-researched catalogue. Most private collections did not meet these criteria. For example, the Bathurst Museum in Cirencester was open to the public, but when Arthur Church wrote its first catalogue in 1867 he described the arrangement as 'unsatisfactory' and the absence of a catalogue 'had been felt as a drawback to the value and usefulness of the collection'.[62] At the Archaeological Institute's annual meeting in 1855, the president listed a number of private collections that were open to students of antiquity and, by implication that offered some of the best material for study. They belonged to William Rolfe,[63] Thomas Bateman,[64] Richard Neville, Lord Londesborough,[65] Joseph Mayer and the 'late Mr Charles at Maidstone'.[66]

It is instructive to look at what was actually offered in these collections. None of them was open to the general public. A prospective visitor would have to know both of the museums' existence and the nature of their contents, and they would also have to have an introduction to their owners. One of the advantages of membership of an archaeological association was that it did open the door to such collections. But to those who were outside this exclusive circle, the collections remained essentially unknown and unavailable. They were also often poorly catalogued: only one of the museums cited by the Archaeological Institute, Bateman's, was properly catalogued.[67] Joseph Mayer's Egyptian collection was catalogued when his museum opened in 1852, but all the objects added subsequently, including Rolfe's, remained uncatalogued, except for a very crude system of acquisition numbers.[68] No catalogue for Neville's collection was ever published which doubtless prompted a some-

[62] Church, *Roman remains at Cirencester*, preface.
[63] William Rolfe (1779–1859) was a farmer, town councillor and antiquarian from Sandwich in Kent. He did some excavating in Roman Richborough, but his collection consisted mainly of Anglo-Saxon and medieval remains. Most of his collection was bought in 1857 by Joseph Mayer, with Roach Smith and Joseph Clarke acting as intermediaries.
[64] Thomas Bateman (1821–61) was a non-conformist from a wealthy family in Derbyshire. He was primarily involved with the excavation of barrows and was nicknamed the 'barrow knight' by a fellow antiquarian, Stephen Isaacson. He was very interested in ethnology and the new 'science' of phrenology. His son sold large parts of his collection, but some artefacts and his papers were bought by Sheffield Museum in 1893 for £1,600.
[65] Lord Albert Conyngham, first president of the BAA, was an enthusiastic excavator of Anglo-Saxon barrows assisted by Akerman. After inheriting a fortune in 1849 he bought a country estate, including its museum of antiquities. He had the contents drawn by Fairholt and described by Wright in a private publication, *Miscellanea graphica*, London 1854.
[66] These were by no means the only good local collections. Others that the president might have mentioned were John Clayton's Museum of Roman Antiquities at Chesters and the duke of Northumberland's collection of British antiquities that he had offered to the British Museum if they would create a British Room.
[67] Anon., *A descriptive catalogue of the antiquities and miscellaneous objects preserved in the museum of Thomas Bateman at Lomberdale House, Derbyshire*, Bakewell 1855. The contents were divided into five sections: Britannic, ethnological, relics, arms and armour and collections illustrative of arts and manufacture. The Britannic section was subdivided into Celtic, Roman and Romano-British.
[68] See Gibson and Wright, *Joseph Mayer*, 43.

what pious hope in the *AJ* that 'It were much to be desired that this spirited antiquary should be disposed to produce a description or catalogue of the Audley End Museum, the creation of his zeal and intelligence in the cause of national archaeology.'[69] In view of his active role in archaeological matters the lack of a catalogue is rather surprising and it is possible that he felt that his numerous, illustrated articles in the journals should suffice.

Apart from detailed knowledge, the great advantage offered by a catalogue was that it ensured, at least on paper, that the material contained in a collection would remain intact. The greatest drawback of private collections was that their future was never assured: they were frequently broken up and dispersed when the owner died. As the antiquarian Vere Irving pointed out in 1859, 'It often seems impossible to account for the way in which articles in private collections, the existence of which was at one time well known among antiquaries, disappear without leaving a trace behind.'[70] Once dispersed, objects could no longer be linked to a particular site and to other objects, with a consequent loss of information.[71] Roach Smith used a large collection of Roman artefacts from the Cirencester area owned by a Mr Purnell as an example of what often happened to private collections: 'Now it had passed through the hands of the London auctioneer and is lost to science. I, in vain, urged him to print an illustrated catalogue. He was a man of affluence and could well have afforded the cost and the collection was worthy of permanent record.'[72] In his preface to the catalogue of his own collection, Roach Smith complained that of all the collections of London antiquities obtained as a result of building work in the 1830s and 1840s, only his own remained intact; all the rest had been sold at auction.[73] William Wire only produced a catalogue of the objects in his collection in order to inform potential purchasers and facilitate their sale.[74]

Some serious collectors did try to ensure that their collections were not dispersed. A review of Bateman's catalogue stated that 'Fully alive to the uncertainty attending the preservation and transmission of all private collections, Mr. Bateman has wisely determined to leave a record of that which he has brought together.'[75] When financial pressures meant that collections had

---

69 Anon., 'Proceedings', *AJ* xi (1854), 399.

70 G. Vere Irving, 'On treasure trove', *JBAA* xv (1859), 93.

71 The great importance attached to Faussett's collection was the result of the fact that he had kept a careful record of his excavations, recording sites and which objects had been found together. This was almost unique in the mid eighteenth-century and was still often neglected in the 1850s.

72 Roach Smith, *Retrospections*, i. 39. In the preface to *Remains of Roman art*, Buckman thanks Purnell along with the Revd W. F. Powell, T. C. Brown and a Mrs Mullings for lending their 'valuable relics' to be drawn for the illustrations.

73 C. Roach Smith, *Illustrations of Roman London*, London 1859, preface. He lists the other collectors as Alfred Kempe, John Newman, George Gwilt, Mr Price and Mr Chaffers.

74 Wire mentioned the catalogue in a letter to the engraver Charles Clarke, 30 Jan. 1852: Wire letter book.

75 Anon., 'Mr Bateman's museum of antiquities', *JBAA* xii (1856), 201.

to be sold, these owners searched for individuals willing to buy the whole collection, rather than single objects. Mayer was probably projecting his own feelings as a collector when he wrote to Rolfe that 'I cannot bear the idea of breaking up and scattering a collection that must have been a source of pleasure to you to collect.'[76] But the ultimate example of a collector striving to protect his collection must be Roach Smith. When financial difficulties and ill health forced him to consider the sale of his collection he produced a catalogue 'to ensure its integrity and to serve for reference and authentication'.[77] He refused Lord Londesborough's offer of £3,000 in favour of the British Museum's £2,000 because he believed that the museum was more likely to keep it together.[78]

Another way of avoiding dispersal of private collections was by the establishment of locally-based public museums that could act as collection centres for a whole locality. The four areas in this study demonstrate the various ways in which such museums came to be founded, differing approaches reflecting different social structures. Indeed, the significance of the semantic change from 'collection' to 'museum' is an indication of how the locus of control was moving from private individuals to the wider community. In Chester, although there were some rather half-hearted attempts on the part of the archaeological society to create a museum, there was no real movement away from a proliferation of small privately-owned collections until the 1880s. In Cirencester, the museum was concentrated in one set of private hands, although, by offering a place to objects owned by other people, it did make some gestures towards being representative of the town as a whole. In Caerleon, the museum was created by a local archaeological society with no assistance from the local authority. In Colchester, although the town council initially tried to form a collection, the local archaeological society came to play an increasingly dominant role and the museum was eventually financed and administered by the two bodies acting in tandem. Despite their initial differences the museums in Caerleon, Cirencester and Colchester could all be recognised as suitable repositories for local artefacts. But they could be a mixed blessing as Augustus Franks pointed out in 1852: 'Local museums are institutions of great value, as they rescue from destruction many relics which would otherwise be lost, and they encourage a local feeling of reverence for the memorials of the past.' But there was a sting in the tail: 'Objects of great importance to the archaeologist often lie buried in these far distant recepta-

---

[76] J. Mayer to W. Rolfe, 8 Sept. 1857, cited in Gibson and Wright, *Joseph Mayer*, 12.

[77] Roach Smith, *Retrospections* ii. 224.

[78] Roach Smith's collection came on the market only a year after the British Museum's failure to buy the Faussett collection had provoked such fury: ibid. 224–36, and see ch. 1 above. The former includes the petition to parliament supporting the sale to the national collection. It is signed by all the 'great and good' in the contemporary archaeological world. Roach Smith's collection formed the nucleus of the museum's Romano-British collection.

cles, affording him facts of the highest value as links in a great chain, but in their isolation perfectly useless.'[79]

The market

The increased interest in British antiquities and the sheer number that was being discovered meant that collecting, previously regarded as the exclusive province of the wealthy upper class, became a possibility for many more individuals. So, whilst the historian John Kemble could declare that 'we are collectors even as our predecessors were; but we are collectors with a definite purpose and in a definite method',[80] there were many other collectors whose interest was anything but archaeological and whose collecting activities were frequently at odds with the scientific and preservation concerns of the antiquarians. As Roach Smith commented in 1857

> This taste for collecting has been fostered by the increased attention paid to archaeology. But it has not only grown with the science, it has far outstripped its audience... The possibility of applying antiquities to historical, artistic or any useful purpose is too often lost sight of in the eagerness of competition and in the race for obtaining possession.[81]

To emphasis his point, Roach Smith cited the tourists who visited the Roman *pharos* (lighthouse) at Dover merely because it was old, or worse still those who 'chip off pieces of ancient walls and pick out tesserae from pavements to carry away as trophies'.[82]

Given the level of interest in antiquities both amongst the antiquarians who wanted to study them and a general public who wanted to possess them as curiosities, it was probably inevitable that a brisk market in antique objects should be created. Charles Wellbeloved commented on the high prices paid for 'the most worthless articles from persons not able to appreciate the value of what they were eager to possess'.[83] But the race for possession and the consequent inflation of prices was not confined to the ignorant; it was also found among dealers and more knowledgeable collectors. In a letter to William Wire, Roach Smith told him that one coin displayed at a meeting of the Numismatic Society had disappeared: 'In my opinion it was purloined by someone (God knows who). Mr. Pindall at Sotheby's the auctioneer, states that the thefts that are perpetuated in his rooms by coin collectors are most

---

[79] A. Franks, 'The collection of British antiquities in the British Museum', *AJ* ix (1852), 14. Franks was the first curator of the British Room in the British Museum and gave an annual report to the Archaeological Institute on new acquisitions.
[80] J. M. K. [Kemble], 'Introduction', *AJ* vi (1849), 2.
[81] Roach Smith, *Collectanea antiqua*, iv. 197.
[82] Ibid. iv. 214.
[83] C. Wellbeloved, *Eburacum or York under the Romans*, London 1842, 144.

scandalous. He has detected two persons, rich collectors in the actual fact.'[84] There was often fierce competition between potential owners, as happened in the case of the ninth-century Aethelswith ring, dug up by an agricultural worker and hung on his dog's collar. The Yorkshire Philosophical Society had wanted to buy it, but was beaten at the sale by Canon W. Greenwell, who promised to leave it to the society in his will, but instead sold it to Augustus Franks.[85] And there was the obsessive book collector, Thomas Phillips, whose zeal to buy was reputed to have inflated prices at auctions and caused many books of national importance to be lost to public bodies which could not match his bids.[86]

The booming market ensured that workmen, who were usually the first to unearth artefacts, tried to profit from their discoveries. This presented a dilemma to the archaeologists who, on the one hand, wanted to alert the men to look out for artefacts because of their archaeological value, but in so doing raised awareness of their potential monetary value. As in Colchester, these differences led to frequent disagreements between the men, the antiquarians and the owner of the site. In London, Roach Smith encouraged the workmen 'by the most persuasive of all arguments, to preserve, and also to understand what to preserve'.[87] He adds, 'For this I was summoned before the Lord Mayor as a receiver of stolen property.'[88] In Chester, Massie seems to have been more successful in persuading the workmen to bring him the artefacts they found.[89]

As they realised the market potential of objects workmen attempted to sell their discoveries, often destroying artefacts in the process. For instance a vase filled with coins that had adhered together in a large mass was broken open and the coins separated with spades: 'In this way several hundreds had disappeared before the fact of the treasure trove was known.'[90] A misunderstanding between a finder and a local antiquary helps to illustrate the difficulties experienced by the antiquarians in their dealings with the workmen. Vases had been discovered near to the site of a tessellated pavement and the antiquary asked to see some coins in the hope that they would assist him in dating it. But the workman assumed that this would lead to him being prosecuted for selling them, so he refused. And the exact spot where Roman and Celtic

---

[84] Roach Smith to Wire, 26 Jan. 1844.

[85] Franks gave the ring to the British Museum: Wilson, *Forgotten collector*, 30.

[86] A. N. L. Munby, *The catalogues of manuscripts and printed books of Sir Thomas Phillips: their composition and distribution*, iv, Cambridge 1951, 35, 169.

[87] Roach Smith, *Museum of London Antiquities*, p. v.

[88] Idem, *Retrospections*, ii. 207.

[89] Massie was probably more tolerant in his attitude than an antiquary in Colchester who described the workmen on the cloaca site as 'knavish but lavishly paid': Duncan, 'Roman cloaca', 223.

[90] Mr Hartland, 'Proceedings', *JBAA* xii (1856), 236. Hartland reported that the market price was 2*d*. each, more than most of them were worth and many of them had been bartered for beer.

skulls had been discovered on the banks of the Thames 'has been most jealously concealed by both workmen and curiosity dealers'.[91]

Given the high demand and rising prices, it was probably inevitable that some individuals would turn to forgery as a way of exploiting the market. Letters and journal articles indicate that the antiquarians were aware of the danger, as Richard Neville told the Archaeological Insitute in 1857:

> I am afraid that so long as the present keen research after antiquities continues and so many collectors are in the field, so long will such a state of things [as forgery] exist. This keenness of research is of course a necessary consequence of the spread of archaeological knowledge ... It is the great eagerness shown by collectors which has led to the results we now experience.[92]

However the definition of forgery was often unclear. It had been accepted practice in the eighteenth century for broken fragments of antique statues and ornaments to be restored and for unrelated pieces to be moulded together to 'create' a new whole object.[93] As late as the 1840s, Roach Smith found it acceptable to add a nose to 'a very fine antique bust of Marcus Aurelius, before presenting it to Lord Londesborough for display in his sculpture gallery.[94] The problem was highlighted in a letter Fairholt wrote from Rome in 1857:

> Rome is not the place to get antiquities, if they are genuine they are absurdly dear and forgeries of all kinds abound. In fact the making of antiquities is a regular trade in Italy, conducted with much ingenuity and talent by really clever people who carefully study genuine antiques and imitate their peculiarities ... Travellers will eagerly buy there what they would not care to purchase from honest traders at home.[95]

Sometimes workmen attempted to sell miscellaneous collections of objects as Roman antiquities from a specific site. When Thomas Gutson visited a newly-revealed stretch of Roman wall in London, he asked whether any pottery had been discovered. He was immediately presented with an earthen lamp, a bronze fibula, two brass coins of Nero and Hadrian, several necks of amphorae, portions of Samian ware, a beautiful Etruscan head of Vesta, a fragment of a Venus and three others in terracotta, besides two small bronze

[91] H. Syer Cuming, 'On the discovery of Celtic crania in the vicinity of London', *JBAA* xiii (1857), 237.

[92] R. Neville, 'Proceedings', *AJ* xiv (1857), 172.

[93] An example was the imported Greek vase displayed to the BAA in 1855. A penknife scratch revealed that: 'the ancient Greek cup is mounted upon the foot of a Venetian goblet and the rich handles were manufactured at Murano in the seventeenth century': J. Syer Cuming, 'On frauds in archaeology', *JBAA* xi (1855), 68. Cuming, pointed out that 'Italy had ever been the hotbed of forgery'.

[94] Roach Smith, *Retrospections*, i. 114. The middle years of nineteenth century was also the high point of the Victorian passion for restoring Gothic churches, another indication that the 'old' was not always what it appeared to be.

[95] Cited in idem, *Collectanea antiqua*, v. 61, 82.

Egyptian figures of Osiris. Unsurprisingly, Gutson smelled a rat: 'Knowing it to be utterly impossible for such a collection to be discovered in the heart of the city, I watched the excavations but I have only been able to trace two men engaged in this system of deceit.'[96] More typical were the activities of dealers who travelled around the country selling wares to unsuspecting antiquarians. The archaeological journals are full of general warnings and, where possible, the specific details of the individuals concerned.

The importance of these forgeries to the antiquarians was not so much the monetary fraud as the question it cast over the validity of the objects themselves, and therefore on their value as evidence. Material objects were so highly valued by the antiquarians because they were seen as a direct link with the past and conveyed knowledge that was not available through any other source. As Roach Smith remarked on the inscriptions found on the Roman Wall, 'They are historical records of unquestionable authority, free from interpretation or fraud of any kind.'[97] More than that, they were the source of evidence of the past that was unique to antiquarians and gave them a claim to be taken seriously as students of the past, alongside historians and their texts. Seyer Cuming summed up the difficulties posed by faked objects: 'They inflict a wrong upon our faith, rob us of our money, create suspicion and distrust, and heap ridicule, discredit and contempt upon the science of archaeology.'[98]

Objects as symbols

The previous section examined the ways in which objects were used to study the Romans and Roman Britain. However tenuous or fanciful, the focus of study was always on the past. This section will examine the ways in which objects were used in a present in which they were owned by somebody and could be displayed and arranged in a number of different ways, or could be props in the creation of an historical narrative. In other words, rather than describing the Roman past, such objects were descriptive of their owners and of contemporary beliefs about the past.

The objects an individual surrounds himself with in everyday life help to create the public persona he presents to the world. They are an act of self-definition, an autobiography even, through which the individual can proclaim a sense of 'self'. To some extent this applies to all the objects in one's surroundings, but it is particularly applicable to those objects that are chosen in a self-conscious manner for a collection or display. Seen in this

[96] T. Gutson, 'Proceedings', *JBAA* x (1853), 85. Wire reported a similar disparate collection that was supposed to have been unearthed in Colchester. 'It is said by some antiquarians that the whole of the above, excepting the urn, were of modern fabrication': WWJ, entry for 19 Mar. 1844.
[97] Roach Smith, *Retrospections*, i. 170.
[98] Syer Cuming, 'On fraud in archaeology', 73.

light, historical objects are divorced from the past and instead represent personal attributes of their owner in the present. Susan Pearce has described this as a process whereby the symbolic qualities of objects are used to 'create an idea of our essential selves in the past, present and future'.[99] The cultural historian, Walter Benjamin, described ownership as 'the most intimate relationship that one can have to objects; not that they come alive in him, it is he who lives in them'.[100] Probably because of the passionate interest shown by collectors, the act of collecting has attracted a great deal of psychoanalytic attention. Susan Pearce used Joseph Mayer as an example of an individual whose collection appeared to 'have grown up around him as an extension of his person'.[101] And there are many other collectors who would seem to fit her description. For instance, Augustus Franks, who in addition to his work in the British Museum was also a great collector, wrote that 'Collecting is an hereditary disease, and I fear incurable.'[102] Another inveterate collector was Lady Charlotte Schreiber, who was reported as touring the pawnbrokers of Liverpool in her quest for acquisitions to add to her collection of ceramics.[103]

In nineteenth-century Britain (as now to some extent) a collection had value as a symbol of its owner's prestige and standing in his community. This was as true of small collectors in the provinces such as Charles in Maidstone, as it was of major collectors such as Charles Townley in London. As though to emphasise the identification between owner and collection, several of the larger collectors, such as Townley, had their portraits painted surrounded by their artefacts, a process which created the impression that the owners were 'a part of', rather than merely the 'owners of' their collections. Joseph Mayer chose to have his portrait painted with his collection twice. The two pictures provide interesting visual proof of changing trends in the fashion for antiquities. In 1840 William Daniels portrayed him sitting in a 'Gothic' chair, surrounded by an eclectic collection, including both Roman and medieval artefacts (see plate 5). By 1856 John Harrison is picturing him against a background entirely composed of Egyptian artefacts, a sign of his increasingly specialised interests. The fact that Roach Smith did not choose to be portrayed in such a manner is probably an indication of his more objective interest in the artefacts, although it could also have been be due to his limited finances.

---

99 S. Pearce, 'Symbols of ourselves: objects of possession', paper given at a conference on 'Material memories', Victoria and Albert Museum, April 1998.

100 W. Benjamin, 'Unpacking my library', in H. Arendt (ed.), *Illuminations*, London 1970.

101 S. Pearce, *Archaeological curatorship*, Leicester 1990, 21. See also Gibson and Wright, *Joseph Mayer*. Jas' Elsner and Roger Cardinal describe the most obsessive collectors as 'teetering between mastery and madness': *The culture of collecting*, Cambridge MA 1994, 6.

102 A. W. Franks, 'The apology of my life', in Caygill and Cherry, *A. W. Franks*, appendix II, p. 318.

103 *Diaries of Lady Charlotte Guest*, 59.

The personalised object

Thomas Bateman believed that 'The emotional character so obvious in nearly every relic that has come down to us, addresses us almost with the distinctness of vocal sounds.'[104] But the problem for the antiquarian was to understand what it was that the antiquities were 'saying', for one effect of their dual nature was to blur the element of time, so that an ancient object can appear to make the past seem either distant or almost contemporary. Austen Layard drew attention to this 'dual nature' in some comments about Rome: 'The sight of Rome, while it brings us near, as nothing else can in the same degree, to the men and the actions of the city's ancient days, it makes us at the same time, realise in a manner altogether peculiar the vastness of the interval which separates us from them.'[105]

Starting in the early nineteenth century scholars began to research the details of everyday life in the original medieval documents. It was seen as important that the details of objects, such as furniture, clothing and domestic utensils, should be correct for the period. According to an 1842 article in the *Edinburgh Review*, 'We can no longer tolerate Plantagenet princes and princesses in the garb and character of modern courts.'[106]

A major factor in the trend towards greater accuracy was the influence of the enormously popular historical novels of Sir Walter Scott. Scott created vivid images of the past by assembling a mass of small and accurate details, in much the same way that antiquarians concerned themselves with the minutiae of archaeological and historical detail. The resemblance was acknowledged by a speaker to the Archaeological Institute in 1856: 'The impulse to which we may trace the growing taste for archaeological investigation is to be sought in the wizard's spell which emanated from Abbotsford.'[107] According to the *Edinburgh Review*, 'Scott's pre-eminent success had changed the whole tone and character of historical literature. He has substituted the picturesque for the philosophical style.'[108] The emphasis on accurate detail increased the 'felt distance' from the past. As the *Edinburgh Review* remarked, 'We acquire a habit of contemplating our ancestors, certainly not as ignorant barbarians; but as quaint respectable oddities, very much to be admired and studied, but altogether incommensurable with ourselves.'[109]

On the other hand, some objects seemed to connect at a human level in such a way as to make sense of the past in quite a different way from that of contemporary traditional history. Such objects evoked human sympathy as they tended to be those that held some imprint of a human presence and

[104] T. Bateman, 'Notices of archaeological publications', *AJ* xiii (1856), 420.
[105] Anon., 'Book review', *QR* cxv (1864), 200. The author was probably Layard.
[106] Anon., 'Book review', *Edinburgh Review* (Jan. 1842), 430.
[107] Anon., 'Notice of archaeological publications', *AJ* xiii (1856), 199.
[108] Anon., 'Book review', *Edinburgh Review* (Jan. 1842), 434.
[109] Ibid. 435.

activity. A literary example is in Dickens's description of Pompeii which he visited in 1844:

> We see at every turn the little familiar tokens of human habitation and every day pursuits; the chaffing of the bucket-rope in the stone rim of the exhausted well; the track of carriage-wheels in the pavement of the street; the marks of drinking-vessels on the stone counter of the wine shop.[110]

By drawing attention to the impact of human activity on the surroundings, Dickens emphasised the reality of human presence very much more powerfully than by merely describing the buildings. Fanny Trollope was also impressed by the immediacy of the Pompeii ruins compared with those in Rome: 'I shall never feel sent back to ages past by the columns and pediments of ancient Rome as I did by the shop counters, the oil jars and the ovens of Pompeii.'[111] It seems to have been much the same evidence of human activity that had impressed Syer Cuming when he talked about the remains discovered in the mud on the Thames embankment. They seemed to indicate that there had been a battle between Celtic and Roman forces in the area. The artefacts included examples of armour and even some skulls, but what finally brought the scene to life for Cuming was the discovery of a sandal:

> Though the tides of eighteen centuries have swept the warrior's footprint from the shore, the covering of that foot has again been gathered from the deep: so that if we have not yet confirmations strong as proofs of holy writ … we have at least sufficient to transmute that which at first loomed as an ill-defined shadow, into a visible and tangible reality.[112]

It is interesting that it should be the sandal and not the skulls that had touched Cuming's imagination. The contemporary interest in phrenology had meant that skulls had become like any other object, a subject for scientific measurement and as a result they had been rendered less suggestive as triggers for the imagination.[113] Cuming's article included a detailed description of a skull, including its measurements, which he described as having 'an ebonized appearance'. Given this description it is perhaps hardly surprising that he could not relate to it emotionally.

The same detachment did not seem to apply to whole skeletons, often discovered in circumstances suggesting a violent end and therefore inviting an explanation. Again Pompeii provided many of the most powerful examples whose presence can be detected even where it was not mentioned. Giuseppe

---

110 Dickens, *Pictures from Italy*, 411.
111 This is cited in M. Liversidge and C. Edwards (eds), *Imagining Rome: British artists and Rome in the nineteenth century*, Bristol 1996, 15.
112 H. Syer Cuming, 'Further discoveries of Celtic and Roman remains in the Thames off Battersea', *JBAA* xiv (1858), 330.
113 Cuming compared the Celtic skulls, 'a long oval form with elevated backs, and rather depressed foreheads' with the Roman, 'shorter proportions and thicker substance': ibid. 238.

Fiorelli, who was in charge of the excavations, devised a method of pouring liquid plaster into the hollows left by disintegrated remains, including human ones. The resulting plaster casts were electrifying, as a writer in the *Quarterly Review* pointed out: 'A more ghastly and painful, yet deeply interesting and touching object it is difficult to conceive. We have death itself moulded and cast – the very last struggle, the final agony brought before us. They tell their story, with a horrible dramatic truth that no sculptor could ever reach.'[114]

Although there were no comparable casts in Britain, there were several skeletons that evoked similar imaginative descriptions. When Thomas Wright, excavating the Roman remains at Wroxeter, found three skeletons in a hypocaust, he speculated on the circumstances surrounding their deaths:

> In the midst of the massacre of Roman Uriconium, these three persons, perhaps two terrified women and an old man had sought to conceal themselves by creeping into the hypocaust and perhaps they were suffocated there. Or when the house was delivered to the flames, the falling rubbish may have blocked up the outlet, so as to make it impossible for them to leave.[115]

Another skeleton had been found near Colchester lying face down and with a patera beside it. Jenkins appears to have used the very scanty evidence afforded by the artefact as the basis upon which he could create a fanciful tale: 'From the emblem of his office, and the most mortal aversion with which the Britons regarded the priests of Claudius, we may almost imagine this skeleton to have been that of a priest, who in his attempt to escape during the insurrection, had been seized by the Britons and buried alive.'[116]

There was frequently a tension between the antiquarians' search for historical accuracy based on evidence, and their desire to tell a story based on their emotional responses to ordinary people from the past. Thomas Wright's description of the violent end of Uriconium included references to a 'dreadful massacre' and survivors 'dragged away to captivity'. Given the antiquarians' comparative lack of excavation skills, Wright can have had only two sources for his account: his imagination and the early Christian texts by Gildas and Bede, written many years after the events they describe. Wright himself had this to say about events as described by Gildas: 'The whole story, built apparently on some slight notes in an old continental chronicler, displays the most

---

[114] [A. Layard], 'Review of books about Pompeii', QR cxv (1864), 332. The article contained several graphic descriptions, for instance this of a woman of about twenty-five: 'Her linen head-dress falling over her shoulders like that of a matron in a Roman statue, can still be distinguished. She had fallen on her side overcome by the heat and gasses; but a terrible struggle seems to have preceded her last agony. One arm is raised in despair; the hands are clenched convulsively. Her garments are gathered up on one side, leaving exposed a limb of beautiful shape. So perfect a mould of it has been formed by the soft and yielding mud that the cast would seem to be taken from an exquisite work of Greek art.'
[115] Wright, *Uriconium*, 39.
[116] H. Jenkins, 'On the site of Camulodunum', *Arch.* xxix (1842), 14.

profound ignorance of the period to which it relates.'[117] But the emotive way in which he describes the events owes much to Gildas, who was primarily responsible for the view that Roman Britain had met a violent end as a result of raids by the Picts. Presumably, in spite of Wright's doubts about the accuracy of the text, its contents resonated with his own emotional response to the human remains he had encountered in the ruins at Wroxeter.[118]

The object as narrative

One of the main uses served by objects was the role they played in helping to create a narrative of the past, to tell a story. Accounts of excavations and artefacts, however 'scientifically' accurate, could appear to be very dull and dry. But the associations brought to mind by particular objects helped to provide a structure, what Massie called 'a peg', around which the imagination could weave a story. And a story is what many people, both then and now, want history to provide. They look to the past to help to explain their origins and to create a picture of the characters and events that had helped to create their locality and their nation. Objects were one of the means through which such stories could be created. Their very physicality was a direct link with the past and could be used to create a sense of that past.[119] Professor Marsden emphasised this characteristic of objects when he suggested that the associations they evoked were the greatest pleasure offered by archaeology: 'The object before us, formed a part and parcel in scenes of bygone days, and imagination presents the actors to the mind's eye.'[120] He illustrated his argument by describing a scene brought to mind by the chance find of a coin:

> The coin is seen at once to be early British and Roman. From that moment the scene around you, however tame and uninteresting it may have been before, starts into life with a newly created interest. On a sudden, the hollows around are peopled with bivouacking legions and you hear the clangour of the litus and the tuba. In the stream that winds around the foot of the declivity, shaggy horses laden with trappings are quenching their thirst. In the midst stands the Praetorium encircled by the banners. The white

[117] Wright, Celt, Roman and Saxon, 397.
[118] Current archaeological thought is that far from being destroyed, there was in fact considerable rebuilding at the site after the Roman period. Gildas had a strong 'political' purpose in writing as he did as he was arguing that the Anglo-Saxons were 'God's punishment on the British' for their wickedness: R. White and P. Barker, Wroxeter: life and death of a Roman city, Stroud 1998.
[119] Objects that were either known to be, or thought to be associated with particular characters from the past were especially valued. For instance Lee was reported as owning a table and chairs belonging to Sir Thomas More (MM, 8 Aug. 1851), whilst a purse in the Charles Museum in Canterbury was said to have belonged to Oliver Cromwell: G. Syer Cuming, 'Proceedings', JBAA xv (1859).
[120] Marsden, 'Inaugural lecture', 14.

sand that glitters among the fern, has rubbed bright many a dingy breast plate; and the turf beneath our feet has been moistened with the crimson stain of bloodshed, by invaders fighting for conquest and sturdy barbarians standing up in defence of their homes and liberty. From yonder hill, the swarthy crowd rushed down furiously upon their opponents, in the hope of surprising them off their guard. At a word every Roman is at his place. A few fierce struggles ensue and then the combat begins to slacken. The barbarians retreat in confusion from the field. In a brief spate however the rout is ended and the returning legion pile up their blood-stained arms.[121]

This is a good example of the sort of vivid imaginative narratives that were prompted by simple objects. Marsden gives no details of the coin. He merely observes that it was ancient. But its discovery allowed him to bring together a whole range of other sources and impressions, supplied in great abundance through the classical texts, to create a vivid story set in a particular local landscape. The stimulus was the coin, but the story it evoked was a great deal larger than the whole. It illustrates one advantage of an object as opposed to a text as historical evidence, namely that it does allow the observer's imagination free rein. In effect it is the observer telling the story rather than the text.

Colchester is an example of a place in which the ambiguity of the remains and the vividness of what little was known could constitute a powerful stimulus to the imagination. For many local antiquarians the search for clues to substantiate and dramatise the well-known stories was at least as important as historical accuracy. In fact it could be argued that it was even more important, as Jenkins's response to the skeleton illustrates. Roach Smith was obviously aware of the dangers when he warned that 'This town is so full of ancient remains, so pregnant with historical connections and associations, that it is difficult to avoid being led into an essay, which however entertaining it might be made, would be out of place in our present proceedings.'[122] But in spite of this warning, the Colchester antiquarians continued to use the most mundane objects as evidence to support their imaginative pictures of the past. When Roach Smith, in his capacity as an expert, expressed the opinion that some finds from a burial site, which were thought to be Roman, were in fact late Iron Age from Gaul, local antiquarians were displeased. Wire tried to explain to Smith why his opinion had so annoyed his fellow townsmen:

Had you stated that the ninth legion was routed and the infantry slain by Boudicea: that the common soldiers bodies were gathered and burnt on the Druidical altars; that the remains were afterwards collected ... and that the ox head irons were the trestles of the legions camp tables and ... the

---

121 Ibid. 14–15. An almost identical passage to Marsden's appears in an article in the QR (Sept. 1843), 377. The article is a review of books on coins by Cardwell and Akerman and is anonymous but the similarity of the words would suggest that the author was Marsden.
122 Roach Smith, 'Roman remains at Colchester', 30.

iron bar was the staff of their standard ... then you would not have given offence.[123]

In other parts of Britain not mentioned by the ancient historians, all the antiquarians had to rely on to recreate the Roman past were the objects that they had left behind. It was the manner in which they used them that distinguished between the local man whose primary objective was to tell a story and those who sought to create a more objective and factual account of Roman Britain. It was the difference between Wykeham Martin's vivid imaginings of crucifixion and Roach Smith's sober assessment of nails holding a coffin together. But, ironically, it was the mundane domestic nature of many of the objects that had begun to challenge the traditional picture of Roman Britain and caused many antiquarians, possibly unknowingly, to present a different picture of the Roman period in Britain.

In Caerleon, for instance, inscriptions were the only form of written evidence, and therefore the antiquarians had to rely on objects to recreate the fortress and the town. The way in which they went about this helps to illustrate the central part played by objects in such imaginative reconstructions; a paper given by the David Jones at the 1849 AGM of the CAA is a good example. He told his audience that 'We are treading in the steps and repeating the actions of those renowned people who were the intermediate link between the ancient and the modern world.'[124] He put a particular emphasis on the activities of the Romans, so that instead of describing the artefacts he describes Roman people using them: 'You have but to add the stately conqueror to his massive column, the purse to the coin, the garment to the pin and clasp and the young damsel to her water jar and you see the city camp of the second Augustan Legion.'[125]

By stressing the everyday objects and activities of the people in the past, Jones creates a picture of domestic life far removed from games and battles. It is a story of the ordinary and domestic told through 'the imperishable materials of stone, pottery and precious metals', rather than a story of rulers and battle as told in the classic texts. Given the lack of written evidence it was a story that could only be told through the medium of objects and it was the objects that were primarily responsible for the shifting perceptions of Roman rule. Their mundane character meant that they had to start telling the story of Roman Britain rather than imperial Rome. Jones's emphasis on the everyday and domestic looks forward to the excavations of the 1860s when urban sites such as Wroxeter and Chedworth would start to reveal the extent to which the Roman way of life had been adopted by the British population.

---

123 Wire to Roach Smith, 5 June 1851, Wire letter book.
124 Anon., 'Caerleon Archaeological Association', MM, 14 July 1849.
125 Ibid.

9

The Picture Changes

In a guide to Bath written in 1858 the author describes the city's Roman past: 'The Romans made it a military town and the station of a legion on the line of their defences against the incursions of Welsh tribes. Claudius visited after his conquest of the northern tribes and conferred upon it the rights and privileges of a Roman colony.'[1] In that it is purely concerned with military matters, and suggests two separate groups in constant conflict, this is a very traditional view of the Roman occupation of Britain. It is also totally inaccurate. A *guide to the knowledge of Bath ancient and modern*, written only six years later, gives a very different picture of the antiquarians' understanding and interpretation of Roman Bath: 'Whether it was a military station, or only a resort for the seekers of health … all the evidence tends to show that in the Roman period Bath was a place of ease, wealth and luxury.'[2] In its more thoughtful approach and acknowledgement of the need for evidence this second quote reflects both changing knowledge of the Romano-British past and a greater understanding of the methods through which it could be studied.

Greater understanding and the use of new archaeological methods are apparent in a series of large excavations on Roman sites in Britain during the 1860s. There were two urban centres: Uriconium near the Shropshire village of Wroxeter where excavations began in 1859 organised by Thomas Wright, and Calleva near Silchester in Berkshire where work started in 1864, supervised by a local vicar, James Joyce. There was also the Roman villa at Chedworth, discovered by accident in 1864, and finally there was the first attempt to locate the Roman baths at Bath. The number and scale of these excavations illustrate the continuing interest of the Victorians in the Roman period; at the same time, the manner in which they were organised and financed was changing in ways which reflect some of the developments in contemporary Victorian society.

New knowledge

Underlying all the new perceptions and understanding of the Roman past was the realisation that the classical texts were a poor guide to Roman Britain. It followed that the antiquarians' increasing awareness of the importance of the material evidence was very influential in changing their picture of the

---

[1] Anon, *Bath, what to see and how to see it*, Bath 1858, 3.
[2] J. Earle, *A guide to the knowledge of Bath ancient and modern*, Bath 1864, 32.

Roman past. The widespread discoveries of extensive sites and high quality objects meant that the antiquarians could no longer ignore the fact that the way of life of the British population, its upper class at least, had been substantially changed during the Roman period. The antiquarians' somewhat pejorative comments about Romano-British artefacts and their low opinion of the standard of civilised living enjoyed by the Romano-Britons had to be reassessed in the light of these new discoveries. In 1858 Edward Cutts was one antiquarian who acknowledged his changed view of Roman Britain: 'During the five hundred years that the Romans held the island, they appear to have occupied and cultivated and civilized it much more thoroughly than cursory readers of the history of Roman Britain have imagined.'[3] It is, of course, difficult to assess how representative of the Essex antiquarians Cutts's views were, but they do seem to indicate that ideas were changing.

Cutts's reference to the centuries of Roman occupation is important because a sense of the passage of time is largely absent from accounts in the classical texts of Roman involvement in Britain. Their authors' preoccupation with events at the centre in Rome ensured that when they do refer to Britain there is no chronological framework into which those events could be slotted, so rather than a continuing narrative they seem more like a series of snapshots. What is missing is a sense of development and change over the centuries of Roman rule and failure to take this into account could lead to some misleading ideas. The importance of the time dimension was highlighted, appropriately enough, by the geologist Charles Lyell. He pointed out that the period of the Roman occupation was 'for as many years as have elapsed from the first discovery of America to our own time'.[4]

The Norfolk antiquarian, Vere Irving, commented on the changing nature of Roman rule in a paper to the BAA in 1859: 'It has been usual to treat the Roman period as one individual whole, but this I believe to be an error which has led to much confusion.' He outlined the stages of Roman rule from 'an invading army in a hostile country' through 'towns occupied by a mixed military and civilian population' to the final stage when 'freed from all apprehension of insurrection or invasion ... [they] constructed open hamlets and detached villas, the latter often displaying signs of great luxury and magnificence'.[5] The practical application of this greater understanding is to be seen in Joyce's description of a large Roman mansion in the centre of Silchester. His workmen had dug down to the lowest course of masonry (the technique used to determine how far to dig on sites where there were no other standing remains) and they had 'declared that no more was to be found here [and] that the remains had been exhausted'.[6] Joyce was unconvinced and digging

---

3 Cutts, 'Roman remains at Coggeshall', 107.
4 *ILN* report of the BAAS conference in Bath, 24 Sept. 1864.
5 G. Vere Irving, 'Earthworks and ancient fortifications in Norfolk', *JBAA* xv (1859), 196–202.
6 J. Joyce, 'Account of further excavations at Silchester', *Arch.* xlvi, paper read on 9 May 1867.

continued and eventually revealed four separate re-buildings. The four layers were a graphic demonstration of the passing of time, as Joyce pointed out: 'Fourteen hundred years after its burial, it silently records its consecutive occupations by the Romans from the earliest days of the Christian era to the last days of their waning power in 410.'[7]

Diversity and domesticity

Another distortion arising from too great a reliance on the classical texts was that the range of conditions existing in Roman Britain went unnoticed. The picture painted by words was essentially a military one; they record battles, campaigns and military leaders and when British figures such as Boudica and Caractacus appear, they do so as leaders to be defeated in battle. Even the information from inscriptions was heavily weighted towards the military as these were largely used to record the deaths of army personnel or to mark the activities of the legions. There was no British equivalent of the Younger Pliny's description of his villa or the guide to farming in the *Georgics* and though they were occasionally referred to, particularly on the Chedworth site, most civilian aspects of life in Roman Britain had to be discovered through excavation and material remains. And what these revealed was a diverse society including a considerably larger civic and domestic sector than had previously been imagined.

Collingwood Bruce, the antiquarian most well known for his detailed work on the military remains along Hadrian's Wall, was most struck by the range and luxury of the sites in the southern counties. In 1860 he delivered a paper to the Archaeological Institute in which he compared the artefacts and sites he was used to finding in the north with those found more commonly in the south: 'The first thing that strikes one is the comparative security and luxury of those fortunate enough to live in the South.' He contrasted 'the mill stones, stone troughs and mortars' with the works of art, precious metals and hoards of coins found in the south. Bruce attributed the differences to the fact that the northern stations were primarily military, there to guard the frontier against 'an active and powerful enemy', whereas in the south Roman towns and villas were built in the countryside, 'covering a space large enough to show that their architects knew nothing of catapults and ballistae, and that the dreams of their occupants were never disturbed by an onslaught of Picts or Scots'.[8] In other words the sites in the south suggested a civil and domestic Romano-British society, which, apart from Tacitus' comments in the *Agricola*, was completely absent from the classical texts, but which had become increasingly visible as material evidence from the excavations in the 1860s began to accumulate.

[7]   Ibid.
[8]   J. Collingwood Bruce, 'Proceedings', *AJ* xvii (1860), 343.

Villas and towns

It was the civilian and domestic sites that enabled the antiquarians to create a vision of Roman Britain as settled, peaceful and civilised. When it was discovered in 1864 the Chedworth villa site was the latest in a long line of Roman villas discovered in the countryside since the eighteenth century. There had been so many that Wright observed that 'The objects which must have struck the traveller as he passed along the roads were the numerous country villas or mansions, many of them magnificent palaces, covering as much ground as a whole town.'[9] Even if these villas were only inhabited by Roman occupiers they suggested a level of peace and security which did not accord with a view of Roman Britain as a purely military outpost. As an article in the *Journal of the Somerset Archaeological and Natural History Society* observed, villa sites were often far away from military stations and 'costly and elaborate ornamentations afforded clear evidence that the Romans held a quiet and peaceful possession of these districts and had no fear of being disturbed'.[10]

It could be argued that villas were usually inhabited by high-ranking military personnel, but this argument could not extend to whole town sites like Wroxeter and Silchester. So it was these urban sites that were particularly important, as they suggested that the benefits of Roman rule had spread more widely into the British population than had hitherto been imagined. Before the large scale excavation at Wroxeter started in 1859, the Bath antiquary the Revd Harry Scarth had argued that the site was a military base: '[It] would have contained at least twenty times as many soldiers as any of the other stations in the area.'[11] But no evidence of a military presence was found and even when an inscription recording a soldier's death was recovered, Wright argued that 'It would be very rash to take the presence of a single tomb stone as a proof that a body of troops to which the deceased had belonged was stationed at that place, unless we had some other information to confirm it.'[12] Instead the baths, the basilica and the forum of a Roman civil centre were all identified along with rows of shops and a forge. Wright emphasised what could be learned from the buildings and objects 'of the degree to which they enjoyed the luxuries of life' and concluded that they 'possessed a great majority of the refinements of modern society; far more than can be traced among the population of the middle-ages'.[13] Roach Smith agreed, citing as evidence 'A spacious and noble building of numerous rooms ... well supplied

---

9 Wright, *Celt, Roman and Saxon*, 188.
10 W. Jones, 'Roman villas in Great Britain', *Journal of the Somerset Archaeological and Natural History Society* xiii (1865), 62.
11 H. M. Scarth, 'Proceedings', GM xliv (1855), 294.
12 T. Wright, 'Uriconium: second article: the inscriptions', JBAA xv (1859), 314.
13 Idem, *Uriconium*, 84.

with hypocausts … the mode of heating [which allowed] the skilful spreading of the heated air up the walls'.[14]

The excavations at Silchester were even more successful in revealing life in a Romano-British town. Several small streets were uncovered and attempts made to 'ascertain with as much exactitude as the exposed walls permit the general plan of the laying out of the streets'.[15] Joyce also located the complex of public buildings, the forum, basilica and the associated arcades of shops and offices, including fishmongers, butchers and money-changers. He describes some of the smaller artefacts which had enabled him to identify the use of each space: 'children's playthings' were found in one shop and in another 'a very small bar of silver for repairing some little silver articles'. He identified 'the favourite luncheon bar of the forum' from the huge pile of oyster shells found along one side and the sandal-makers by several awls.[16] An interesting example of the way in which the material evidence could sit uncomfortably with older, more stereotypical conceptions of the Roman past is to be seen in Joyce's view of the large mansion mentioned earlier. He suggested that it could have been the home of a high-ranking official, if not of the Emperor Carausius himself.[17] However, despite this claim to an association with a military leader, all the evidence from Silchester was concerned with civil and domestic life and Joyce did not attempt to argue otherwise.

Both Wright and Joyce had a model of Roman civilian life based on excavation reports from Pompeii. As Wright explained, 'We have few opportunities for examining the internal arrangements of a Roman town and until the uncovering of Pompeii our knowledge was very limited.'[18] In 1860 the king of the newly-united Italy had appointed Giuseppe Fiorelli to excavate the Pompeii site systematically. His reports and methodology were very influential and it is impossible to read the reports of the Wroxeter and Silchester excavations without realising the absolute centrality of the Pompeii site as a guide and an inspiration. For Joyce the main benefit was that it had not experienced a slow decline: 'At Pompeii alone it [Roman culture] was smitten in an instant into the stillness of death, preserving intact every feature of life … Pompeii alone bears a perfect example on her scorched bosom, and one which recalls with a startling reality the description of Vitruvius.'[19] But although Wright also made many references to Pompeii, he was concerned that too close an analogy with Italian examples would obscure that 'differences in climate and many other causes existed in this island which should

[14] C. Roach Smith. 'Roman city of Uriconium, GM ccxxiv (1868), 665.
[15] J. Joyce, On the excavations at Silchester', Arch. xi. 413.
[16] Idem, 'Further excavations at Silchester', 354–6.
[17] Idem, 'Third account of excavations at Silchester', ibid. 340 (paper read 9 May 1867). Carausius was a low-born soldier in the Roman army who proclaimed himself emperor and seized the province of Britain in AD 286.
[18] Wright, Celt, Roman and Saxon, 173.
[19] Joyce, 'Third account', 349. Vitruvius was the only remaining classical text on Roman architecture.

make us cautious in applying to Roman houses in Britain the rules which we know were observed in Italy'.[20] Wright's comment is an example of the more nuanced and thoughtful approach which allowed Roman Britain to emerge from the shadows cast by the classical texts' concentration on Rome itself.

The Romano-Britons and Romanisation

Another indicator of changing perspectives is to be found in the antiquarians' descriptions of the end of Roman rule. For instance, Wright's comments about the 'comforts and luxuries of life' enjoyed by the inhabitants of Wroxeter is followed by his account of the sacking of the city in the fifth century: 'Abundant traces of burning in all parts of the site leave no doubt that the city was plundered and afterwards burnt by some barbarian invaders of Roman Britain.'[21] Joyce also noted a violent end at Silchester: 'The central part of the Forum clearly underwent destruction and re-building prior to its ultimate ruin, and … this destruction was accompanied by extreme violence.'[22] What is striking about these accounts is that they do not picture the cities being destroyed by the local population turning on the depleted and weakened Romans; rather they fall to outsiders, barbarians from beyond the frontiers of Roman rule. For instance: 'In the fifth century the Roman soldier goes away; the barbarians rush from their mountains in the North, the Irish pirates follow in their wake, ruin and desolation mark their track.'[23] The implication is that those within the frontier are in some way 'Roman'. Roach Smith, reviewing John Buckman's book in 1850, was already of this view: 'When the Romans retreated from the Northern provinces they left to their successors the villa and other buildings, and although in some instances they may have been destroyed, there can be but little doubt that by far the greater number were preserved and tenanted for many generations.'[24] His statement acknowledges that Roman life continued after the legions withdrew and, as in Rome itself, only ceased when the 'barbarians' from outside invaded. But in 1850 Roach Smith's was a lone voice; much more common were the antiquarian accounts in Chester and Cirencester that pictured two extremes, Roman soldiers and ancient Britons in mud huts. It was largely due to the excavations at Wroxeter and Silchester that a much more complex view of life in Roman Britain was beginning to emerge.

The confusion surrounding the antiquarians' use of the word 'Roman' in a British context and the increasingly common assumption that imperial Britain was a natural heir of imperial Rome has already been discussed. The way in which these changing views had begun to permeate the antiquarians' view

---

20 Wright, *Celt, Roman and Saxon*, 161.
21 Idem, *Uriconium*, 84.
22 Joyce, 'Third account', 360.
23 J. Grover, 'Verulam and Pompeii compared', *JBAA* xxv (1869), 47.
24 C. Roach Smith, 'Roman art at Cirencester', *GM* xxxiv (1850), 243.

of the Roman past can be detected in the reports of site visits to Chedworth. Several of them read almost as though their authors were peopling the villa with country gentlemen of nineteenth-century Somerset rather than fourth-century Romano-Britons. For instance Harry Scarth told the Bath Field Club that 'these villas appear to have been comfortable country residences and the owners engaged in agricultural pursuits as well as the pleasures of hunting'.[25] And when the BAA visited in 1869, its journal reports that 'the party then proceeded to the drawing room' and a pavement design was likened to 'a beautiful Brussels carpet'.[26] Another antiquarian, J. W. Grover, pushed the analogy further: 'Can the architectural taste implanted by the Latin lords eighteen hundred years ago have descended to these modern times in the modern mind?'[27] Grover went on to make the association even more explicit: 'The historical and archaeological student is gradually coming to the conclusion that we may as well and as correctly call ourselves Anglo-Roman as Anglo-Saxon.'[28]

It is probable that the changing view of the Roman occupation in Britain and the increasing willingness of the Victorians to identify themselves as Romano-Britons was, in part at least, a reflection of Britain's altered view of itself as a world power with large overseas colonies. There can be little doubt that as Britain's own empire expanded, a model of empire-building that emphasised the benign affects of the imperial role would be a more comfortable model to live with than one based on the subjection of a native population by harsh military rule. Furthermore, whereas ruined military structures such as Hadrian's Wall could be seen as evidence of 'the decline and fall' of a mighty military empire, contemporary Victorian towns and country houses could be seen as the natural heirs of a peaceful and civilised Romano-British society and therefore as evidence for the benefits conferred by empire.

New methods

The difficulties presented by excavations under crowded houses and streets such as in Colchester, Cirencester and Chester made it impossible to obtain a clear picture of the layout of Romano-British towns. The excavations at Wroxeter and Silchester were so significant because they combined two important changes in archaeological method: they were chosen rather than happened upon by accident and, apart from Caerwent, they were the first to be carried out on green-field sites.[29] The antiquarians knew the approxi-

[25] H. M. Scarth, 'Remains of a Roman villa at Cold Harbour Farm', *Proceedings of the Bath Field Club* i (1867–9), 16.
[26] Anon., 'Proceedings', *JBAA* xxv (1869), 404.
[27] J. Grover, 'On a Roman villa at Chedworth', *JBAA* xxiv (1868), 133.
[28] Ibid.
[29] In the opinion of George Boon 'Caerwent, had the Caerleon Society persevered, would have been the first of the green-field Romano-British town sites to be tackled systemati-

mate locations of most Roman towns from Roman road maps, although as in Colchester this topic could still arouse considerable disagreement. But both Wroxeter and Silchester had sufficient remains to indicate their precise position under open fields and therefore offered an opportunity to explore a Romano-British town site. Roach Smith explained the advantages:

> Wroxeter presents the site of an ancient city under circumstances unusually favourable to the researches of the antiquary. A very small portion of the ground has been disturbed by modern buildings; while the position and nature of the ground have rendered it unnecessary to have recourse to the process of deep draining which would have broken up the ruins below.[30]

James Joyce was also aware of the benefits of a green-field site: 'Silchester has never been lived upon, or built over, by any subsequent civilization. It remains exactly as it was when the hand of destruction first overtook it.'[31] Wright was quick to point out the advantages of a planned dig: 'They already show us what may be done by continuous research, instead of digging here and there at hap-hazrp [sic].'[32]

The excavations at Bath were an intriguing combination of chance discovery and informed excavation. It was known that the healing springs at Bath had been used by the Romans. The third-century writer Solinus had written about a temple to Minerva on the site and the discovery of a large bronze head of the goddess in 1727, and the remains of Roman carvings unearthed in 1790, appeared to confirm his account. But the head and carvings were chance finds, uncovered as a result of quite unrelated activities. They had been deposited in the museum of the Bath Royal Institution and formed a part of a possible plan of the temple in Samuel Lysons's volumes of the *Reliquae Romano Britannicae* (1813).[33] However the modern city completely covered the site and therefore large-scale planned excavation, such as had been carried out at Wroxeter and Silchester was impossible.

When the architect James Irvine arrived in the city in 1864 to be clerk of works for Gilbert Scott's restoration of Bath abbey, he found the artefacts in much the same state of disarray as Roach Smith had described in 1848. Furthermore they were not just neglected, they had never been carefully examined or intelligently related to possible sites on the ground; instead they

cally ... as it was, when Fox and Hope presented their Silchester project to the Society of Antiquaries in 1900' Caerwent was not mentioned: E. I .P. Boon, 'Archaeology through the Severn Tunnel: the Caerwent Exploration Fund, 1899–1917', *TBGAS* cvii (1989), 6. Lack of funds was probably an important factor in the decision to cover over the Caerwent site after only one season.

30 C. Roach Smith, 'The Roman city of Uriconium', GM ccvi (1859), 448–58.

31 J. Joyce, 'The excavations at Silchester', AJ xxx (1873), 26.

32 T. Wright, 'Uriconium', *JBAA* xv (1859), 223.

33 *The original Bath guide* suggests that the reader should 'consult a most splendid work from the classical pen and correct pencil of that profound antiquarian the late Samuel Lysons' (p. 9). Barry Cunliffe has described Lysons's work as 'A landmark not only in printing but also in archaeological recording': *Roman Bath discovered*, London 1984, 225.

had been cut and displayed to satisfy the assumptions of previous antiquarians. Irvine declared that 'It is lamentable to see the fragments at present fixed up, with the lower half sawn off and destroyed only to produce a miserable uniformity with the other piece and the new slabs on which a modern and certainly erroneous attempt (as the old letters testify) at restoration of the inscription is perpetuated.'[34] He re-examined and measured the fragments and compared them with some foundations found on the site of an extension to the United Hospital in 1865. He concluded that 'there remained enough of the fragments found in 1790 wherewith to construct the elevation of two buildings'.[35] He thought that the other building was the entrance hall to the Roman public baths and that the reconstruction in the museum had served only to confuse: 'These, the ancient stones of the attempted restoration … have been frequently most erroneously described as the "Inscription on the Great Temple at Bath", but never had any connection with it.'[36]

Some idea of the level of confusion prompted by the fragmentary and ill-understood Bath remains is to be found in Scarth's *Aquae Solis* published in 1864, the year Irvine arrived in the city. The book was the first attempt to collate the existing information on Bath's Roman past. Scarth analysed the temple remains in Bath by comparing them with the 'Roman temple' in Chester described by William Tite in 1863. But the Chester remains were the foundations of a large hypocaust and Tite had only hypothesised a temple because of apparent similarities between the Chester remains and the better known examples in Bath.[37]

Irvine used the 1790 discoveries to inform his belief that the site of the Roman temple lay beneath the derelict White Hart Inn, a belief that proved correct when he dug there and discovered a part of the massive concrete podium of the temple under the cellar.[38] He made another excavation on the north side of the Kingstone Buildings and became the first to locate the main Roman drain.[39] Although relatively small scale, both Irvine's excavations were planned and based on his close analysis of the fragments and the

---

[34] J. Irvine, 'Remains of the Roman temple and entrance hall to Roman baths found at Bath in 1790', *JBAA* xxix (1873), 393.

[35] Ibid. 379.

[36] Ibid. 392.

[37] H. M. Scarth, *Aquar Solis, or Notions of Roman Bath*, London 1864, 17–18. Wright described Scarth's book as 'very disappointing, but he is a very worthy fellow and I mean to review it kindly in the Athenaeum': Wright to Roach Smith, 20 Nov. 1864, BL, MS Add. 33346.

[38] See Cunliffe, *Roman Bath discovered*, 19–21.

[39] Who actually found the drain and thus provided the impetus to locate the main Roman baths was disputed. Irvine's papers include a bill he received from a Bath building firm 'To opening ground and searching for the Roman baths in Kingstone Buildings' (dated 6 Oct. 1865). Irvine wrote on the bottom 'I think this will fairly settle the question of its recovery.'

foundations which he used as a guide to inform his decision as to where he should dig.[40]

The same careful observation and attention to detail is to be seen in James Joyce's excavation at Silchester, for instance in his description of the discovery of the large mansion:

> The discovery was not accidental; the line of a small street ... had been previously ascertained by prolonging the direction of the northern wall of the first house opened ... the point of intersection where this minor road cuts the great road across was ascertained, allowance was made for the width of the streets and a corner house at each side was searched for, and both were found.[41]

Joyce used coins found at the different levels of the mansion to date the successive re-buildings even though he recognised that they could be problematic as evidence: 'I am aware that strictly speaking such a deduction is incapable of proof, because coins may have been in circulation a long time subsequent to their original issue ... my object is not to prove a theory but merely to approximate to a period.'[42] Joyce's methods were sufficiently robust to be copied by Wilfred Cripps in Cirencester thirty years later and are in stark contrast to the Caerleon Society's somewhat cavalier decision to put a modern building on top of what they knew to be an important site.

Organisational changes

Not only was the picture of Roman Britain and the methods used to investigate it changing, so also were the ways in which excavations were organised and financed. Obviously large-scale excavations such as those at Wroxeter and Silchester required more time, administration and money than Irvine's small digs, and the potential demands of a project aimed at uncovering the major Roman buildings in Bath were even larger. The different responses to these demands and the variety of ways in which they were met draws attention to the fact that the antiquarian world itself was beginning to change. However it is important to note that there was no direct relationship between the type of excavation, its complexity and the organisational methods used at any particular site. Instead each excavation was a unique combination of different approaches dictated by the particular circumstances at each site.

Cirencester had been typical of a traditional excavation. It was precipitated by an accidental discovery in the course of unrelated building activity, it was carried out by amateurs and it was financed and the finds appropriated

---

[40] Irvine's collection of drawings, plans and observations made during his stay in the city (1864–72) are still available in two unbound volumes in Bath Reference Library.
[41] Joyce, 'Further excavations at Silchester', 330 (letter read 9 May 1867).
[42] Ibid. 332–3.

by the local magnate. It is probably no coincidence that the level of interest, both on the part of the general public, the antiquarian world and the magnate was directly related to the nature of the finds, beautiful and well-preserved tessellated pavements, for when John Buckman attempted to organise further research in the town, he failed to get the support of Lord Bathurst and to a lesser degree the townsfolk.

Although the Silchester excavation was on a planned green-field site, in many ways the excavations there and at Chedworth followed the traditional pattern. Both were on the land of the local magnate who paid for the excavations and who, as a result, was seen as 'owning' the remains. This was particularly apparent at Silchester which was on land owned by the Arthur Wellesley, 2nd duke of Wellington, whose generosity Joyce praised in much the same manner as Bathurst had been praised in Cirencester: 'The discoveries were possessed of so much interest that by the generous liberality of the Duke the excavations have been carried on ever since.'[43] But the duke still proclaimed his ownership by having the large tessellated pavements found on the site, lifted and removed to his own hall at Stratfield Saye, where they remain to this day. However there was one significant organisational development at Silchester: Joyce lived near the site and kept a daily watch over activities which he carefully recorded in his excavation journal.[44] This was a level of supervision and recording carried out over a number of years which had previously been almost unheard of and was still notable in the 1860s.

The organisation at both Wroxeter and Bath differed significantly from the traditional pattern. Although the local landowner in Wroxeter, the 2nd duke of Cleveland was supportive, the actual excavation was organised by a local committee set up by Thomas Wright and the local MP, Beriah Botfield, and the work was financed by a public subscription. In contrast to Joyce at Silchester, Wright's role was largely that of a figurehead, only visiting the site to show visitors around and leaving the day-to-day supervision to Henry Johnson, the secretary of the Shropshire Antiquarian Society. Perhaps inevitably, given the lack of a sponsor, finance was an ever-present worry and Wright's role was increasingly that of a populariser and fund-raiser. He set up a metropolitan committee 'so that we can make a direct appeal to the country by advertising ... I hope to get a good show of noblemen and MP's with a few names of our leading families in different parts of the country'.[45] In a letter to Joseph Mayer he described an activity which was to take up more and more of his time: 'We will have a little meeting in Shrewsbury when I will give a

---

43 Idem, 'The excavations at Silchester', AJ xxx (1873), 15.
44 According to his obituary in the Proceedings of the Society of Antiquaries, Joyce entered into his journal 'every fact and measurement ... noting with skill and discrimination every surface laid bare, every object exhumed, every coin discovered'. The journal is now in Reading Museum.
45 Wright to Mayer, 10 May 1859, BL, MS Add. 33347. Wright's 'name chasing' is particularly interesting when it is remembered how much he and Roach Smith criticised similar activities during the split with the AI in 1844.

popular lecture on the Roman towns in Britain and the way in which they were destroyed and gradually covered up, so as to explain exactly our object and what we hope and expect to find.'[46] Wright's letters record a number of such lectures around the country and even if his main purpose was to raise money, they are a testament to the continuing interest in the Romans and Roman Britain in the country at large.[47]

In his attempts to keep the excavation going Wright appealed for public funds but was turned down: 'The Commissioners of the Treasury saw no reason for employing public money on any excavation, as if it had not been employed on excavations abroad and foreign to our history as at Carthage.'[48] It sounds like the battle for the British Room all over again and demonstrates that there was still a long way to go before the preservation of the national past would attract public money.

In Bath the situation was different again. The actual excavation was carried out under the supervision of one individual, first Irvine and after he left the city, by Major Charles Davis, the city's engineer. But the antiquarians' desire to find the remains of Roman Bath was both supported and frustrated by the city council itself. Bath's fortunes had declined sharply since their heyday in the eighteenth century and, despite the claims of a local guide that 'No town in England can offer such telling proofs of ancient splendour as Bath has to show in these Roman remains', the reality was that Roman Bath was more talked about than seen.[49] A large part of the difficulty was that, as in Chester, the traces of the Roman presence remained in the shadow of a later era. The fabric of the city was redolent of the Georgian period when the classical buildings of the two John Woods and the social life dictated by Beau Nash attracted many of the most well known in the land to take the waters at Bath. Such was the dominance of the Georgian past that the Roman remains had been neglected, as Irvine complained. They were 'huddled at present into any out of the way corner or dark receptacle in which it strangely seems Bath hopes to cause to be forgotten these remains of her ancient grandeur'.[50]

The Bath city council decided that one way to revitalise the local economy and attract more visitors was to build a new spring bath and a luxury hotel. In 1866 work was started on the bath and a plaque recorded that it was 'Laid on Roman masonry seventeen hundred years old, the cornerstone of new baths, thus connecting in work and object the modern with the ancient

46 Ibid. 21 Dec. 1858.
47 The lectures are mentioned in letters to Mayer and during 1859–61 were usually on Roman topics and especially the excavation at Wroxeter. Apart from the desire to raise funds for the excavation, they were also an important part of his attempts to earn his living as an antiquarian writer.
48 Wright to Mayer, 10 Dec. 1860, BL, MS Add. 33347.
49 Earle, *Guide to Bath*, 32.
50 Irvine, 'Remains of the Roman temple', 394. This was probably the same display so heavily criticised by Roach Smith in 1848. Roach Smith had concluded that 'I find nobody knows; and it seems equally clear that nobody cares': Anon., 'Proceedings', *JBAA* iv (1848), 148–9.

world'.[51] The plaque's wording indicates that the council was aware of the potential advantages of using the Roman past as a tourist attraction, but the desire to maximise the benefits was in conflict with the council's other aim of promoting Bath as a modern and up-to-date spa: the new bath had to utilise the same springs as the old and therefore had to be built on top of the Roman remains. The next twenty years were to see Bath at the centre of a major archaeological battle between the council's plans and the archaeologists' concern to preserve the remains of the Roman baths.[52]

Developments in Wroxeter and Bath demonstrate that there was sufficient interest in the Roman past to aid economic recovery in Bath and attract subscribers to excavation funds as at Wroxeter. Roach Smith had been arguing the economic case for financial help for excavations for years. In 1850 he persuaded the London and Southeast Railway to give him a free pass to travel to the site of his excavations in Lymne: 'They soon found that that the excavations attracted hundreds weekly; and that it was in their interests to encourage them.'[53] In 1854 he wrote to the *Essex Standard* that financial help could lead to discoveries in Colchester that 'would doubtless be advantageous to the town at large, and increase its prosperity'.[54] Wright's lectures and articles appear to have been very successful in attracting visitors to the Wroxeter site as a report in the AJ suggests: 'The buildings, now cleared of debris, are left open for the gratification of numerous visitors who resort daily to the spot, and have shown remarkable interest in the undertaking.'[55] To encourage visitors Wright wrote a guide and a museum of the finds was created on site. He told Meyer that he was hoping that 'four or five acres of buildings be kept permanently open as a more interesting ruin than a castle or an abbey'.[56]

These excavations illustrate some of the ways in which antiquarian activity was changing. In the 1840s the main focus had been on the preservation of remains discovered accidentally as the result of unrelated building work and to this end the provision of a safe depository such as a museum was a priority; as Lee explained to the CAA, no excavation could be even contemplated until the new museum was built. However by the 1860s the focus had changed: rather than concentrating solely on the artefacts, there was a growing interest in excavation of the sites themselves as the means whereby the Roman past could be better understood. The information gained from excavating green-field sites indicated the extent to which Roman Britain was significantly different from the traditional picture of a country under military occupation. Questions were raised which could only be answered by further planned excavations such as those carried out by Irvine in Bath. This is not to suggest that there was no interest in conservation or that all excavations

51 B. Cunliffe, 'Major Davis: architect and antiquarian', *Bath History* i (1986), 46.
52 See idem, *Roman Bath discovered*, 99–105.
53 Roach Smith, *Retrospections*, i. 207.
54 Idem, 'Roman antiquities of Colchester', GM xlii (1854), 70.
55 Anon., 'Proceedings', AJ xvii (1860), 350.
56 Wright to Meyer, 21 Aug. 1859, BL, MS Add. 33346.

were planned, far from it. But there was a growing awareness that the sites themselves, not only the objects found in them, contained vital information which could only be made available by systematic and planned excavations such as those carried out in Bath by James Irvine and in Silchester by James Joyce.

However the extent to which these new methods and ideas were accepted by local antiquarians and societies is debatable. None of the excavations discussed in this chapter were carried out by local antiquarian societies; even the Wroxeter site, where the Shropshire society did supply the labour, was planned and managed by outsiders. In Chester there were no excavations at all and in Colchester and Cirencester there were only small-scale digs, usually prompted by chance finds. John Buckman failed to get significant support for further exploration and after the excitement created by the mosaics all the articles about Roman Corinium were written by outsiders. The only exception was the Caerwent dig, carried out by the CAA on a green-field site in 1855, although once again the work was supervised by an outsider and was very limited in scope.

Given their lack of involvement in the excavations is it possible to discover what local antiquarians felt about the new techniques or the picture of Roman Britain which they revealed? The short answer is 'no', as the ordinary membership remains the silent majority and even the main players, such as Edward Lee and John Buckman restricted themselves to detailed non-analytical descriptions of objects. But their passive role would suggest that it was not the challenge and excitement of new ideas concerning the past which drew the membership into the local antiquarian societies. Rather they offered another venue in which they could meet their equals and confirm their position in the local community. The fact that the subject of the meetings was the past of their locality and that its importance was usually emphasised, was an added bonus. Lee in Caerleon, who was clearly in touch with new classification systems and was an early and vigorous exponent of the need to conserve Roman antiquities, still presided over museum plans which were responsible for building on top of the crucial centre of the Roman fortress. This could indicate that he failed to persuade his fellow antiquarians that the museum should not be built over an important site. Alternatively it could be that he was unwilling to take up the cudgels on behalf of the site because his priority was the conservation of smaller remains. In the absence of any evidence we will never know, but it would be interesting to speculate whether the museum would have been built on that site in the 1860s. The wider conclusion has to be drawn that to a very large extent the changing methodology and new ideas were developed by individuals outside the antiquarian societies, men such as Charles Roach Smith, Thomas Wright and James Joyce.

Conclusion

This study has argued that the Victorians' rediscovery of Roman Britain was important because it represented a shift in the way in which the British past, and in particular its relationship with Rome, was conceptualised. Antiquarians used the material remains of more than four hundred years of Roman occupation to create a rich and detailed image of 'Roman Britain' in which the Romano-Britons were allowed to emerge from the shadow cast by the Roman presence. This new version of Roman Britain was largely a nineteenth-century creation, in which the rather scanty material remains were used as triggers for the antiquarians' imagination, enabling them to construct a Roman past better suited to the purposes of contemporary society. The very scarcity of textual evidence, rather than being a drawback, allowed the antiquarians to call upon 'the rich and flexible vocabulary'[1] of the whole Roman tradition and to use it in discussions and debates about national origins, social organisations and the social and professional standing of individuals.

Just as Tacitus' description of Rome's encounters with the native British can be seen as his commentary on political and social events in the city of Rome in the first century CE, so the British antiquarians' description of the relationship between the Romans and Britons was influenced by contemporary events and changing circumstances in the nineteenth century. But in the process, the analogies were reversed. The imperial power was British, not Roman, and the subject race was no longer British but the native populations of India and Africa.[2]

What both the Roman and the British accounts had in common was the use of conventional descriptions, based on rhetorical stereotypes, such as 'the freedom-loving Celts' or 'the civilising Romans', what was referred to earlier as 'shorthand'. Rather than being objective observations, these phrases were used as devices to further internal debate by setting up comparisons through which incidents and individuals could be evaluated. For modern historians they are a useful source of information about the society that used them.

Throughout much of the eighteenth century classical Rome had been used as a model for many aspects of social and cultural life in Britain. It is perhaps

---

1 The phrase is from Vance, *The persistence of Rome*, 270.
2 David Cannadine has argued that the crucial divisions were not so much racial as based on class and therefore that the 'native other' included the working class in Britain: *Ornamentalism*, 5–6. Bernard Porter's recent work on Britain's imperial role also stresses that attitudes towards the empire were class-related and that it was only when the empire appeared to be threatened that the ruling upper class encouraged some broader popular support: 'What did they know of empire?, *History Today* (Oct. 2004), 42–8.

not surprising therefore that this Roman inheritance should assume such cultural significance and should become an important arena within which various types of authority could be contested. For instance, the frequent references to the civilising effect of the Roman occupation, and the claim that the British had inherited that civilising role, suggest the contemporary belief that Britain had a similar responsibility to carry civilisation overseas.

In Britain itself the debates were complicated and revolved around questions of ownership of the Roman artefacts which were perceived as the 'markers' of civilised living. There were the overt questions about who had both the right and the duty to preserve the vestiges of the national past and the best way in which this could be achieved. But there were also covert differences between individuals and groups, in which the classical inheritance was used as a symbol of the right to rule of some, and the exclusion of others. In effect, these debates were about the redistribution of authority and influence at both national and local level. They were between the established ruling groups and an increasingly important and vocal middle class. The debates were essentially about shifting authority at a time of rapid social change. It is probably no coincidence that they occurred at the same time as other issues, such as the extension of the franchise and central government's involvement in local affairs, were being debated.[3] They all involved questions of participation and ownership that were at the root of claims to authority and the right to rule.

As the traditional ruling groups felt their authority being challenged, they reacted by closing ranks, even in those areas that were not directly political. A collection of objects could signify ownership, not just of the objects themselves, but of the history of a particular locality, suggesting a link between the locality, the objects and the owner. From Camden in the sixteenth century to the Victorians of the nineteenth century, antiquarians had been concerned with the topography and landscape of their piece of countryside. By their searching and minute examination of all the features of that landscape, they identified themselves with every hedge and ditch, and through such intimate acquaintance could claim an identity with the land that went beyond ownership. They were the land and its history personified, and the collection was the embodiment of that identity.

For local groups in mid-Victorian Britain anxious to maintain their authority, the study of the past appeared to confirm their position, as it seemed to demonstrate continuity between the past and the present. In those areas where there had been a significant Roman presence, familiarity with the Classical stories and accounts made the Romans seem almost contem-

---

[3] The 1867 Reform Act extended the vote to many more householders. The risk to health posed by poor urban living conditions was forcing the government to become more pro-active and involved in local affairs through such measures as the 1848 Public Health Act.

porary, especially where there were allegedly identifiable connections with well-known figures. The more magnificent the part that the locality had played in past national events, the greater the glory attached to the current elite. Even in those areas where there was no textual evidence, artefacts such as the mosaics in Cirencester were able to conjure up a wealth of associations through their likeness to other examples in the Roman world. The sense of familiarity was based on an assumed similarity between the Romans and contemporary individuals: a similarity that rested, above all else on their literacy.

Local antiquarians were not interested in philosophical theories of history; rather they wanted to tell the local story. In order to do so, they were willing to consider all types of evidence, both textual and material, and to take account of local traditions and myths, however improbable. To use Michael Dietler's description, they were the guardians of 'the collective memory'. There was more than a hint of idealisation in their attitudes, a sense that in some lost 'golden age' society had been ordered and everyone had known his place. This parochial and inward-looking approach to the study of the past, reinforced by the socially exclusive inclinations of the local groups, successfully fended off both the lower classes in the locality and those antiquarians and historians with more general interests. Although lip-service might be paid to inclusion, essentially the local antiquarians used their groups to maintain their social position and confirm their identity as the rightful rulers.

Despite these parochial attitudes, developments in the 1860s, such as Thomas Wright's lectures and the number of visitors to excavation sites, do suggest that there was a continuing interest in the Roman past and that this was more extensive than could have been imagined at the beginning of the nineteenth century. Potentially it could be harnessed by antiquarians anxious to further the development of their subject, as justification for their demands for public money and sponsorship.

By concentrating on just four areas this book has been able to provide a clearer understanding of some of the complex processes underlying the attitudes and social organisations involved. By highlighting the often conflicting views on the study of the Romano-British past it has been possible to avoid at least some of the stereotypes so often used to describe the Victorians. This mirrors the way in which the Victorian antiquarians' greater knowledge of Roman Britain enabled them to achieve a more nuanced view of the Roman past and to see beyond some of the contemporary stereotypes of that past.

Arguably, the social functions of these local groups were even more important than the study of the past. The published books and journals provide very little evidence of the interests of 'the historically invisible majority' as, without exception, they are written by a small number of the most active. Even a prominent figure like William Wire in Colchester was inhibited from writing publicly about his interests and it is only through pure chance that his journal and letters have survived. However, the fact that they did survive allows a clearer picture of some of the underlying factors at work to emerge.

This would seem to suggest that it is only through examining individuals in specific situations and in as much detail as possible that a deeper understanding can be achieved.[4]

Those individuals who were not accepted into the local societies for social reasons, or who had wider intellectual horizons, had to look elsewhere for stimulation and companionship. They were outside the ruling elite and in some cases they sought to use their interest in the past as a way of earning their living and gaining social and intellectual recognition among like others. They wanted to become professional historians. Unlike the local antiquarians who identified themselves by their association with a particular area and their social connections, these 'would-be' professionals were specialists and used their knowledge to gain acceptance in the metropolitan world of learning and science. So, as a result of being spurned by one elite group, they effectively created or joined another. The change was symbolised by their use of the term 'archaeologist' rather than 'antiquarian' to identify themselves and their activities.

In the years after 1860 the term 'amateur' acquired a distinctly pejorative connotation, as the Roman archaeologist, Francis Haverfield suggested in 1911:

It is a peculiar result of our dominant classical education, which is after all, a general and not a specialising education, that in such branches of science as history or literature, the average Englishman is comparatively indifferent to accurate and scientific training, and practically believes that an untaught and unprepared writer can produce first-rate work by his intelligence.[5]

It is therefore ironic that the current, popular image of the Romans is not dissimilar to that envisioned by the local antiquarians in the middle of the nineteenth century. Today's popular archaeology books, and in particular television programmes, which attempt to link our world with that of the Romans, are still based on the premise that the Romans and ourselves are essentially similar and that contemporary civilisation is built upon Roman foundations. Indeed the very images conjured up by the term 'Roman' today are much as they might have been in 1850, namely the games, the Coliseum and a well-organised army marching to conquest along straight roads. Significantly, just as in the 1850s, these images owe as much to the city of Rome itself as they do to Roman Britain. And again, as in 1850, the estimation of the Romans' similarity to ourselves is at odds with some of these images. Perhaps what these developments demonstrate is that people will continue

---

[4] Charles Wallace has argued the need for a biographical approach to the study of archaeology which could provide context and a cast list of others involved. Essentially this is what I have striven to achieve. There is a lot of potential for further work in this area: 'Writing disciplinary history, or why Romano-British archaeology needs a biographical dictionary of its own', *Oxford Journal of Archaeology* xxi (2002), 381–92.

[5] F. Haverfield, 'Inaugural address to the Society for the Promotion of Roman Studies', *Journal of Roman Studies* i (1911), p. xii.

to look to history to provide a story that will help them to make sense of their own experience in any given place and time. The current popularity of genealogical and local history would seem to support this view. It would also seem to vindicate the antiquarians' activity.

Bibliography

[This book draws extensively on contributions to mid nineteenth-century periodicals, in particular *Archaeologia, Archaeologia Cambrensis*, the *Archaeological Journal* and the *Journal of the British Archaeological Association*. Owing to limited space individual journal articles are not listed. The reader is referred to the first footnote to each article for full bibliographical information.]

Unpublished primary sources

Bath Reference Library
James Irvine: notes, drawings and miscellaneous letters

Caerleon, Legionary Museum
Minute book of the Caerleon Archaeological Society (held by the secretary of the Monmouthshire Antiquarian Society)

Cheshire Record Office
Minutes of the Chester Architectural, Archaeological and Historical Association
CAAHS accessions book

Cirencester Museum
Uncatalogued manuscripts including Buckman's plan of the layout of the museum, the original accessions book and the visitors' book, in a box marked 'early museum' in a museum storeroom.

Cirencester Public Library
Minute book of the library committee, 1838–47, Box L2–1 (9)

Colchester, Essex Record Office
William Wire letter book

Colchester Museum Service
Colchester museum contribution book
Correspondence of William Wire and Charles Roach Smith
Minutes of the Colchester Archaeological Society
Minutes of Essex Archaeological Society
William Wire journal

Gwent Record Office
Manuscripts concerning the Dos works and Edward Lee, D 169, D 372

London, British Library
MSS Add. 30277–300   Correspondence of Thomas Hugo
MSS Add. 33346–7   Correspondence of Thomas Wright and Joseph Mayer

Saffron Walden Museum
Correspondence of Joseph Clarke and Charles Roach Smith, drawer 4.

Published primary sources

Newspapers and periodicals
Antiquary
Archaeologia
Archaeologia Cambrensis
Archaeological Journal
Art Journal
Athenaeum
Courant
Edinburgh Review
Essex Standard
Gentleman's Magazine
Illustrated London News
Journal of the British Archaeological Association
Journal of the Chester Architectural, Archaeological and Historical Society
Journal of the Somerset Archaeological and Natural History Society
Monmouthshire Merlin
Penny Magazine
Proceedings of the Bath Field Club
Proceedings of the Cotteswold Naturalists' Field Club
Proceedings of the Historical Society of Lancashire and Cheshire
Proceedings of the London Society of Antiquaries
Proceedings of the Somerset Natural History and Archaeological Society
Quarterly Review
The Times
Transactions of the Bristol and Gloucestershire Archaeological Society
Transactions of the Essex Archaeological Society
Wiltshire and Gloucestershire Standard

Books and articles
Akerman, J. Y., *An archaeological index*, London 1848
—— *Pagan Saxondom*, London 1852–5
Ammianus Marcellinus, trans. John C. Rolfe, Cambridge, MA 1938
Anon., *The stranger in Chester*, Chester 1816
Anon., *A descriptive catalogue of the antiquities and miscellaneous objects preserved in the museum of Thomas Bateman at Lomberdale House, Derbyshire*, Bakewell 1855
Anon, *Bath what to see and how to see it*, Bath 1858
Anon, *The original Bath guide*, Bath 1856
Arnold, T., *The history of Rome*, 5th edn, Oxford 1848

———— *Introductory lecture on modern history*, 4th edn, London 1849

———— *The Second Punic War: being chapters of the history of Rome*, ed. W. T. Arnold, London 1886

Bateham, G., *Stranger's companion in Chester*, Chester n.d.

Bathurst, H., *Roman antiquities at Lydney Park, Glos*, London 1879

Beecham, W. K., *The history and antiquities of the town of Cirencester*, London 1842

Broster, J., *A walk round the walls and city of Chester*, Chester 1822

Bruce, J. C., *The Roman wall*, London 1851

Buckman, J., *A guide to Pittville: containing an analysis of Pittville's saline waters*, Cheltenham 1842

———— *Our triangle: geology, archaeology and botany of the most picturesque and interesting spots of Cheltenham*, Cheltenham 1842

———— *Proceedings and papers of the Historical Society of Lancashire and Cheshire*, Liverpool 1849–9

———— *An address to E. Holland Esq. M.P., chairman of the Agricultural College, Cirencester*, Cirencester 1863

———— *Notes on the Roman villa at Chedworth*, Cirencester 1872

———— and C. Newmarch, *Remains of Roman art in ancient Corinium*, London 1850

Budge, E. W., *An account of the Roman antiquities preserved in the museum at Chesters*, London 1903

Bulwer-Lytton, E., *The last days of Pompeii*, London 1834

Camden, W., *Camden's Wales; Being the Welsh chapter taken from Edmund Gibson's revised and enlarged edition of Camden's Britannia, trans. from the Latin by Edward Lhuyd*, London 1722

Church, A. H., *A guide to the Roman remains at Cirencester*, Cirencester 1867

Cliffe, C. F., *The book of south Wales, Bristol Channel, Monmouthshire and the Wye*, London 1847

Cowper, W., *Poetical works*, ed. H. S. Milford, Oxford 1967

Coxe, W., *A historical tour through Monmouthshire*, 1st edn, Brecon 1801; 2nd edn, Brecon 1904

Cromwell, T., *History of Colchester in Essex*, London 1825

Cutts, E., *Colchester castle not a Roman temple*, Colchester 1853

Darwin, C., *The voyage of the Beagle* (1839), London 1989

Davis, J. B. and J. Thurnam, *Crania britannica: delineations and descriptions of the skulls of the early inhabitants of the British Isles*, London 1856.

Defoe, D., *A tour through the whole island of Great Britain* (1724–6), London 1971

Dickens, C., *Pictures from Italy* (1846), London 1938

Earle, J., *A guide to the knowledge of Bath ancient and modern*, Bath 1864

Earwater, J. P. (ed.), *Roman remains in Chester: recent discoveries of Roman remains found in repairing the north wall in the city of Chester*, Manchester 1888

Edwards, E., *Lives of the founders of the British Museum*, London 1870

Fairholt, F. W., *Miscellanea graphica*, London 1854

Fletcher, [?], *A stranger in Chester*, Chester 1816

Franks, A. W., 'The apology of my life', in Caygill and Cherry, *A. W. Franks*, appendix II

Freeman, E. A., 'The unity of history', in *Comparative politics: six lectures read before the Royal Institution*, London 1873

Gell, W., *Pompeiana: the topography, edifices and ornaments of Pompeii*, London 1819

Geoffrey of Monmouth, *The history of the kings of Britain*, trans. Thorpe Lewis, London 1966

Gibbon, E., *Memoirs of my life*, ed. B. Radice, London 1984
—— *The decline and fall of the Roman empire* (1776–88), abridged D. M. Low, London 1960

Giraldus Cambrensis, *The journey through Wales*, trans. Thorpe Lewis, London 1978

Gomme, G. R., *The Gentleman's Magazine library: Romano-British remains*, London 1887

Green, J. R., *The making of England*, London 1885

Guest, Lady C., *The diaries of Lady Charlotte Guest*, ed. Frederick Posonby, Lord Bessborough, London 1950

Hall, S. C. and A. M. Hall, *The book of South Wales, the Wye and the coast*, London 1859

Hansell, J., *A stranger in Chester*, Chester 1816

Hawthorne, N., *English notebooks*, Boston 1884

Hemingway, J., *History of the city of Chester from its foundation to the present time*, Chester 1831
—— *Panorama of the city of Chester*, Chester 1836

Henty, G. A., *Beric the Briton: a story of the Roman invasion*, London n.d

Hughes, T, *Stranger's guide to Chester and its environs*, Chester 1856

Hunt and Co., *Directory of Gloucestershire and Bristol*, Bristol 1849

James, H., *English hours* (1905), ed. L. Edel, London 1981

Jenkins, H., *Colchester castle built as a temple of Claudius Caesar*, Colchester 1852
—— *A lecture on Colchester castle*, Colchester 1853

Kemble, J. M., *The Saxons in England: a history of the English commonwealth until the Norman conquest*, London 1849

Kingsley, C., *The Roman and the Teuton*, London 1864

Lee, J. E., *Delineations of Roman antiquities found at Caerleon and neighbourhood*, London 1845
—— *Description of a Roman building and other remains lately discovered at Caerleon*, London 1850
—— *Isca Silurum: an illustrated catalogue of the museum of antiquities at Caerleon*, London 1862
—— *Supplement to Isca Silurum*, Newport 1868
—— *Notebooks of an amateur geologist*, London 1881

Macaulay, T. B., *The lays of ancient Rome*, London 1842

Merivale, C., *A history of the Romans under the empire*, London 1850–64

Morant, P., *History of Colchester*, Colchester 1748

Morgan, O., *Excavations prosecuted by the Caerleon Archaeological Association within the walls of Caerwent in the summer of 1855*, London 1856

Murray's handbook for southern Italy, London 1862

Neville, R. C., *Antiqua explorata*, Saffron Walden 1847
—— *Sepulchra exposita*, Saffron Walden 1848

Nyerup, R., *Oversyn over faedrelandets mindesmaerker fra oldtiden*, Copenhagen 1806

Ormerod, G., *History of Cheshire*, Chester 1819

Parry, E., *The railway companion from Chester to Holyhead*, Chester 1848
——— *The railway companion from Chester to Shrewsbury*, Chester 1849
Phillips, Sir T., *Wales: The language, social conditions, moral character and religious opinions of the people considered in relation to education*, London 1849
Planche, J., *Recollections and reflections: a professional autobiography*, London 1872
Price, J., *Catalogue of the collection of Romano-British, medieval and miscellaneous antiquities in the museum at Colchester*, Colchester 1884
Pugin, A. W., *Contrasts: or parallels between the architecture of the fifteenth and nineteenth centuries*, 2nd edn, London 1841
Roach Smith, C., *Collectanea antiqua: etchings and notices of ancient remains, illustrations of the habits, customs and history of the past ages*, i–iv, London 1848–80
——— *Report on excavations made on the site of the Roman castrum at Lymne in Kent in 1850*, London 1852
——— *Catalogue of the Museum of London Antiquities*, London 1854
——— *Illustrations of Roman London*, London 1859
——— 'Chester: its Roman remains', *Collectanea antiqua*, vi. 28–47
——— *Retrospections: social and archaeological*, i–iii, London 1883–91
——— (ed.), *Inventorium sepulchrale*, London 1856
Roberts, H., *Chester guide*, 2nd edn, rev. J. Hicklin, Chester 1858
Rudder, S., *History and antiquities of Cirencester*, Cirencester 1780
Scarth, H. M., *Aquae Solis, or Notices of Roman Bath*, London 1864
——— *Roman Britain*, London 1883
Scott, Sir W., *The antiquary* (1816), London 1955
——— *Introduction to Waverley novels*, XVI: *Ivanhoe* (1820), Edinburgh 1860
Seacome, J., *The Chester guide*, n.p. 1836
Slater's royal, national and commercial directory, 1858–9, Newport 1860
Smith, H. E., *Reliquiae insurianae*, London 1851
Smith, W. (ed.), *Dictionary of antiquities*, London 1843
Stanley, A. F., *Life and correspondence of Thomas Arnold* (1844), 6th edn, ed. B. Fellowes, London 1846
Stephens, W. R. W., *Life and letters of E. A. Freeman*, London 1895
Stubbs, W., *Constitutional history*, Oxford 1873–8
Tacitus, *The Agricola and The Germania*, trans H. Mattingly, Harmondsworth 1970
——— *Annals*, trans. J. Jackson, London 1969
Taine, H., *Taine's notes on England*, New York 1957
Tennyson, Alfred Lord, *Letters of Alfred Lord Tennyson*, II: *1851–1870*, ed. C. Y. Lang and E. F. Shannon, Oxford 1987
——— *Tennyson: poems*, ii, ed. C. Ricks, London 1987
Thomsen, C., *Kortfattet udsigt over mindesmaerker oldsager fra nordens fortid*, Copenhagen 1836, trans. by Francis Egerton, 1st earl of Ellesmere as *A guide to northern antiquities*, London 1848
Trollope, A., *The New Zealander* (1855–6), Oxford 1972
Trollope, E., *Illustrations of ancient art, selected from objects discovered at Pompeii and Herculanaem*, London 1854
Vaux, W. S. W., *Handbook to the antiquities of the British Museum*, London 1851
Watkin, W. T., *Roman Cheshire: a description of Roman remains in the county of Chester*, Liverpool 1886

Wellbeloved, C., *Eburacum or York under the Romans*, London 1842

Willis, N., *Pencillings by the way*, 1st edn, London 1844

Worsaae, J., *Danmarks oldtid oplyst oldsager og gravhoie*, Copenhagen 1843, trans by W. T. Thoms as *The primeval antiquities of Denmark*, London 1849

Wright, T., *The archaeological album*, London 1845

—————— *Ruins of the city of Uriconium*, Shrewsbury 1860

—————— *The Celt, the Roman and the Saxon* (1852), 2nd edn, London 1861

York Museum handbook, 8th edn, York 1891

Secondary sources

Altick, R. A., *The English common reader: a social history of the mass reading public, 1800–1900*, Chicago 1957

—————— *The shows of London*, Cambridge, MA 1978

—————— *Writers, readers and occasions: selected essays on Victorian literature and life*, Columbus 1989

Anderson, B., *Imagined communities: reflections on the origins and spread of nationalism*, London 1983

Andrews, M., *The search for the picturesque landscape: aesthetics and tourism in Britain, 1760–1800*, London 1989

Ayres, P., *Classical culture and the idea of Rome in eighteenth-century England*, Cambridge 1997

Bann, S., *The clothing of Cleo: a study of the representation of history in nineteenth-century Britain and France*, Cambridge 1984

—————— *Romanticism and the rise of history*, New York 1995

Beer, G., *Darwin's plots: evolutionary narrative in Darwin, George Eliot and nineteenth-century fiction*, London 1983

—————— *Science in cultural encounter*, London 1996

Benjamin, W., 'Unpacking my library', in H. Arendt (ed.), *Illuminations*, London 1970, 59–67

Best, G., *Mid-Victorian Britain, 1851–1875*, London 1971

Block, E., 'T. H. Huxley's rhetoric and the popularization of Victorian scientific ideas, 1854–1874', VS xxix (1986), 363–86

Boase, T. S. R., 'The decoration of the new Palace of Westminster, 1841–1863', *Journal of the Warburg and Courtauld Institutes* xvii (1954), 319–59

Bolt, C., *Victorian attitudes to race*, London 1971

Boon, G. C., *Silchester: Roman town of Calleva*, Newton Abbot 1957

—————— *The legionary fortress of Caerleon, Isca*, Cardiff 1987

—————— 'Archaeology through the Severn Tunnel: the Caerwent Exploration Fund, 1899–1917', TBGAS cvii (1989), 5–26

Bowen, E. I. P., 'Presidential address', AC cxx (1971), 2–9

Brand, V. (ed.), *The study of the past in the Victorian age*, Oxford 1998

Braund, D., *Ruling Roman Britain: kings, queens, governors and emperors from Julius Caesar to Agricola*, London 1996

Brewer, R., *Caerwent Roman town*, Cardiff 1993

—————— 'Caerleon and the archaeologists', *Monmouth Antiquary* xvii (2001), 1–10

Briggs, A., *Victorian people*, London 1965

———— *Saxons, Normans and Victorians*, Hastings 1966

———— *Victorian cities*, London 1968

Brown, A. F. J., *Essex people, 1750–1900* (Essex Record Office lix, 1972)

———— *Colchester, 1815–1914* (Essex Record Office lxxiv, 1980)

Bruce-Mitford, R. L. S. (ed.), *Guide to the antiquities of Roman Britain*, London 1951

Burrow, J. W., 'The village community', in McKendrick, *Historical perspectives*, 259–69

———— *A Liberal descent: Victorian historians and the English past*, Cambridge 1981

Cannadine, D., *Patricians, power and politics in nineteenth-century towns*, Leicester 1982

———— 'Civic ritual and the Colchester oyster feast', *Past & Present* xciv (1984), 107–13

———— *Ornamentalism: how the British saw their empire*, London 2001

Caygill, M. and J. Cherry (eds), *A. W. Franks: nineteenth-century collecting and the British Museum*, London 1997

Chandler, A., *A dream of order: the medieval ideal in nineteenth-century literature*, London 1971

Chapman, W., 'The organisational context in the history of archaeology: Pitt Rivers and other British archaeologists in the 1860's', *Antiquaries Journal* lxix (1989), 23–42

Colley, L., 'Whose nation? Class and national consciousness in Britain, 1750–1830', *P&P* cxiii (1986), 97–118

———— *Britons: forging the nation, 1707–1837*, London 1992

———— *Captives: Britain, empire and the world, 1600–1850*, London 2002

Collingwood, R. G., *The idea of history*, Oxford 1946

Cook, B. F., 'British archaeologists in the Aegean', in V. Brand (ed.), *The study of the past in the Victorian age*, Oxford 1998, 139–55

Cornell, T. J., *The beginnings of Rome*, London 1995

Cowling, M., *The artist as an anthropologist: the representation of type and character in Victorian art*, Cambridge 1989

Crook, J. M., *The Greek revival: neo-classical attitudes in British architecture, 1760–1870*, London 1972

———— *The dilemma of style*, London 1987

Crosby, A. G., *The Chester Archaeological Society: the first one hundred and fifty years*, Chester 1999

Crummy, P., *City of victory: the story of Colchester, Britain's first Roman town*, Colchester 1997

Culler, A. D., *Victorian mirror of history*, New Haven 1985

Cunliffe, B., 'Images of Britannia', *Antiquity* lviii (1984), 175–8

———— *Roman Bath discovered*, London 1984

———— 'Major Davis: architect and antiquarian', *Bath History* i (1986), 27–60

Daniel, G., *The origins and growth of archaeology*, London 1967

———— *A hundred and fifty years of archaeology*, London 1975

Daunton, M. J., *Progress and poverty: an economic and social history of Britain, 1700–1850*, Oxford 1995

De La Bedoyere, G., *The buildings of Roman Britain*, London 1991

Desmond, A., *Huxley: the devil's disciple*, London 1994

Dietler, M., 'A tale of three sites: the monumentalization of Celtic *oppida* and the politics of collective memory and identity', *World Archaeology* xxx (1998), 72–89

Dowling, L., 'Roman decadence and Victorian historiography', *VS* xxviii (1985), 579–607

Dresser, M., 'Britannia', in Samuel, *Patriotism*, iii. 26–49.

Drury, P. J., 'The temple of Claudius at Colchester reconsidered', *Britannia* xv (1984), 7–50

Dudley, D. R. and G. Webster, *The rebellion of Boudica*, London 1962

Dumville, D. N., 'Sub Roman Britain: history and legend', *History* lxii (1977), 173–92

Ebbatson, L., 'Context and discourse: Royal Archaeological Institute membership, 1845–1942', in Vyner, *Building on the past*, 22–74

Edwards, C., 'Translating empire? Macaulay's Rome', in Edwards, *Roman presences*, 70–88

——— (ed.), *Roman presences*, Cambridge 1999

Edwards, O. D., *Macaulay*, London 1988

Elsner, J., 'A collector's model of desire: the house and museum of Sir John Soane', in J. Elsner and R. Cardinal (eds), *The culture of collecting*, Cambridge, MA 1994, 155–77

Evans, J., *A history of the Society of Antiquaries*, Oxford 1956

Fleming, L. (ed.), *Memoir and selected letters of Samuel Lysons*, Oxford 1934

Foster, R., 'Philanthropy and patronage', in Gibson and Wright, *Joseph Mayer*, 28–43

Fraser, D., *Power and authority in the Victorian city*, Oxford 1979

Gathorne-Hardy, J., *The public school phenomenon, 597–1977*, London 1977

Gerrard, C. and L. Viner, 'Archaeological endeavour and data sources', in T. Darville and C. Gerrard (eds), *Cirencester: town and landscape*, Cirencester 1994, 17–22

Gibson, M. and S. M. Wright (eds), *Joseph Mayer of Liverpool, 1803–1886*, London 1988

Girouard, M., *The return to Camelot: chivalry and the English gentleman*, New Haven 1981

Grafton, A., *Forgers and critics: creativity and duplicity in western scholarship*, Princeton 1990

Griffiths, T., *Hunters and collectors: the antiquarian imagination in Australia*, Cambridge 1996

Hall, R., *English heritage book of York*, London 1996

Harrison, J. F. C., *Early Victorian Britain, 1832–1851*, London 1979

Haskell, F., *History and its images: art and the interpretation of the past*, New Haven 1993

——— and N. Penny, *Taste and the antique*, New Haven 1981

Haverfield, F., 'Inaugural address to the Society for the Promotion of Roman Studies', *Journal of Roman Studies* i (1911), pp. xi–xx

——— 'Roman Cirencester', *Arch.* lxix (1920), 161–200

Helmstadter, R. and B. Lightman, *Victorian faith in crisis: essays on continuity and change in nineteenth-century religious belief*, London 1990

Henig, M., 'Graeco-Roman art and the Romano-British imagination', *JBAA* cxxxviii (1985), 1–22

—— The art of Roman Britain, London 1995

Herson, J., 'Victorian Chester: a city of change and ambiguity', in Swift, *Victorian Chester*, 13–53

Hess, J. P., *George Ormerod: historian of Chester*, Whitchurch 1989

Hingley, R., *Roman officers and English gentlemen: the imperial origins of Roman archaeology*, London 2000

Hobsbawm, E., 'Inventing traditions', in Hobsbawm and Ranger, *Invention of tradition*, 1–15

—— *Nations and nationalism since 1780*, Cambridge 1990

—— and T. Ranger (eds), *The invention of tradition*, Cambridge 1983

Hockey, P., *Caerleon past and present*, Risca 1981

Hodder, I., 'Writing archaeology: site reports in context', *Antiquity* lxii (1989), 268–74

—— *Archaeological theory in Europe: the last three decades*, London 1991

Horseman, R., 'Origins of racial Anglo-Saxons in Great Britain before 1850', *Journal History of Ideas* xxxvii (1976), 387–410

Houghton, W. E., *The Victorian frame of mind, 1830–1870*, New Haven 1957

Howell, R., 'Roman survival, Welsh revival: the evidence of re-use of Roman remains', *Monmouthshire Antiquary* xvii (2001), 55–60

Inkster, I., 'Introduction', in Inkster and Morrell, *Metropolis and province*, 1–41

—— and J. Morrell (eds), *Metropolis and province: science in British culture, 1780–1850*, London 1983

Ireland, S., *Roman Britain: a source book*, London 1986

Isbell, J., *The birth of European romanticism: truth and propaganda in Stael's De l'Allemagne, 1810–1813*, Cambridge 1994

Jann, R., 'From amateur to professional: the case of the Oxbridge historians', *Journal of British Studies* xxii (1982), 122–47

Javed, M., 'Comparativism and references to Rome in British imperial attitudes to India', in Edwards, *Roman presences*, 88–110

Jeffes, K., 'The Irish in early Victorian Chester: an outcast community?', in Swift, *Victorian Chester*, 85–119

Jeffrey, K. (ed.), *Audley End*, London 1997

Jenkins, I., *Archaeologists and aesthetes in the sculpture galleries of the British Museum, 1800–1939*, London 1992

—— and K. Sloane, *Vases and volcanoes: Sir William Hamilton and his collection*, London 1996

Jones, M., *Fake? The art of deception*, London 1990

Kendrick, T. D., *British antiquity*, London 1950

Kidd, A. and D. Nicholls, *The making of the English middle class*, Stroud 1998

Klindt-Jensen, O., *A history of Scandinavian archaeology*, London 1975

Knight, J., *Caerleon, Roman fortress*, Cardiff 1994

—— 'The Caerleon Museum and the association', *Monmouthshire Antiquary* xiii (1997), 1–3

—— 'City of Arthur, city of the legions: antiquaries and writers at Caerleon', *Monmouthshire Antiquary* xvii (2001), 47–54

Kwint, M., C. Breward and J. Aynsley (eds), *Material memories: design and evocation*, Oxford 1999

Levine, J. M., *Dr. Woodward's shield: history, science and satire in Augustan England*, Ithaca 1991

Levine, P., *The amateur and the professional*, Cambridge 1986

Liversidge, M. and C. Edwards (eds), *Imagining Rome: British artists and Rome in the nineteenth century*, Bristol 1996

Lowenthal, D., *The past is a foreign country*, Cambridge 1985

—— 'Classical antiquities as national and global heritage', *Antiquity* lxii (1988), 726–35

—— *The politics of the past*, London 1990

Macaulay, B., *The complete works of Lord Macaulay: history of England*, i, London 1898

Macdonald, S., 'Boudicea: warrior, mother and myth', in S. Macdonald, P. Holden and S. Ardener (eds), *Images of women in peace and war*, London 1987, 40–61

McDougall, A., *Racial myths in English history*, Montreal 1982

Macfarlane, A., *Reconstructing historical communities*, Cambridge 1977

McKendrick, N. (ed.), *Historical perspectives: studies in English thought and society*, London 1974

Mackenzie, J., *Orientalism: history, theory and the arts*, Manchester 1995

McWhirr, A. D., *Roman Gloucestershire*, Gloucester 1981

Mandler, P., *The fall and rise of the stately home*, New Haven 1997

Mann, J. C. and R. G. Penman, *Literary sources for Roman Britain*, London 1977

Marchand, S., *Down from Olympus: archaeology and philhellenism in Germany, 1750–1970*, Princeton 1996

Mattingly, D. J., 'Dialogues in Roman imperialism: power, discourse and discrepant experience in the Roman empire', *Journal of Roman Archaeology*, s.s xxiii (1997), 7–24

Mellor, R., *The Roman historians*, London 1999

Millett, M., *The Romanization of Britain: an essay in archaeological interpretation*, Cambridge 1990

Momigliano, A. D., *Studies in historiography*, London 1966

—— 'Eighteenth-century prelude to Mr Gibbon', in *Storia della storiografia metodo storico*, Rome 1975, 249–63

—— *The classical foundations of modern historiography*, Berkeley, CA 1990

Moore, J., 'Theodicy and society: the crisis of the intelligentsia', in Helmstadter and Lightman, *Victorian faith in crisis*, 153–86

Morgan, P., 'From a death to a view: the hunt for the Welsh past in the romantic period', in Hobsbawm and Ranger, *Invention of tradition*, 15–43

—— 'From long knives to blue books', in R. R. Davies, R. A. Griffiths, I. G. Jones and K. O. Morgan (eds), *Historical essays presented to Glanmore Williams*, Cardiff 1984, 199–216

—— 'Keeping the legend alive', in T. Curtis (ed.), *Wales the imagined nation*, Cardiff 1986, 20–63

Morley, N., *Writing ancient history*, London 1999

Morrell, J. B., 'Professionalisation', in R. C. Olby, G. N. Cantor, J. R. R. Christie and M. J. S. Hodge (eds), *Companion to the history of science*, London 1990, 980–9

—— and A. Thackray, *Gentlemen of science: the early years of the BASS*, Oxford 1981

Morris, R. J., *Class, sect and party: the making of the middle class in Leeds*, Manchester 1990

———— and R. Rogers (eds), *The Victorian city: a reader in British urban history*, *1820–1914*, New York 1993

Munby, A. N. L., *The catalogues of manuscripts and printed books of Sir Thomas Phillips: their composition and distribution*, Cambridge 1951

Nash Williams, V. E., *The Roman legionary fortress at Caerleon*, Cardiff 1940

———— (ed.), *One hundred years of Welsh archaeology: centenary volume, 1846–1946*, Cardiff 1946

Neve, M., 'Science in a commercial city; Bristol, 1820–1860', in Inkster and Morrell, *Metropolis and province*, 179–204

Newsome, D., *The Victorian world picture*, London 1997

Orange, A. D., *Philosophers and provincials: the Yorkshire Philosophical Society, 1822–1844*, York 1973

Pearce, S. M., *Archaeological curatorship*, Leicester 1990

Piggott, S., 'William Camden and the Britannia', *Proceedings of the British Academy* xxxvii (1951), 199–217

———— *Ruins in the landscape: essays in antiquarianism*, Edinburgh 1976

———— *William Stukeley: an eighteenth-century antiquary*, London 1985

———— *Ancient Britain and the antiquarian imagination: ideas from the Renaissance to the Regency*, London 1989

Plumb, J. H., *The death of the past*, London 1969

Porter, B., 'What did they know of empire?', *History Today* (Oct. 2004), 42–8

Porter, R., 'Gentlemen and geology: the emergence of a scientific career, 1660–1920', *Historical Journal* xxi (1978), 809–36

Pugh, C. W. (ed.), *The Wiltshire Archaeological and Natural History Society, 1853–1953*, Devizes 1953

Rainger, R., 'Race, politics and science: the Anthropological Society of London in the 1860s', *VS* xxii (1978–9), 51–70

Rankin, H. D., *Celts and the classical world*, London 1987

Richmond, I. A., 'British section of the *Ravenna cosmography*', *Arch.* xciii (1949), 1–50

Rivet, A. L. F., 'The British section of the *Antonine itinerary*', *Britannia* i (1970), 34–82.

———— 'Rudyard Kipling's Roman Britain', *The Kipling Journal* (June 1978), 1–10

———— and C. Smith, *Place names of Roman Britain*, London 1979

Royle, E., *Revolutionary Britannia? Reflections on the threat of revolution, 1789–1848*, Manchester 2000

Rudsdale, E. J., 'Colchester Museum, 1846–1946', *Essex Review* lvi (1946), 1–10

Said, E. W., *Orientalism: western conceptions of the orient*, London 1978

Salmon, F., 'The impact of the archaeology of Rome on British architects and their work, 1750–1840', in C. Hornsby (ed.), *The impact of Italy: the grand tour and beyond*, Rome 2000

Samuel, R., *Patriotism: the making and unmaking of the British national identity*, III: *National fictions*, London 1989

———— *Theatres of memory*, II: *Island stories: unravelling Britain*, London 1998

Sandys, J. E., *A history of classical scholarship*, Cambridge 1908

Sayce, R., *History of the Royal Agricultural College, Cirencester*, Stroud 1992

Schnapp, A., *The discovery of the past*, London 1993

Sealey, P., *The Boudican revolt*, Princes Risborough 1997

Secord, A., 'Corresponding interests: artisans and gentlemen in nineteenth-century natural history', *British Journal of the History of Science* xxvii (1994), 383–408

—— Science in the pub: artisan botanists in early nineteenth-century Lancashire', *History of Science* xxxii (1994), 269–315

Secord, J. A., 'King of Siluria: Roderick Murchison and the imperial theme in nineteenth-century British geology', *VS* xxv (1978), 413–42

—— *Victorian sensation: the extraordinary publication, reception and secret authorship of Vestiges of the natural history of creation*, Chicago 2000

Sewell, E. C., 'The Corinium Museum Cirencester and its curators', *TBGAS* lv (1933), 317–21

Shanks, M., *Classical archaeology of Greece: experiences of the discipline*, London 1996

Smiles, S., *The image of antiquity: ancient Britain and the romantic imagination*, New Haven 1994

Smith, B., *European vision and the south Pacific*, New Haven 1985

Smith, C. S., 'Museums, artefacts, and meanings', in Vergo, *The new museology*, 6–21

Stewart, P. C. N., 'Inventing Britain: the Roman creation and adaptation of an image', *Britannia* xxvi (1995), 1–10

Stocking, G., *Victorian anthropology*, London 1987

Stray, C., *Classics transformed: schools, universities and society in England, 1830–1960*, Oxford 1998

Strong, R., *Recreating the past: British history and the Victorian painter*, London 1978

Summerson, J., 'The architecture of British museums and galleries', in J. Chapel and C. Gere (eds), *The fine and decorative art collections of Britain and Ireland*, London 1985, 9–20

Swift, R. (ed.), *Victorian Chester*, Liverpool 1996

Thompson, E. A., 'Gildas and the history of Britain', *Britannia* x (1979), 203–15

Thompson, F. H., *Roman Cheshire*, Chester 1965

Tillotson, K., *Novels of the 1840s*, Oxford 1954

Treuherz, J., *Victorian painting*, London 1993

Trevor-Roper, H., *The romantic movement and the study of history*, London 1969

Trigger, B. G., *A history of archaeological thought*, Cambridge 1989

Turner, F. M., 'The Victorian conflict between science and religion: a professional dimension', *Isis* lxix (1978), 356–76

—— 'The Victorian crisis of faith and the faith that was lost', in Helmstadter and Lightman, *Victorian faith in crisis*, 9–39

—— *Contesting cultural authority: essays in Victorian intellectual life*, Cambridge 1993

Vance, N., *The persistence of Rome: the Victorians and ancient Rome*, London 1997

VCH, Essex, IX: *Borough of Colchester*, ed. J. Cooper, Oxford 1994

Vergo, P. (ed.), *The new museology*, London 1989

Vyner, B. (ed.), *Building on the past: papers celebrating 150 years of the Royal Archaeological Institute*, London 1994

Wacher, J., *The towns of Roman Britain*, London 1974

Wallace, C., 'Writing disciplinary history, or why Romano-British archaeology needs a biographical dictionary of its own', *Oxford Journal of Archaeology* xxi (2002), 381–92

Webster, G., *Boudica: the British revolt against Rome AD 60*, London 1978

Weinbrot, H. T., *Britannia's issues: the rise of British literature from Dryden to Ossian*, Cambridge 1993

Wetherall, D., 'From Canterbury to Winchester: the foundation of the Institute', in Vyner, *Building on the past*, 9–21

Wheeler, T. U. and R. E. M. Wheeler, *The Roman amphitheatre at Caerleon Monmouthshire*, Oxford 1928

White, R. and P. Barker, *Wroxeter: life and death of a Roman city*, Stroud, 1998

White R. H., 'Mayer and British archaeology', in Gibson and Wright, *Joseph Mayer*, 118–37

Williams, D., *A history of modern Wales*, London 1950

Williams, D., *Romans and barbarians: four views from the empire's edge*, London 1998

Wilson, D. M., *The forgotten collector: Augustus Wollaston Franks of the British Museum*, London 1984

Wilton, A. and I. Bignamini (eds), *Grand tour: the lure of Italy in the eighteenth century*, London 1996

Wilton-Ely, J., *Apollo of the arts: Lord Burlington and his circle*, Nottingham 1973

Woolf, G., *Becoming Roman: the origins of provincial civilisation in Gaul*, Cambridge 1998

Wright, P., *On living in an old country: the national past in contemporary Britain*, London 1985

Unpublished dissertations and papers

Jones, G., 'John Edward Lee: a Monmouthshire antiquary', MA diss. University of Wales 1991

Miele, C., 'Conservation and the enemies of progress', paper given at a conference on 'The idea of heritage: past, present and future', London Guildhall University, September 1999

Pearce, S. M., 'Symbols of ourselves: objects of possession', paper given at the Material Memories Conference, Victoria & Albert Museum, April 1998

Rhodes, M., 'Some aspects of the contribution to British archaeology of Charles Roach Smith, 1806–1890', PhD diss. London 1993

Index

Johnson, Henry, 180
Joyce, James, 170, 171–2, 174, 175, 177, 179, 180

Kemble, John, 13, 15 n. 35, 21, 43, 44, 159
Kingsley, Charles, 35 n. 28, 43 n. 67, 45, 74
knowledge, sources of, 10–13; increasing importance of material evidence, 170–1. *See also* Bede; classical texts; Geoffrey of Monmouth; Gildas; Richard of Cirencester; topographical accounts

Layard, Austen, 144, 164
Lee, Edward, 4, 53: antiquarian activity, 89, 90, 144, 154, 182, 183; *Delineations of Roman antiquities found at Caerleon*, 81, 84; social background, 55, 62–3, 87–8. *See also* Caerleon; Caerleon Archaeological Association
libaries: local, 77–8, 79, 105, 131; Muddies, 78
local identity, 46, 52–4, 94, 122–3, 186, 187. *See also* myths
local societies, *see* place names
Londesborough, 1st baron, *see* Conyngham
London Corporation, 20
London Museum of Antiquities, *see* Roach Smith, Charles
Lyell, Charles, 9, 171
Lysons, Samuel, 24 n. 71, 97, 128, 129, 177

Macaulay, Thomas Babington: *Lays of ancient Rome*, 8
Malahide, James, 4th Baron Talbot de, 26, 58, 145
Marsden, John Howard, 53, 61, 115, 116, 142, 155, 167–8
Massie, William: archaeological activities and views, 129, 132, 134–5; social background, 57, 60, 133, 138, 160
Mayer, Joseph: collector, 26, 72, 151, 156, 158, 163; supporter of archaeological activity, 32, 71, 75
Meyrick, Sir Samuel Rush, 50
Morant, Philip: *History of Colchester*, 123
Morgan, Octavius, 4, 53, 65, 89, 90, 148
mosaics: as art, 102; conferring prestige,

65, 155, 180; as object, 144. *See also* Cirencester
museums, local: catalogues, 93–4, 106–7, 154, 156–7; curators, 66, 70, 71, 74, 75, 106–7, 117; 1845 Museums Act, 91, 118; importance of, 21, 88, 158–9, 182; layout, 74 n. 62, 93, 105, 153, 154–5; as tourist attractions, 106, 136, 182. *See also* individual collections: Bath, Bathurst, British, Charles, Colchester, Cripps, Disney, Faussett Collection; London Museum of Antiquities, Saffron Warden
myths, 7–9, 45 n.79, 50, 54, 187; Arthur, 51–2, 82, 84; Coel, 47–8, 122, 123; Helena, 122; Vortigen, 12, 49

national origins, 5, 46–50, 185; Celtic, 31–7; Roman, 38–41; Saxon, 41–5; stereotypes, 3, 48, 185, 187
nationalism, 24, 29, 46; Danish, 15; French, 19, 27, 54; German, 8 n.5, 41–2, 43; Welsh, 49–50. *See also* archaeology, support for
Neville, Richard Cornwallis: archaeological activity, 17–18, 31, 44, 51, 153, 156 n. 57, 161; social background, 18, 53
Newton, Charles, 8, 25, 146, 151
Niebuhr, Barthold Georg, 8, 12, 43
Northumberland, Algernon Percy, 4th duke, 24
Numismatic Society, 73, 146, 159. *See also* coins

Percy, Algernon, *see* Northumberland
Pettigrew, Thomas, 70, 73
Phillips, John, 63
phrenology, 34, 165
Pompeii: as domestic evidence, 90, 135, 165, 174–5; influence of, 38, 145, 147–9, 155
Price, Edward Bedford, 70, 114
professionalism, 2, 50, 52, 55, 66, 68, 72–6, 130, 185, 188

racial attitudes: *see* empire
Raikes, Arthur: archaeological views, 46, 53; social background, 60, 133, 138
railways: facilitating travel to archaeological sites, 58, 71, 77, 99, 131, 140, 182; revealing archaeological remains, 19, 112, 140
Richard of Cirencester, 12, 78